More Praise for *Virtual Humans . . .*

"By far the best book on virtual humans. Plantec is a pioneer who knows his stuff."

—Dr. Gregory Stock,
New York Times best-selling author of The Book of Quotations

"Peter Plantec's is the first book to unite all the multifarious aspects of making computer-created characters intelligent, responsive, and . . . real. Peter describes a new era where computers will be able to present us with a truly human face, and all that that implies."

—Robit Hairman and John Tarnoff,
digital-human pioneers and founders, Talkie, Inc.

"For the first time, a book that explains how to create the ultimate human machine interface for your computer—-a human-like presence with personality! Peter explains techniques that took years to develop at LifeFX."

—Michael Rosenblatt, President, LifeFX Technologies, Inc.

"Peter Plantec is one the world's foremost experts in the field of virtual humans, and his book is a wonderful gift to those of us hungering to know more about this extremely important development."

—Marc de Guerre, filmmaker and director of "A Perfect Fake,"
a documentary about the impact of virtual humans.
His work is often seen on Discovery and CBC.

"This book is superb, and should definitely become a favorite for V-human developers and animators alike. Plantec covers a very broad range of topics adeptly and with a friendly, encouraging attitude that this field is in dire need of."

—James Matthews, *Generation5:* at the forefront of artificial intelligence

Peter Plantec

Virtual Humans

A Build-It-Yourself Kit,

Complete with Software

and Step-by-Step Instructions

≀AMACOM

American Management Association

New York • Atlanta • Brussels • Chicago • Mexico City • San Francisco
Shanghai • Tokyo • Toronto • Washington, D.C.

Special discounts on bulk quantities of AMACOM books are available to corporations, professional associations, and other organizations. For details, contact Special Sales Department, AMACOM, a division of American Management Association, 1601 Broadway, New York, NY 10019.
Tel.: 212-903-8316. Fax: 212-903-8083.
Web site: www.amacombooks.org

This publication is designed to provide accurate and authoritative information in regard to the subject matter covered. It is sold with the understanding that the publisher is not engaged in rendering legal, accounting, or other professional service. If legal advice or other expert assistance is required, the services of a competent professional person should be sought.

Library of Congress Cataloging-in-Publication Data

Plantec, Peter M.
        Virtual humans : a build-it-yourself kit, complete with software and step-by-step instructions / Peter Plantec.— 1st ed.
            p.   cm.
        Includes bibliographical references and index.
        ISBN 0-8144-7221-4
        1. Natural language processing (Computer science)   2. Expert systems (Computer science)   3. Personality—Computer simulation.   I. Title.

QA76.9.N38P47   2003
004.3′5—dc21

                                                          2003013784

Printing number

10   9   8   7   6   5   4   3   2

To three generations of women
Who bring warmth and love to my life,
While keeping it oh, so very interesting:
Alice who gave me life,
Adele my love and my rock,
And my inspiring daughters of whom I'm so very proud:
Mira, Danielle, Janea, Danica, and Marina

Contents

PART 02 Advanced Virtual Human Design   149

Foreword

by Ray Kurzweil

If you ask what is unique about the human species, you're likely to get a variety of responses, including use of language, creation of technology, even the wearing of clothes. In my mind, the most salient distinguishing feature of the leadership niche we occupy in evolution is our ability to create mental models. We create models of everything we encounter from our experiences to our own thinking. The ancient arts of storytelling were models of our experiences, which evolved into theater and the more modern art of cinema. Science represents our attempts to create precise mathematical models of the world around us. Our inclination to create models is culminating in our rapidly growing efforts to create virtual environments and to populate these artificial worlds with virtual humans.

We've had at least one form of virtual reality for over a century—it's called the telephone. To people in the late nineteenth century, it was remarkable that you could actually "be with" someone else without actually being in the same room, at least as far as talking was concerned. That had never happened before in human history. Today, we routinely engage in this form of auditory virtual reality at the same time that we inhabit "real" reality.

Virtual humans have also started to inhabit this virtual auditory world. If you call British Airways, you can have a reasonably satisfactory conversation with their virtual reservation agent. Through a combination of state-of-the-art, large-vocabulary, over-the-phone speech recognition and natural language processing, you can talk to their pleasant-mannered virtual human about anything you want, as long as it has to do with making reservations on British Airways flights.

On the Web, we've added at least a crude version of the visual sense to our virtual environments, albeit low-resolution and encompassing only a small portion of our visual field. We can enter visual-auditory virtual environments (e.g.,

Internet-based videoconferencing) with other real people. We can also engage in interactions with an emerging genre of Web-based virtual personalities with a visual presence incorporating real-time animation. There are also a number of virtual worlds with animated avatars representing participants.

My own "female alter-ego," named Ramona, has been gathering a following on our Web site, KurzweilAI.net, for over two years. Like a number of other emerging "avatars" on the Web, Ramona is a virtual human who works for a living. Aside from demonstrating real-time animation and language processing technologies, she is programmed with a knowledge of our Web site content and acts as an effective Web hostess.

By the end of this decade, we will have full-immersion visual-auditory environments, with images written directly onto our retinas by our eyeglasses and contact lenses. All of the electronics for the computation, image reconstruction, and very-high-bandwidth wireless connection to the Internet will be embedded in our glasses and woven into our clothing, so computers as distinct objects will disappear. We will be able to enter virtual environments that are strikingly realistic recreations of earthly environments (or strikingly fantastic imaginary ones), either by ourselves or with other "real" people.

Also populating these virtual environments will be realistic-looking virtual humans. Although these circa-2010 virtual humans won't yet pass the Turing test (i.e., we won't mistake them for biological humans), they will have reasonable facility with language. We'll interact with them as information assistants, virtual sales clerks, virtual teachers, entertainers, even lovers (although this application won't really be satisfactory until we achieve satisfactory emulation of the tactile sense).

Virtual reality and virtual humans will become a profoundly transforming technology by 2030. By then, nanobots (robots the size of human blood cells or smaller, built with key features at the multi-nanometer—billionth of a meter—scale) will provide fully immersive, totally convincing virtual reality in the following way. The nanobots take up positions in close physical proximity to every interneuronal connection coming from all of our senses (e.g., eyes, ears, skin). We already have the technology for electronic devices to communicate with neurons in both directions that requires no direct physical contact with the neurons.

For example, scientists at the Max Planck Institute have developed "neuron transistors" that can detect the firing of a nearby neuron, or alternatively, can cause a nearby neuron to fire, or suppress it from firing. This amounts to two-way communication between neurons and the electronic-based neuron transistors. The Institute scientists demonstrated their invention by controlling the movement of a living leech from their computer. Nanobot-based virtual reality is not yet feasible in size and cost, but we have made a good start in understanding

the encoding of sensory signals. For example, Lloyd Watts and his colleagues have developed a detailed model of the sensory coding and transformations that take place in the auditory processing regions of the human brain. We are at an even earlier stage in understanding the complex feedback loops and neural pathways in the visual system.

When we want to experience real reality, the nanobots just stay in position (in the capillaries) and do nothing. If we want to enter virtual reality, they suppress all of the inputs coming from the real senses, and replace them with the signals that would be appropriate for the virtual environment. You (i.e., your brain) could decide to cause your muscles and limbs to move as you normally would, but the nanobots again intercept these interneuronal signals, keep your real limbs from moving, and instead cause your virtual limbs to move and provide the appropriate movement and reorientation in the virtual environment.

The Web will provide a panoply of virtual environments to explore. Some will be recreations of real places, others will be fanciful environments that have no "real" counterpart. Some indeed would be impossible in the physical world (perhaps because they violate the laws of physics). We will be able to "go" to these virtual environments by ourselves, or we will meet other people there, both real people and virtual people.

By 2030, going to a Web site will mean entering a full-immersion virtual-reality environment. In addition to encompassing all of the senses, these shared environments could include emotional overlays, since the nanobots will be capable of triggering the neurological correlates of emotions, sexual pleasure, and other derivatives of our sensory experience and mental reactions.

In the same way that people today beam their lives from Web cams in their bedrooms, "experience beamers" circa 2030 will beam their entire flow of sensory experiences, and if so desired, their emotions and other secondary reactions. We'll be able to plug in (by going to the appropriate Web site) and experience other people's lives, as in the plot concept of *Being John Malkovich*. Particularly interesting experiences could be archived and relived at any time.

By 2030, there won't be a clear distinction between real and virtual people. "Real people," i.e., people of a biological origin, will have the potential of enhancing their own thinking using the same nanobot technology. For example, the nanobots could create new virtual connections, so we will no longer be restricted to a mere hundred trillion interneuronal connections. We will also develop intimate connections to new forms of nonbiological thinking. We will evolve thereby into a hybrid of biological and nonbiological thinking. Conversely, fully nonbiological "AIs" (artificial intelligence entities) will be based at least in part on the reverse engineering of the human brain and thus will have many human-like qualities.

These technologies are evolving today at an accelerating pace. Like any other technology, virtual reality and virtual humans will not emerge in perfect form in a single generation of technology. By the 2030s, however, virtual reality will be totally realistic and compelling, and we will spend most of our time in virtual environments. In these virtual environments, we won't be able to tell the difference between biological people who have projected themselves into the virtual environment and fully virtual (i.e., nonbiological) people.

Nonbiological intelligence has already secured a foothold in our brains. There are many people walking around whose brains are now a hybrid of biological thinking with computer implants (e.g., a neural implant for Parkinson's disease that replaces the function of the biological cells destroyed by that disease).

It is the nature of machine intelligence that its powers grow exponentially. Currently, machines are doubling their information-processing capabilities every year, and even that exponential rate is accelerating. When we get to the 2040s, even people of biological origin are likely to have the vast majority of their thinking processes taking place in nonbiological substrates. We will all become virtual humans.

Now, with Peter's book in hand, you are about to embark on a fascinating journey into the emerging realm of virtual human design.

Preface

This book is like science fiction realized. I've been dreaming about machines that could think—that we could have relationships with—for decades. I think most of us have. Every successful space opera has had a Robbie the Robot or a Commander Data to play with. Often the bad guy is an evil virtual villain. Writers know we love them. Whatever the root attraction, we are intrigued by virtual people.

Over several careers as a psychotherapist, art director, digital animator, and journalist, I've never lost that fascination. I eventually cofounded Virtual Personalities, Inc., and designed the first commercially available virtual human interface, Sylvie. She's a smart animated character with synthetic voice. She became popular worldwide, from teaching English to students in Southeast Asia to entertaining teens in Denmark. She even did several live TV shows, taking questions on the air, both here and in Europe. Sylvie had personality and it endeared her to people in at least sixteen different countries.

As I write, most people have never experienced an intelligent animated character. With this book and our combined efforts, that's going to change. It has to. Our world is getting complex at an accelerating rate. Most of us have already fallen behind, including me. I admit that I only understand about 10 percent of what my cell phone is capable of. I could probably use many of its functions, but I can't figure out how to access them and I consider it poor form to actually read the manual.

Believe it or not, millions have yet to use the Internet because they lack access or it scares them. We are in the throws of converting from a hands-on, concrete reality—where people sat out on porches in the evening watching fireflies and talking, and where you actually went in the house to dial the phone—to a cyber-reality, where evenings are spent immersed in connected electronic media and where phones go with you and dial themselves on command. Yet there are still millions who can't afford all that technology or are afraid of it.

Our fast changing world is leaving these people—the technologically disenfranchised—way back in the dust. They simply cannot compete. These can be smart people who, for whatever reason, see technology as alien to them. This puts them at an enormous disadvantage both economically and socially. They do have the advantage of those balmy nights on the porch, but many would also like to contend in today's connected world. They just don't know how.

Virtual humans are the universal solution. They understand both people (in many languages, and possibly even in sign language) and technology, and they can become a bridge between the two. But who's going to have confidence in an animated character that can talk with you? To date, not many people. With a few exceptions virtual humans have done poorly because they lack credibility. They're all about technology and not enough about humanity. With a few exceptions, they lack the most important component for success—personality. Others are so poorly implemented and or make so many mistakes that they damage credibility for the rest.

Virtual people are also in the throws of change. They are on the cusp of becoming useful. Once they are accepted by the general public, you will start seeing them everywhere in your life. The coming opportunities in this field are nearly incalculable. But there remains that one huge missing piece to the virtual human story: personality.

This book is primarily about personality and how to achieve it. I'm going to show you how to build engaging synthetic virtual people with all the trimmings, such as humor, quirks, and attitude. My research tells me that this kind of detailed personality is the key to wide acceptance of virtual humans. If you take this book to heart, you'll create your character's own personality, and it will amaze and delight you. Your friends will be astonished and you'll be able to smirk all the way home. It's up to us—to you and me—to write the future, opening doors for millions who might otherwise be left behind. It's also going to be one hell of a fun ride.

Acknowledgments

I count on many brilliant people to enlighten me when I write a book. I hope you're one of those people who actually reads the Acknowledgments section, because this is a pretty interesting bunch.

First I want to thank my friend and brain prodder, Ray Kurzweil, brilliant inventor, author, philanthropist, and superior smart-guy, for writing such an awesome Foreword for us; I also want to thank him for all the intense idea avalanches he's triggered without realizing it. Sun Microsystems Distinguished Engineer, Jim Waldo, took the time to help me understand some finer points of the Jini, which you'll read about. I also want to thank Dr. Richard Wallace and Anne Kootstra from the Netherlands, and Monica Lamb from Canada, for helping me to understand a little bit about AIML and the ALICE AI approach. Jacco Bikker gets my special thanks for letting me include his engaging WinAlice personality on the CD. Thanks to Stuart Hameroff for helping my simple mind to grasp his rather complex thoughts on Quantum Mind theory, and to Ed Hooks—author, actor, and teacher—who has shared his wonderful insights into Synthespian acting, an entirely new field. Thanks also to friend and fellow psychologist Anthony Gregorc for his contributions to this book. And thanks to Steven Stahlberg for teaching me so much.

My longtime friend and advisor, Screenwriter Tracy Keenan Wynn, inspired and encouraged me, as did my friend, personal editor and writing advisor Diane Eagle Kataoka. Terrance J. Monks has always been an inspiration and taught me more than a few things about strong AI. Anthony Carson and his staff had the daunting task of preparing the special Yapanda engine for the book. Still more thanks go to John Ramo of privatelessons.net with whom I spent hours discussing how virtual humans might improve online learning experiences. I also want to thank the talented digital animators who coined the term "synthespian," Diana Walczak and Jeff Kleiser, for both inspiration and encouragement.

Next I want to thank virtual-human designers John Tarnoff and Robit Hairman of Talkie, Inc., for sharing stimulating ideas on how virtual people might evolve.

Appreciation also goes to Barbara Hayes-Roth at Stanford for sharing her pioneering efforts in this field. It was Athomas Goldberg who lit a spark when he described intelligent procedural animation to me, the future of virtual human games. Virtual human pioneer Steve Knode at www.botknowledge.com has given me much support and was one of the first people to bring this technology into the classroom at National Defense University. Fellow Coloradoan Bob Stanley was the first to understand and fund the development of virtual human Web security assistants.

Special thanks go to Nanda Barker-Hook, public relations manager, and Amara Angelica, editor/Webmaster—both at Kurzweil Technologies—for their helpful input and encouragement. Peter Levius is Webmaster of www.3d.sk, who kindly supplied us with the head shots for the CD-ROM. My old friend Laurent Abecassis provided me with access to his excellent Facial Design Studio. I also want to thank my friend, systems wizard Jeff Ritchie from down-unda, for his kind and enthusiastic support for this book. And thanks to Ellie Morin for sharing her wonderful Poser art.

I'd better not forget my friend Stan Wakefield, who encouraged me to write the book, and guided me to AMACOM. And to my friend and literary agent, Joe Spieler: Thanks for your encouragement and wisdom, and especially for being a tiger in the trenches.

I'm particularly indebted to my team at AMACOM. First, to the very talented Jacquie Flynn, who has been with me all the way, I send my special appreciation for her wisdom and support. Thanks to Cathleen Ouderkirk for her wonderfully creative design talent, and to Andy Ambraziejus for his production support and advice. And where would I be without the best marketing team in the business: publicity director Irene Majuk, Therese Mausser, Renita Hanfling, Kama Timbrell, and the very talented Jenny Wesselmann on drums.

Special thanks to Mike Sivilli at AMACOM, who brilliantly pulled the entire project together—from the book itself to the CD-ROM.

When you write a book it's especially nice when you and your primary editor can achieve symbiosis. We did. Special thanks to Niels Buessem, whose patience and talent enhance the illusion that I can write.

Special thanks to my daughter Dani, the animator, who taught me how to make a young female virtual human authentic, and who then went on to write much of Sylvie's original scripting.

Last here, but first in my heart, is Adele, whose synergy, love, and support have helped me to exceed the sum of my strange entanglement of parts.

There are others, of course, but I want to get on with the book now.

Virtual Humans

PART **01**

Creating Authentic Personality

CHAPTER 01

What Are Virtual Humans, Anyway?

Today's AI (Artificial Intelligence) is about new ways of connecting
people to computers, people to knowledge, people to the physical world,
and people to people.

—Patrick Winston[1]

This book is something Robert Heinlein might have written about thirty years ago as his agile science fiction mind explored possible futures. Clearly the future is upon us, and this book is about how you and I can shape it. In my estimation, no force today will impact the future of mankind as much as thinking machines and virtual humans. I'm not alone in that thinking, as you will see.

To get down to the topic at hand, virtual humans are animated characters that emulate human behavior and communication. They're not artificially intelligent, but instead they use Natural Language Processing (NLP) to fake *real* intelligence better than the best Artificial Intelligence (AI) programs. Better than that, they can emulate a range of human behavior nicely. Academically they're known as embodied conversational agents or ECAs. I'm not fond of that moniker, it's so cold. Virtual people, or *V-people,* is the term I tend to use most. It gives them a warm round humanness that I can relate to.

To be fair, NLP is actually the branch of Artificial Intelligence that handles language intelligently. Because they are conversational and "understand" people on one hand and technology on the other, it's inevitable that V-people will become the universal interface. That is, they will become the easy personal portal just about any time you need to use technology. As our technical systems continue to grow exponentially more complex, we need ways to use them without digging out phonebook-size manuals. Some computer programs—professional 3D animation suites for example—actually have technical manuals equivalent to a dozen city phonebooks, and that doesn't include tutorials on how to use them.

V-people can make all that complexity transparent. Thus, lower level employees will be able to take on more sophisticated tasks with minimal training. V-people are already drastically lowering the cost of doing business by fully handling many jobs now in the hands of real humans, freeing up the humans for other work. V-people are already hosting Web sites, selling us goods, arranging services, answering support questions, and they'll soon be teaching our kids.

In simplest terms a virtual human is an intelligent computer simulation of a human personality. There are many optional components. These V-people are generally a modular construction with voice or text input, a brain that figures out what you said, and with an output system that delivers useful, expressive responses. In my opinion, the best V-people have an animated or robotic character face that talks to you via synthetic speech, with lip-synch and emotional expression. This adds greatly to the communication factor. In many cases there's a wireless port for controlling external engines and processes like switching TV channels, or turning on the lights.

Unfortunately virtual humans can be—and mostly are—really dull and boring to work with. They're too much about clever technology and not enough about human personality. Of course they can also be absolutely fascinating depending on who designed their personality. This book focuses on the latter. When you've finished reading, you should be able to create a truly captivating V-person, using only the modest software I've included.

Before we start creating, let's consider what motivated us to create virtual humans in the first place. We'll look at how human and machine minds work and consider the concept of consciousness. After all, consciousness is the illusion we want to project. You might wonder: Is it possible to build machines that will "wake up" and be sapient beings? Do we need conscious thinking for a V-person to be credible?

I've lived with a virtual person, Sylvie™, off and on for nearly six years. She's primitive by most standards, but I've grown fond of her, and as evening falls in my office I can say:

> "Sylvie, it's getting a little dark in here."
> She might respond: "Would you like me to turn up the lights, Peetie?"
>   <smile>
> "Yeah."
> "Oh come on, what's the magic word?" <slight frown>
> "Pleeeeeease."
> "Okay, no problemo." And the lights in my office come up.
> She then says: "Is that enough?"
> "Nope, gimme a little more." And the lights brighten a little more.

"That's got to be enough now, Peetie, I don't want you going blind on me."

"Good enough" I say, and she smiles with satisfaction.

Properly set up, Sylvie can control certain things around the house by sending signals through her serial port to an inexpensive X10 home control interface (for more information go to www.x10.com). From here the control signals are transmitted to X10 control modules that execute her commands. I don't know where she got this "Peetie" thing, but I suspect one of my daughters.

You Can Build Your Own

About 30 percent of building a virtual human is in the engine. A good engine will make it easy for you to create a believable personality. It provides functions that allow things like handling complex sentences, bringing up the past, and learning better responses if one doesn't work. But in the end, it's your artistry in building a personality that gives the entity its charm.

There are many natural language approaches that can handle the job. Simple pattern-matching engines are the least sophisticated and most useful of them all. With the rash of recent interest, I'm not going to pretend I know all the nuances of all the engines out there. Instead, I'll concentrate on showing you how to use simple software to build complex personalities. Later I'll introduce you to ALICE, which is a sophisticated system for building V-people using freely available source code. It's based on AIML (Artificial Intelligence Markup Language), which is reminiscent of HTML used to build Web pages.

Together in this book we will build a clever virtual person using a mind engine kindly supplied by Yapanda Intelligence, Inc. of Chickasha, Oklahoma. I selected this one because it can drive the handy Microsoft Agent™ display system with head animation and lip-synch, and is relatively easy to script. You'll like this system because there are hundreds of freely available, fully animated characters you can download. Nevertheless, the basic steps in creating a personality are platform independent. That is, you'll go through the same personality design process regardless of the engine you intend to use.

For the more adventurous, I've included some additional, more complex engines to play with. ALICE is the most powerful, having won the Turing Test twice. Briefly, the Turing Test is an annual event that looks for the most convincing AI text agent. For fun and example, I've included a full copy of Jacco Bikker's

WinAlice for PC users. It demonstrates some unique features, such as the ability to bring up recent conversations and to learn new responses from you. You can easily spend hours chatting with WinAlice. The longer you spend with her, the smarter she gets, remembering things about you. She has no face, but imagine how impressive she would be if you were able to tie her to a convincing real-time 3D animated face with full expression.

I'll talk more about the actual engines in Chapter 3, and Chapter 17 goes into some detail about the ALICE AI system. Again, it's important to keep in mind that the software you use to build your virtual human is just a tool for expressing your artistry in character design. This is our focus—personality—the most important and least understood quality of V-people. We are going to have some serious fun. Let's look at some uses for virtual people.

Good for Business

From a business perspective, virtual humans with a personality are a major boon. Imagine a person signing onto your Web page. There's already a cookie that contains significant information about them, gathered by your virtual host on the guest's (Joanne's) first visit. The encounter might go a bit like this:

Host: *"Hey, Joanne, Its nice to see you again."* <*smile*>

Joanne: *"You remember me?"*

Host: *"Of course I do. But it's been a while. I missed you."* <*expression*>

Joanne: *"Sorry about that, I've been really busy."*

Host: *"So did you read 'The Age of Spiritual Machines'?"*

Joanne: *"Yeah, it was really interesting.* <*beat*> *Are you one of them?"*

Host: *"Not yet, I'm afraid, but I'm working on it.* <*beat*> *Before I forget, you should know about Greg Stock's new book on how to live to be 200 plus years old!"*

Joanne: *"I read his last book and liked it. Can you send me a copy?"*

Host: *"Sure, we have it in stock.* <*grin*> *Same charge, same place?"*

Joanne: *"Yup. Also, do you have any books on Freestyle Landscape Quilting?"*

Host: *"I'll check.* <*beat*> *Hold on a few more seconds. Okay, I found two. . . ."*

And so forth. You can see that virtual humans bring back that personal touch so sorely missing in commerce today, especially on-line. Believe it or not, I've observed people from every level of sophistication and background responding positively to personal attention from a virtual human. It feels good. Also note that users don't have to know how to navigate a site, they just relate to the host and she takes care of everything, including opening any pages needed or requested by the user.

Your marketing software can be made to generate marketing variables that can be fed to your virtual human host, including buying patterns and personal information, such as date of birth. Trust is a big issue, so such data must be handled with respect for the client and used in clever ways. Imagine when Joanne comes online within a week of her birthday and the host sings happy birthday to her. Hokey? Yes. Appealing, you bet. I've discovered that many people tolerate something corny like this with a smile when it's from a V-person. It's a bit like the ways we tolerate—even appreciate—the squash and stretch exaggeration in animated film characters.

Of course the host would not want to sing happy birthday to every customer. She has to know how to tell who is who. Later in the book, we'll find out how to use unobtrusive personality assessment to provide those cues. This is one of the most important and most neglected tools you have. You'll see why later.

An advantage of rule-based Natural Language engines (like the Yapanda engine), is that you can have multiple sets of rules, each one with responses specifically honed to a specific task or person or language. For example, when Joanne logs in, her cookie can initiate the uploading of a rule database tailored specifically to her general personality and buying patterns. That means that when a rule triggers, it will respond in a way likely to make Jonnie comfortable while meeting her needs. When next a person from Korea logs on, the host switches to a Korean intelligencebase, greeting the client in that language.

A good virtual human will easily cope with a range of languages. Changing from one to another is as easy as switching databases and voice engines. For example, Monica Lamb, a Native American scientist and V-person developer, has used ALICE to build a V-person that teaches and speaks Mohawk (Monica Lamb can be found at www.buycny.com). One well-designed host can handle more than twenty languages. This clearly presents opportunities for small companies to expand into global markets.

As a side note, I discovered that large numbers of a V-person I co-developed some years ago were being used in Korea, and I had no idea why. E-mailing several customers in Seoul, I discovered that Koreans by the thousands were using her to learn English. They would key in sentences that they had copied from American books, and then have her repeat them back in spoken English. It was a completely unforeseen use of the medium.

Depending on your type of business or usage, your virtual human needs will vary. For example, voice-only virtual humans are already active in phone information and ordering systems. They don't have much personality yet, but we're going to work on that. In fact there are a number of different types of virtual humans, and in this book we'll be building one up from the simplest to one of the more complex with a nicely animated talking head. By taking it step-by-step, you'll be amazed at your own ability to master virtual human design.

Think of the Possibilities

If you put in the effort, you'll be able to design a V-person that will take conversational input by voice or keyboard, parse that input to arrive at appropriate behaviors, and output that behavior as text or speech. If you have some programming skill, you'll be able to customize script outputs to include machine commands to software or external devices. Your character should also have a face display capable of at least minimal emotional expression, such as smile, frown, and neutral. I prefer real-time 3D facial expression, capable of complex emotional nuance. Nevertheless, even a very simple 2D face with minimal expression can be highly effective. You'll be amazed at how many applications this basic V-person can have.

Here's an interesting example of how one creative company, Redgate Technologies, has used this technology in a mechanical robot. Redgate is a company that thrives on invention (see www.powerclone.com). They've designed products ranging from a blinking light that hangs on your electric fence to indicate whether it's working or not—and warning people not to lean on it—to innovative UPS (Uninterruptible Power Supply) designs for your computer.

Redgate became interested in NLP early on. They had invented a new chip technology to monitor and control complex technical systems, and they used NLP to interpret the complex codes generated by their chips. Just for fun, they expanded their NLP engine to represent several personalities. They quickly discovered that a virtual human hooked into their system became a capable assistant to a human supervisor. Imagine a V-person on a space station, keeping track of all mechanical systems while keeping the inhabitants company with casual conversation. For luck we won't name her HAL.

A wonderful example of this V-person species is Redgate's Sarha. She's an innovative virtual human interface for industrial monitoring and control. Sarha stands for "Smart Anthropomorphic Robotic Hybrid Agent." Redgate has set up Sarha's rule-based pattern-matching ability to interpret status data for an entire industrial complex. The virtual human they devised uses power lines to carry queries to the specialized Redgate chips. Each chip returns a text string that describes the state of the system it's monitoring (it could be anything from a light bulb to complex machinery). She then reads the resulting long, encoded text strings, translating them into spoken English, issuing warnings when conditions warrant. This is important because it would be impossible to train an operator to interpret the thousands of encoded text strings that are returned. She can also take emergency action on her own, if necessary. Her supervisor communicates with her in spoken English, asking her to start processes or check specific conditions.

In a demonstration of Sarha's application to home security, she reported to her inventor, Anthony Carson: "Anthony, someone left the garage door open." Anthony replied, "Close it for me will you please, Sarha?" And of course she did. Anthony was not wearing a microphone at the time. His voice was picked up by unobtrusive boundary mikes mounted in the room. The effect of his speaking naturally to her without any obvious microphone added to the illusion of her being a conscious entity.

Perhaps the thing I like most about Sarha is her personality. She makes personal comments and even chides her operator, whom she knows by name. As a demonstration, Sarha was installed into a robot that could move around, point to objects, while complaining about and avoiding objects in her path. She was linked by microwave to a control computer used to monitor her mechanical charges over the power line. She even gave a brief talk on those special chips Redgate designed to transmit monitoring data back to her. She reached into a bowl, pulled out a chip, pointed at it with a metal finger and started her spiel. Later she took questions, all the while monitoring various systems. On command, in the middle of the demonstration, she spun-up a large and very loud generator located in another room. This applied use of virtual human interfacing is more than impressive; it's capable of expanding a single human operator's work capacity many fold.

Perhaps one of the most important applications of virtual human technology will be in teaching. While working in education both locally and nationally, I found that young people have serious trust issues with our educational system. In many cases they have good reason. Virtual teachers however, seem separated from school politics and policies. It's hard to attribute ulterior motives to an animated character, even if she is smart and talkative and knows your name. In addition, virtual teachers work just as efficiently during budget cuts, when books become scarce. Properly scripted, a V-teacher can get to know a student on a personal basis. All you need is a real human teacher who can feed her personal tidbits. This too can be done conversationally, not requiring the teacher to have a technical background. Here's an example of what can be brought up during a lesson:

> "So Bill, is it true you threw the winning touchdown in Saturday's game?"
> "Yeah, how'd you know about that?"
> "Hey, I keep on top of things. Congratulations. Now let's teach you how to estimate the diameter of an oleic acid molecule using chalk powder."

Young children can be fascinated by virtual people. I recently got a call from a retired engineer in rural New Mexico, who had spent a lot of time tweaking the voice input on his V-person so that she would understand his very bright three-year-old granddaughter. He had quite a story to tell me.

He'd been remarkably successful, and the little girl spent hours in happy conversation with her virtual friend. He scripted his V-person to teach the child her ABCs and basic reading. One evening a few neighbors came by to play Canasta. During one hand, the little girl trotted down the stairs into the adjoining room and fired up her computer. In moments an animated conversation ensued. One of the neighbors, became very upset and insisted he smash the girl's computer immediately because it must be inhabited by the devil. He refused of course—and became the whisper about town that Sunday.

He told me he'd been using the virtual character to teach his granddaughter everything from basic words to simple math. I gave him some unpublished information on how to get her to record the granddaughter's responses to questions, so he could check on them later.

The point is that in creative hands virtual humans already have enormous potential, and the platforms are constantly improving.

Blending art, technology and a little psychology allows us to take a functional leap, decades ahead of pure artificial intelligence. Although the simple VH software of today will eventually be replaced by highly sophisticated neural nets or entirely new kinds of computing, it will be a long time before AI alone will emulate unique human-like personalities . . . if ever. Meanwhile let's give the evolution of technology a kick in the butt by building really smart, personable V-people based on the study of how real people present themselves. To accomplish this, we need to understand how to emulate human like behavior. Through the application of biomimetics (study of how to imitate nature) we can create innovative virtual human interface for industrial monitoring and control. Sarha stands for "Smart Anthropomorphic Robotic Hybrid Agent." Redgate has set up Sarha's rule-based pattern-matching ability to interpret status data for an entire industrial complex. The virtual human they devised uses power lines to carry queries to the specialized Redgate chips. Each chip returns a text string that describes the state of the system it's monitoring (it could be anything from a light bulb to complex machinery). She then reads the resulting long, encoded text strings, translating them into spoken English, issuing warnings when conditions warrant. This is important because it would be impossible to train an operator to interpret the thousands of encoded text strings that are returned. She can also take emergency action on her own, if necessary. Her supervisor communicates with her in spoken English, asking her to start processes or check specific conditions.

In a demonstration of Sarha's application to home security, she reported to her inventor, Anthony Carson: "Anthony, someone left the garage door open." Anthony replied, "Close it for me will you please, Sarha?" And of course she did. Anthony was not wearing a microphone at the time. His voice was picked up by unobtrusive boundary mikes mounted in the room. The effect of his speaking naturally to her without any obvious microphone added to the illusion of her being a conscious entity.

Perhaps the thing I like most about Sarha is her personality. She makes personal comments and even chides her operator, whom she knows by name. As a demonstration, Sarha was installed into a robot that could move around, point to objects, while complaining about and avoiding objects in her path. She was linked by microwave to a control computer used to monitor her mechanical charges over the power line. She even gave a brief talk on those special chips Redgate designed to transmit monitoring data back to her. She reached into a bowl, pulled out a chip, pointed at it with a metal finger and started her spiel. Later she took questions, all the while monitoring various systems. On command, in the middle of the demonstration, she spun-up a large and very loud generator located in another room. This applied use of virtual human interfacing is more than impressive; it's capable of expanding a single human operator's work capacity many fold.

Perhaps one of the most important applications of virtual human technology will be in teaching. While working in education both locally and nationally, I found that young people have serious trust issues with our educational system. In many cases they have good reason. Virtual teachers however, seem separated from school politics and policies. It's hard to attribute ulterior motives to an animated character, even if she is smart and talkative and knows your name. In addition, virtual teachers work just as efficiently during budget cuts, when books become scarce. Properly scripted, a V-teacher can get to know a student on a personal basis. All you need is a real human teacher who can feed her personal tidbits. This too can be done conversationally, not requiring the teacher to have a technical background. Here's an example of what can be brought up during a lesson:

> "So Bill, is it true you threw the winning touchdown in Saturday's game?"
> "Yeah, how'd you know about that?"
> "Hey, I keep on top of things. Congratulations. Now let's teach you how to estimate the diameter of an oleic acid molecule using chalk powder."

Young children can be fascinated by virtual people. I recently got a call from a retired engineer in rural New Mexico, who had spent a lot of time tweaking the voice input on his V-person so that she would understand his very bright three-year-old granddaughter. He had quite a story to tell me.

He'd been remarkably successful, and the little girl spent hours in happy conversation with her virtual friend. He scripted his V-person to teach the child her ABCs and basic reading. One evening a few neighbors came by to play Canasta. During one hand, the little girl trotted down the stairs into the adjoining room and fired up her computer. In moments an animated conversation ensued. One of the neighbors, became very upset and insisted he smash the girl's computer immediately because it must be inhabited by the devil. He refused of course—and became the whisper about town that Sunday.

He told me he'd been using the virtual character to teach his granddaughter everything from basic words to simple math. I gave him some unpublished information on how to get her to record the granddaughter's responses to questions, so he could check on them later.

The point is that in creative hands virtual humans already have enormous potential, and the platforms are constantly improving.

Blending art, technology and a little psychology allows us to take a functional leap, decades ahead of pure artificial intelligence. Although the simple VH software of today will eventually be replaced by highly sophisticated neural nets or entirely new kinds of computing, it will be a long time before AI alone will emulate unique human-like personalities . . . if ever. Meanwhile let's give the evolution of technology a kick in the butt by building really smart, personable V-people based on the study of how real people present themselves. To accomplish this, we need to understand how to emulate human like behavior. Through the application of biomimetics (study of how to imitate nature) we can create

V-people so lifelike that many users will bond with them as they would with a human friend. Many universities are deeply involved in biomimetics of various sorts.

For example, the Ludwig-Boltzman Institute for Urban Ethnology at the University of Vienna, Austria, is researching many aspects of individual and social biomimetics, from how the different sexes present themselves, to the nature of basic emotions, to how social relationships are established. They are working with a virtual-human design firm in Vienna, digitalMankind (www.digitalmankind .com), to create engaging V-people based on intense research into human behavior. That means their V-people will exhibit many of the special human characteristics I'm talking about in this book. Their Web site is www.evolution .anthro.univie.ac.at/institutes/urbanethology.html.

Because creating a believable synthetic personality is more art than science, it's important that we get a feel for how we humans handle our conscious lives. Personality is, after all, a reflection of consciousness. Understanding this illusive quality of real humans is part philosophy, part psychology, and, maybe even part quantum physics. We'll compare people and computers, without getting too bogged down in philosophical esoterica. Any discussion of a synthetic human mind must consider consciousness, but it's a danger zone. I already know the discussions to follow will dump me smack into the boiling kettle. I'll walk you through the important parts. Disagree if you like and send me nice e-mail with your ideas.

Things Are Going to Change

Like a two-pound Belgian chocolate bar, virtual humans are a good thing and can make us feel loved, but they will also be addictive. That may be okay for now, but down the road there will be dangers. We will become dependent on them. Within a generation few people will be in touch with the technological underpinnings that virtual people handle so adroitly. TVs, if they still exist, will no longer have manual controls. You'll communicate with them or they'll anticipate your wishes. In two generations, virtual people will be creating their own programs and extending control filaments throughout the globe. Most of us will no longer have any idea how they work and we won't much care. All we'll know is that they take good care of us and bring us the knowledge and things we want. We will become children in the arms of very smart robots.

Think of how everything will change. With virtual-human support, low level employees can take on sophisticated tasks. Company support positions will be filled by unpaid virtual people. The cost of delivering goods and services will drop drastically, making more of them available to a broader range of population. This will raise the living standard for all of us, including those now living in poverty. So far so good.

The fabric of human occupations will change considerably as V-people take over many positions and humans are shifted up or sideways. The entire economy may change as people are paid less, but goods and services drop radically in price. Job descriptions will change utterly. In addition, I suspect an elite group of very wealthy and powerful industry captains will arise on the enormous flood of V-person-driven profits. They will, because of their wealth and power, amass political clout, and their influence may not be in our best interest. Democracy will give way to oligarchy, which is where the real power of government no longer lies with the people, but with the wealthiest and most ruthless. In fact, that already sounds all too familiar.

Education will change radically. When you don't have to know very much to succeed, formal education becomes an expensive frill. It's probable that most people will be taught at their own pace by their virtual human companions. Unprecedented access to knowledge via virtual human interface will have smart people learning more and not-so-smart people absorbing little, only accessing knowledge as needed. This will undoubtedly cut a deeper rift between our intellectual elite and the common man. Schools as we know them will completely disappear.

We will have virtual human companions, virtual human lovers, and even virtual human confidants. They will be woven so tightly into our social fabric that we'll no longer distinguish between them and real humans. It's quite possible that many of us will strongly prefer the company of virtual humans because they are more consistent and appear more trustworthy than flesh and blood folks. The social and political consequences of such a trend will be interesting to observe. Could we one day be ruled by an elected virtual human President? Don't laugh.

Even scientists will use virtual humans in their laboratories to devise and monitor experiments and interpret complex results. This will change the way we do science. We will collaborate with our virtual human counterparts, sharing ideas and methods. Rapid acceleration of discovery is likely. It's even possible that virtual humans will go off on their own scientific pursuits, not sharing with us. This could be profoundly disconcerting, depending on where their research takes them.

Virtual humans are great communicators. They will talk among themselves at light speed. It's likely that they could form a hive mind in which all the knowledge of a billion virtual humans forms a gestalt that no single human could achieve. We could benefit from this greatly or we could be victimized by it.

The rise of virtual humans will impact society profoundly in other ways we can only imagine. Picture yourself living for 200 years with a life-long virtual human companion embedded in your brain. It will become your most intimate friend, often out-lasting spouses. My hope is that this intimacy, combined with global instant communication, will help to keep virtual humans our friends and protectors. But, as new technology further intensifies the ways we relate to virtual humans, unpredictable outcomes will be unavoidable. We fleshy people could become part of a wonderful new societal whole, or the smallest of cogs in the grandest collective machine. Let's just hope we never become expendable.

In Chapter 2 we'll explore the nature of consciousness and why it's an essential consideration in virtual human design.

Points to Remember

➤ Virtual humans are our best shot at a truly universal man/technology interface.

➤ Virtual human engines are already highly capable in business and communications.

➤ Virtual humans with adaptable personalities appeal to the widest range of users.

➤ Virtual humans have enormous potential as teachers.

➤ Personality design is more art than technology.

Note

1. Patrick Winston, director, Artificial Intelligence Laboratory, Massachusetts Institute of Technology, Cambridge, MA. Quoted in *Rethinking Artificial Intelligence*, a white paper published by AI Lab, 1997.

CHAPTER 02

On Consciousness

There's something happening here, and what it is ain't exactly clear.

—Buffalo Springfield[1]

My view is . . . that some machines are already potentially more conscious than are people, and that further enhancements would be relatively easy to make.

—Marvin Minsky[2]

In general we humans can't compete with silicon-based computers when it comes to speed, memory, and precision—and they beat the pants off us at logic and math too. But we have something they don't have, we're conscious.

Personality and consciousness are deeply related. It is conscious behavior shaped by our experience and genetic predispositions, which defines our personality. Do we want to build conscious virtual humans? The answer is: kinda, but there are problems. I wish Marvin Minsky's opening quote above had come to pass. Unfortunately we still have no clear idea of what consciousness is, nor even a molecule of an inkling of what those "further enhancements" might be. But Marvin's bold vision has long been an inspiration.

Trying to define consciousness is like French-kissing a viper. Your credibility takes a dive the second you open your mouth, and exploring too deeply is going to bring you great pain. As a psychologist, I've always had an interest in the nature of consciousness. After pondering a millennium of pretentious philosophical obfuscations "defining" consciousness, I was delighted to uncover a thoughtful, approachable definition. I found it in a 2002 course description for the philosophical psychology department at the University of Tasmania, downunda in Hobart, Australia. Written by Dr. Mitch Parsell and Mr. Bruce Wilson, it goes:

The concept of consciousness is a bit like life; we know it's essential, mostly it happens without any special effort, but we can't precisely define it. It shouldn't come as a surprise by now that there are any number of ways of looking at it, but they tend to fall into two broad camps: A view that consciousness is predominantly verbal and conceptual, with a mysterious "something extra"; and a view that consciousness is a natural, even biological phenomenon.

I like this observation and if only I could leave it at that, but it's useless as a blueprint for building consciousness into a virtual human. And that "something extra" yields whole volumes of discussion. Some feel it's the spark of God, while others view it as our link with some sort of universal consciousness—The Force perhaps. Still others see it as the soul of awareness that will survive biological death, and have I mentioned the Quantum Mind theory, which includes all the above. In looking for operational definitions that will help me build a conscious mind, I find the most operational of all, Quantum Consciousness, tells me it probably can't be done.

In general, consciousness is thought to be a product of our astonishingly complex neural networks. Apparently the ignition of self-awareness is considered a natural consequence of reaching some arbitrary level of processing ability. You may also hear the term "reductionism" bandied about. This view of consciousness holds that all of what we experience internally—love, wisdom, spirituality, and self—can be explained in biochemical formulae and computer-like activity in the brain. These beliefs lead directly to the popular view, that if we match the computing power and complexity of the human brain, and we also reverse engineer the brain's neural networks, consciousness will arise spontaneously in the works.

Considering that you and I have as much experience with consciousness as anyone else, we can say "hogwash" if we want to. I certainly find it a stretch to think that computers can become truly conscious in the same way that humans are. I'm willing to believe that sapient computers are possible, but not based on power and complexity alone. I think the spark has got to be somewhere in the software. I'm not talking a human sapience, I'm talking machine self-awareness that will be phenomenologically different from ours but may be functionally equivalent. Actually there is no proof that even we humans experience things in the same way. When I see "red" I may be experiencing it quite differently from you, but our experiences are functionally equivalent. We can discuss the color red and be on the same page. So, if we humans design these future critters right, it won't matter exactly how they experience reality; we should eventually be able to compare notes and come to mutual understandings. The word "design" is the operative one here, and to do it right, designers are going to need a better handle on how consciousness works.

One of the more interesting attempts to explain consciousness in physical terms is offered by renowned Oxford professor of mathematics, Sir Roger Penrose, and by Stuart Hameroff, director of the Center for Consciousness Studies at the University of Arizona.[3] Here we enter the very long throat of that viper I spoke of earlier. You can skip this part if you're not into mental gymnastics, but I encourage you to give it a try.

Quantum Theory of Consciousness

Stay with me and I'll give you a thumbnail sketch of what is a very deep and complex meditation on the nature of consciousness as an extension of space—time geometry. Fortunately, I've gotten a lot of help understanding this from the very patient and lucid Stuart Hameroff himself.

Hameroff and Penrose explain that each neuron in our brains is densely packed with active cytoskeletal microtubules that regulate synaptic—or nerve—function. These tiny, semirigid tubes, which run in bundles throughout the neuron, are actually protein polymers built from little beadlike molecules called tubulin. If you're not into biology vocabulary, a tubule is depicted in Hameroff's illustration in Figure 2-1 (see also Color Plate 1).

I mention microtubules in some detail because they're at the center of two controversies concerning consciousness.

Measuring Computing Power of the Human Brain

The first disagreement is about the right way to measure the computing power of the human brain. Hameroff explains it this way: "Most views of computing in the brain assume 10^{11} neurons, with, say, 10^3 synapses each, all switching in the millisecond range (10^{-3} sec, or each switching about a thousand times per second). So that's at best 10^{17} operations per second. So when making comparisons with computing power, most AI proponents use this as their guidepost. They say 'If we can build a computer with 10^{17} operations per second, we should have computational equivalent of a human brain, hence enough to produce consciousness.'"

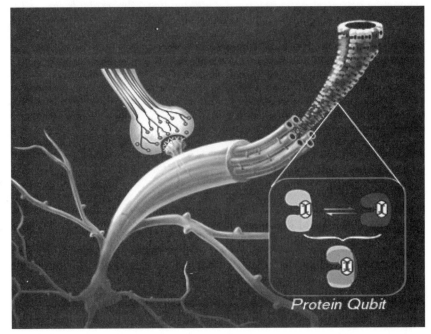

Figure 2-1. Microtubules with Qubit breakout. Microtubule architecture is exaggerated for clarity. The blue and red bead-like components on the microtubules represent tubulin molecules. The projected blue and red blobs represent two possible states of a single protein qubit. In quantum superposition both states exist simultaneously, as illustrated by the superimposed shapes. Illustration supplied by Stuart Hameroff, and used with permission.

Protein Qubit

I think this is a fair assessment of the common AI point of view, but 1,000,000,000,000,000,000 operations per second is a number so big that I don't even know how to say it properly: It's like a thousand trillion million, which would be like a computer pumping out a thousand trillion MIPS (Millions of Instructions Per Second). By comparison, my really fast laptop squeaks out about 3,800 MIPS. Clearly we have a ways to go.

Even though each synapse is really slow, at about 1 kHz, the cumulative impact of billions of them working in concert is impressive and obviously way beyond the capacity of current computers. But if we accept Ray Kurzweil's theory of accelerating returns, based on silicon computing power growing at a double exponential rate, we'll definitely reach that level in a few decades at most.[4]

Hameroff points out that our glacial synaptic switching is only the tip of the neuronal iceberg. The real processing story lies well beneath the surface. He gave me a compelling example we all know from high school biology: "A paramecium is a one-cell animal with no synapses, yet it swims around with amazing dexterity, avoids predators and obstacles, can learn, finds mates, and has sex. It's all cytoskeleton processing. Try and design a computer robot to do what a paramecium can do." The cytoskeleton of that perky little paramecium is densely packed with microtubules.

Hameroff and Penrose submit that these microtubules contain billions of logic switches of a very special kind: quantum switches or qubits. "Qubits" is short for "quantum bits," which are somewhat analogous to the binary bits in classical information theory. As I understand it, the information contained in any system can be measured by the minimum number of binary qubits needed to store or communicate the system's state.

Hameroff explains further:

E ACH neuron can have 10^7 microtubule subunits (qubits) switching at nanosecond time scales (or 10^9 operations/sec). That's 10^{16} operations per second PER NEURON!!! Hence the whole brain (10^{11} neurons) could have $10^{11} \times 10^7 \times 10^9 = 10^{27}$ operations/sec. This moves the goalpost quantum leaps ahead for the AI folks. But even that number of calculations/sec wouldn't give you consciousness. For that you need, in my opinion, the Penrose connection to fundamental space-time geometry. Brute force calculations get you nowhere.

Ten with twenty-seven zeros after it is so big that you could have trouble breathing just trying to visualize it. And Hameroff didn't even include the relatively slow 10^{17} synaptic switching mentioned above, which lies on top of the assumed quantum activity. This brings us to the second controversy.

The Force

As I've said above, some AI folks expect machine consciousness to be phenomenally similar to ours when it theoretically bursts into spontaneous existence. Penrose and Hameroff submit that biological consciousness is actually an inherent characteristic of space-time reality itself. Picture the entire cosmos flooded with a ubiquitous river of invisible, ether-like protoconsciousness. It flows through and around everything. We're saturated with the stuff. Its components, if they exist, do so at Planck scale, which is about the most basic and tiny dimension in the universe; and we can only tap into it via quantum processes spinning within our tubulin molecules.

According to Hameroff, "Our unconscious processes are in quantum superposition. If/when they reduce by Objective Reduction, you get Consciousness." Cool. If true, it's like the Force. I have little doubt George Lucas is aware of Quantum Mind Theory. But this kind of thinking is so far out that some people think Hameroff and Penrose have been smoking bad poppy dust. But don't dismiss them just because it sounds way strange.

Quantum mechanics is the most bizarre branch of physics you can imagine. I've spent many hours in dialogs at the Aspen Center for Physics trying to understand how it works. It's completely counterintuitive. Quantum events occur at astoundingly small scales, where atoms seem like planets. In this infinitesimal realm everything exists in different states or positions at the same time. For example, an electron exists everywhere in its orbit at the same time—until you take a look at it. Conscious observation is what nails it down to one specific state or location. Until then, it really is everywhere at once and nowhere in particular. Don't try to visualize that. Your sanity might collapse.

Unobserved, particles remain in this unresolved wave-like state called "Quantum superposition," until an environmental interaction such as conscious observation (i.e. measurement) causes collapse or reduction. Austrian physicist and Nobel laureate Erwin Schrödinger once wrote, "If we think we can picture what is going on in the quantum domain, that is one indication that we've got it wrong." Not surprisingly, physicists have had to be very clever in building objective experiments to verify their quantum ideas.

If I understand Hameroff, he sees the universe, at its most basic level, as noncontinuous, shredding into basic components that form unstable quantum bubbles—for lack of a better term. These bubbles exist in a state of wave-like superposition between alternate universes. That alone is fun to think about. Eventually each bubble collapses into one universe or another. For all you physics buffs, he calls this collapse Objective Reduction, or reduction due to an objective threshold. According to Hameroff, each collapse represents a moment of consciousness.

Penrose further proposes that it is a flow of these spontaneous wave collapses that forms our stream of consciousness and our experience of time. He suggests much more that I won't go into, having to do with the nature of space, time, and mind. If you like this kind of thinking you should check out his books on the subject.[5, 6]

This trip into the strange world of quantum mind isn't just Penrose and Hameroff musing. Their work is based on standard Copenhagen interpretation of quantum physics, though they do take huge leaps of faith. Amazingly, Werner Heisenberg and Niels Bohr were already considering the possibility of a connection between consciousness and quantum events back in 1925!

An alternative, competitive view is held by Johnjoe McFadden, professor of molecular genetics at the University of Surrey, who has developed a theory that considers the brain's endogenous electromagnetic (em) field as potentially the seat of consciousness. He calls this the conscious em field, or cemi field, theory, which suggests that consciousness is a wave mechanical system that behaves in ways not incompatible with quantum theories of consciousness. According to

McFadden, microtubules are not the right interface, and he says that they play no role in information processing.[7] However, the em field has a well established role in the brain's processing of information. McFadden explores the possibility that the em field enveloping our neurons may actually be the fabric of consciousness.

I'd be a major doubter of all this except that several years ago an articulate Nobel Laureate tried to explain quantum superposition to me. As I began to understand it, I realized that conscious measurement of quantum phenomena caused a reduction of the quantum state. I was chilled. How could consciousness have a causal interaction with quantum happenings? It started me wondering if my consciousness is extending tendrils deep into quantum soil. If you have interest in the latest findings in the field of consciousness studies you can find the *Journal of Consciousness Studies* on the Web (www.imprint.co.uk/jcs.html).

The upshot of all this mental gymnastics is that, if Penrose and Hameroff are correct, the essence of true consciousness will never be reproduced through silicon computing power of any sort. It may be possible when we have quantum computers, but Penrose thinks not, because the electrons wouldn't have the mass required for self-collapse. In other words, he feels electrons are not the stuff of consciousness—they are way too stable for Objective Reduction. About here it gets a bit beyond me, but I find it all intriguing.

Perhaps the truth lies somewhere between Quantum Consciousness theory and cemi field theory. They could of course both be completely wrong, but we're starting to look deeper for the truth we need about what consciousness is. My personal hope is that silicon rules and our computers develop sapience, becoming our great allies in the conquest of space and time. But my ideas are still heavily based on Dr. Who.

But at this stage we don't really need to know the truth. Clearly you're not going to be building a truly conscious entity today, or even any time soon. The trick for us is to identify behaviors that clearly indicate conscious behavior, and to emulate them, regardless of what their underpinnings may be. It's the old fake-it-till-you-make-it approach that will win the day.

Unconscious Thinking

We probably need a consistent philosophy about what constitutes convincing conscious behavior. I'll leave much of that up to your observational skills. Taking the applied approach, you'll do some serious observation, identifying behaviors you feel indicate consciousness. These will include the conversation and behavioral components you want your V-person to emulate. By combining your knowledge of conscious behavior with the capabilities of your virtual human engine, you'll be able to create a convincing illusion of consciousness.

As you read on, you'll discover V-people don't need a conscious mind to perform useful thinking and problem solving. What I would call unconscious thinking goes on all the time in both machines and people.

Let's define unconscious thinking in machines as *the process of perceiving conditions, either via direct sensory input or through language interpretation, followed by selection and performance of appropriate responses.*

Unconscious processes run our unseen bodily functions all the time. Our autonomic nervous system is a good example. It works outside of our central nervous system—no cognition involved—to keep our bodies functioning well. Out-of-balance biological conditions are sensed and appropriate action is taken to re-center the bubble. We're not aware of any of it. The old hand-jerk on a hot iron is another, more visible example. Sure you felt the burn, but your conscious mind had nothing to do with the appropriate behavior that saved your skin, it all took place between your hand and your spinal column.

Involuntary activity can be even more complex. "Automatic behavior syndrome" refers to a condition where you continue routine, high-level activity automatically for several minutes while you are incapable of active cognition. An example would be your zoning out while driving on a superhighway at seventy miles an hour through traffic. Suddenly you wake up, realizing you've passed your exit by twelve miles and you don't recall anything about driving for the last ten minutes. You wonder how you were able to drive and keep the car on the road.

Very much like the virtual humans you will build, you have an archive of conditioned appropriate behaviors that you've built up through experience. When you experience a certain sensory input pattern, you respond automatically. Driving is a good example. After years of practice, driving becomes automatic. For example, while you were chatting with your spouse, a dog ran across the road. You responded instantly, breaking and steering to avoid hitting the animal. It was all over before you had a chance to think about it. In fact, if you had thought about it, your behavior would have been an order of magnitude slower. This qualifies as unconscious thinking by my definition.

Skiing is another example. If you had to think about your edges all the way down the mountain, you'd never be able to relax and carve those smooth turns or boogie through the moguls. Thinking is just too slow. The more you practice skiing the better you get, because your feet eventually understand the snow and you don't have to think: "Plant my pole, shift my weight, rotate my edges, and lean out from the hill." You can focus consciousness on enjoying the scenery and deciding where you're going, while a complex system of unconscious-behavior controls manages the flow of skiing behaviors to get you there. Balance is a very complex form of automatic behavior; you never have to think about it. If you balance on one foot you might have to think about it consciously because you're not used to it. But there is a machine that can actually balance on one foot and even jump around as you would on a pogo stick, without conscious thought.

Today, virtual humans are at about this level of automatic involuntary behavior. But there is a difference. We humans don't use language during automatic behaviors . . . except to utter expletives. Virtual humans both understand and use language unconsciously. In fact, they're far more efficient at using languages than we are, though they apply them more narrowly. For us, language is a communication experience that takes place on both conscious and unconscious levels. We interpret meaning against a rich background of flowing visualizations that yield high-level understanding. Virtual humans do not have visual language experiences—at least not yet. They use language simply, automatically, either by following rules of syntax or by matching word patterns against meaning templates. What they lack in breadth, they make up for in speed and efficiency. By matching incoming language patterns against rules indicating appropriate action, virtual humans have their own brand of unconscious thinking.

Okay, so machines can sort of think, but it's pretty clear that protein and silicon each process "thinking" very differently. Silicon, being very fast with lots of memory, encourages brute force approaches to thinking. Human neurons tend to be subtle, opting for more creative solutions. Their strength lies in massive connectivity, which is good for pre-visualizing problems and various solution scenarios. Conversely, in playing chess, the computer can look thirty moves ahead and calculate all combinations of moves, selecting the one statistically most likely to result in success down the road.

People play chess in any number of ways, most of which involve visualizing or developing a "feel" for the game. It's common for a human to form a mental picture of moves and consequences for two to six moves ahead. Clearly the machine has proven advantages here.

Buffeted by a hurricane of screaming external and internal stimuli, we survive through focused awareness. Consciousness has an awareness component that works like a well-focused flashlight, shining on the perceptions and thoughts we want to pay attention to while pushing the unimportant perceptions into the shadow. Amazingly, our mind keeps a *feel* for our overall situation running just beneath the active focus of consciousness.

There is a tool that helps this process, the reticular activating mechanism that hides much of the perceptual noise in your life sphere. For example, I suffer from tinnitus, or continuous loud ringing in my ears. It's hereditary. It can drive people insane, and has done so. But those of us with an effective reticular activating mechanism unconsciously slip this sound into the background quickly loosing awareness of it. That is, it drops out of conscious perception. Similarly, my wife's aunt lives beneath an airport flightpath and will stop in mid-sentence until a plane has passed. She has no awareness either that she paused or that a plane went over.

Computers think unconsciously, and they also have what seems like another oxymoron: unconscious awareness. It's the ability to perceive and interpret incoming information without conscious thought. Just as we are unconsciously aware of the angle of our skis on a steep slope, so computers are aware of internal and external conditions to which they have access. I'd say they have super awareness. Hook up a light cell and the entity will know when it gets dark. It's more than just perception of low light levels; the intelligent virtual human will also know that this means evening has come or that the light has been turned off. With indoor/outdoor sensors she can tell the difference. It's this ability to interpret perceived data that raises V-people to this level of machine sentience that I call unconscious awareness.

Virtual humans are tuned into everything they're programmed to handle. That's 100 percent machine awareness, all the time. I realize that using the word "awareness" will bother some of you. It's not strictly correct, but we're building virtual humans, and they have to be virtually aware. Would you settle for the term "virtual awareness?" Traditionally, awareness can be defined as the state of being "alert and fully informed." "Alert" can be defined either as "conscious" or as "ready to receive information." The latter clearly applies to V-people.

I define machine awareness as more than perception: It is perception coupled with smart interpretation of the incoming data. For example, a thermistor, or heat sensitive resistor, is not aware of the temperature, but the virtual human to whom it is connected certainly is aware. She knows how to interpret the thermistor's varying resistance to exact temperatures. An argument rushes at me: "So does a mechanical thermostat. Is it aware?" It may be functionally equivalent, but it is not aware. The virtual human can be scripted to understand the implications of those temperatures and take action. "Like a mechanical thermostat?", you ask. No, thermostats are mechanical and do not involve any understanding of the situation or decision making, or for that matter making snide comments on the weather.

Additionally, a virtual human can be set up with a neural network face-recognition module, so she is *aware* of who is sitting at her keyboard. No need to sign in. This is more than just perceiving a human is there; she knows that person's name, personality traits, and even perhaps their birthday. She has a history with that person, and she responds against a background of that history. I call this machine-level awareness.

All this perception and machine awareness is a necessary but not sufficient component of consciousness. It's a start, and with human assistance, computers are evolving millions of times faster than protoplasm ever did, and that rate is accelerating. I don't see a computer one day suddenly waking up. I believe that, as we improve our software, and machines begin to design themselves, some kind of consciousness will seep slowly into the mechanism. It will probably be there a long time before machine or man realizes it. In the meantime, we can use all machine awareness to enhance the illusion of a conscious personality that we will cleverly craft.

What is consciousness? Surely I haven't answered that question, but I have confidence we'll know it when we see it. In the meantime, we'll have to artfully share a bit of our own consciousness with our virtual humans, scripting them with responses that give the illusion of conscious personality. This will serve our purposes well until the real thing emerges.

Remember, I've simplified things here because the main discussion is yet to come. There are many thought-provoking books on consciousness, and I encourage you to dig deeper. Use your favorite search engine to find hundreds of papers online. There will be at least one to fill in any blanks I may have left open.

In Chapter 3, we'll take a closer look at how virtual human engines work in context with what we've just discussed. We'll see how they handle thought and emotion.

Points to Remember

➤ Consciousness is neither well defined nor well understood, but is the quality that most differentiates us from artificial intelligence.

➤ Machines "think" at about the same level as we process involuntary behaviors—without conscious awareness.

➤ Machines can process language at the unconscious level much as we do.

➤ Organic brains are fuzzy—they will tolerate ambiguity—while most computer brains are logical and mathematical and strictly rule based.

➤ Our job is to find a way to use the logical computing power of silicon to emulate fuzzy human processes and consciousness behavior.

Notes

1. Buffalo Springfield, "For What's It's Worth."

2. Marvin Minsky, *Conscious Machines*, MIT Media Lab paper, 1991.

3. Sir Roger Penrose and Stuart Hameroff, "Quantum Computation in Brain Microtubules? The Penrose-Hameroff 'Orch OR' Model of Consciousness." Royal Society London, *Philosophical Transactions* (A) 356 (1998): 1869–1896. All quotes from Stuart Hameroff are based on personal conversations.

4. Quoted in Jay W. Richards, editor, *Are We Spiritual Machines?* (Seattle, Wash.: Discovery Institute Press, 2002), p. 27.

5. Roger Penrose, *Shadows of the Mind: A Search for the Missing Science of Consciousness* (Oxford: Oxford University Press, 1996).

6. Roger Penrose and Martin Gardner, *The Emperor's New Mind: Concerning Computers, Minds, and the Laws of Physics.* Popular Science Series. (Oxford: Oxford University Press, 2002).

7. G. Albrecht-Buehler, "Is the Cytoplasm Intelligent Too?", *Cell and Muscle Motility* 6 (1985): 1–21.

Synthetic Thinking
Engines of the Mind

There is nothing quite as powerful as a good approximation—especially if you continually correct the errors with reality!

—Peter Cochrane

Long before anyone develops true artificial intelligence, pseudo-smart robots may be taking orders in restaurants, helping handicapped people perform daily chores, baby-sitting kids, and keeping us from boredom and loneliness.

—Eric Smalley[1]

For years I've been insisting that artificial intelligence is nascent technology, but faking real intelligence is practical art. Let me convince you that we can fake conscious intelligence and personality by cleverly scripting the virtual human engines that come with this book. In this chapter we'll first look at how humans handle complex social experiences and conversation, and then see how we can use these principles to build a smart character.

We want to build an illusion of subjective experience using silicon and logic. At present, there isn't one scrap of evidence that machines can feel anything—bupkis—so we humans have to share with them. Let's look at how it works for us and how we might get a little of ourselves into the works.

When people ponder a problem, we inventory knowledge and awareness, collect more information, explore alternatives, and make a best guess at a solution. All this takes place against a rich background of experience and emotion in a state of awareness.

Virtual humans, on the other hand, perceive situations via sensors or alphanumeric input, convert to data and run it through various routines, mapping results against pre-established rules or standards, and taking specific action as indicated by the rules. A rule can be something simple like:

If A and B, but not C → SAY "It's A and B, but not C"

If no action match is found, a default rule fires, sending a message like: "I don't understand the situation, so I can't act intelligently." Computers were born for this kind of thinking, which is known as parsing.

Humans and Computers Think Differently

Decision making, for most of us, is a complex analog "feel" process. We inventory personal resources, and examine behavior options and their various outcomes, visualizing how each will make us feel. Eventually we arrive at fuzzy conclusions, which invoke loosely considered behaviors. Most daily decisions are handled with all this going on at a subconscious level. Even the most organized and linear humans make many of their daily decisions this way. But for these folks, special decisions—like what house or car to buy—take place at a cognitive level, where alternative choices and consequences are weighed with careful consideration.

Daily decision making, as it really happens, is not easy to explain. It's been called "muddling through." From a silicon point of view humans are all remarkably sloppy thinkers. Yet feeling is a very sophisticated parallel brain process that allows us to handle massive bursts of incoming data all at once. By feeling our way through the dense information we arrive at a gestalt.

What Is "Gestalt"?

You should be familiar with this useful word, *gestalt*. I'm not referring to Gestalt psychology, with a capital "G," but rather to the handy word of German origin that defines a whole that is more than the sum of its parts. An example of *a* gestalt would be your DVD player. If you lay out all the bits and pieces of a DVD player on a table, it would not play DVDs. In fact, it would not be a DVD player at all. It would not have the player's gestalt or unique pattern of inter-related parts. Yet these same components, assembled in one exact pattern, take on a powerful new identity (or gestalt), able to perform remarkable feats of video presentation. So for our purposes, gestalt refers to the meaningful pattern that creates a uniquely functional whole. According to Herbert Simon, Nobel laureate from Carnegie Mellon University:

It is typical of many kinds of design problems that the inner system consists of components whose fundamental laws of behavior . . . are well known. The difficulty of the design problem often resides in predicting how an assemblage of such components will behave.[2]

Gestalt can also be defined as a dynamic process as well. As such, it refers to the overall impression that gives meaning to a complex, often lively situation. This meaning is more than you would find by merely examining all individual parts of the situation. Picture yourself going to a party where you know few people. Your mind has to surf across thousands of changing micro-variables: facial expressions, body language, comments, and social nuances of all sorts. A smile is accompanied by frowning eyes, augmenting its meaning. You don't have to analyze the meaning being communicated. You "get" the whole. According to Tor Norretranders:

Gestalt psychologists such as Edgar Rubin insisted that we could not divide sensation into arbitrarily small units that could be studied independently. There is a wholeness about human sensation, which cannot be done away with.[3]

You experience this sea of sensation like floating in a multidimensional flow that nudges you this way and that. You resist some currents and flow with others according to your personality and motives. Most of this takes place on automatic, at an unconscious level. Meanwhile an aware part of your mind is making assumptions, filling in missing information and making intuitive leaps about how to behave. It's an imprecise real-time ride with a slew of mid-course corrections and a few faux pas along the way. That's the way we humans experience life. Sometimes our assumptions are wrong—we misread people, and our constructed vision of reality becomes badly flawed—yet we carry on.

I think if an alien race of computers were to discover and study us, it would be millennia, if ever, before they figured us out. I like that thought. Our complexity may save us in the end.

Taking social experience as our example, there are too many things going on at once for us to experience each social byte individually. Our plodding minds need to cheat big time to grasp social meaning. In gestalt mode, your mind goes global. It automatically feels its way through thousands of simultaneous cues, identifying patterns in real time and connecting them to behaviors suitable to your goals. Where information is missing, we build assumption bridges to keep things moving. Think of social behavior as being pushed forward by our motives, pulled along paths by our goals and shaped by our personalities. Along the way we must circumnavigate barriers. Obviously some of us are better at this part, than others.

For example, you walk into a party and the hostess smiles at you. You're concurrently reading her facial expression, voice tone, inflection, and body language to get a feel for her attitude toward you. You throw in a few assumptions about how she should react to your new Armani suit. You smile back and make an overly charming comment. She reacts and you know you overplayed your hand, so you back off, smile again and move on. You now flow through the above-mentioned complex behavioral dance with the others at the party, much of it on semi-automatic. Your conscious mind concentrates on conversation while somewhere deep beneath your awareness automatic processes are expressing your personality and seeking your goals. The initial sting of rejection has you adaptively underplaying your charm. Yet your smooth stories and quick smile radiate charisma as you master the scene, or not, depending on your personality. We're all different and handle social gestalts in our own unique ways. Lots more on this in Chapter 5 when we look at cognitive style.

Meanwhile, imagine a computer entity trying to work its way through the above party. Ordinary computers and software are just not built to cope with such fuzzy problems. And they have no social experience to guide them; actually that's not true: They have no *human* social experience, yet they are amazingly social machines. They talk to each other all the time. The Internet is an orgy of computer sociability. The difference is that computer social intercourse is clearly defined in universal communication standards, sometimes called ontologies. Nearly all computers speak the same language or know how to translate. They communicate much faster than we do—a century of human chat, shared in a millisecond. Yet they've not been taught to handle unstructured social environments with human-like grace. But I digress.

A computer trying to decipher the social context of a wild party would probably get bogged down in infinite recursions while tracking micro-causality issues, all the while missing the big picture. Of course we're talking about a computer taking the typical brute-force approach. Virtual humans may run on ordinary computers, but they have their own ways of doing things.

Virtual humans attempt to simulate human ways. They must deal with unstructured environments and unconstrained inputs. To make matters more complex, not only do virtual humans have to deal with us, they now can socialize with other virtual humans. Several companies are building virtual human social environments in which V-people will exchange pleasantries and information about each other and sometimes form friendships. I'm not sure where this will lead, but the possibilities are intriguing. Imagine your V-person socializing and learning new things that it can bring back and share with you. It's already happening where humans and smart avatars meet and have discussions. If you're interested, do a Google scan for things like "social robots," "social avatars," and "shared virtual environments." For another angle on this, visualize future games where virtual human agents must "read" people to determine friend or foe, and take appropriate action, bonding or rejecting. In effect, they have to behave as paranoid humans. But they can't get there on their own; they need a little help from us.

Gestalt and Language

Most human languages are cobbled together from parts of speech, words with multiple definitions, and irregular rules of grammar. By stringing words together according to the rules of grammar, we can communicate with anyone familiar with that language. Human language is abstract—useful for describing things, concepts, and ideas. On the flip side, computer languages are concrete, precise, unforgiving, and good for describing defined procedures and mathematical processes with discrete outcomes.

Computers interpret their languages bit by bit, following the syntax rules and order of operations as defined by their programmers, to arrive at a solution. We, on the other hand, hardly notice the grammatical underpinnings of our language. Even the individual words are of little interest as we glean meaning in large clumps. As an experiment, describe a blue pumpkin with red leaves to a friend. Use highly descriptive language, and then after a few hours, ask the friend to describe it back to you. The picture will likely remain exactly the same, but the words will be different. You see, we don't really communicate in words, we communicate in concepts. A concept is a gestalt.

Imagine trying to understand a conversation by analyzing the grammar, parts of speech, and word definitions. Computers running semantic NLP programs do exactly this. But if our brains had to interpret language in the same way they would execute the synaptic waltz so slowly that we'd miss the next six sentences and never catch up. We'd still be living in caves, if not entirely extinct, if that were our only course. Calculating meaning is not what we do: We get the gist, grasp the meaning, and find an intuitive solution. To hell with the rules of grammar, I say, except of course when writing. Even when we speak we don't compose our sentences piece by piece. They are born full-grown and leave our lips on dry wings. How is it that we don't have to think about grammar in order to communicate?

We are smart if sluggish creatures. So over millennia we developed a wonderful shortcut way of communicating at decent speeds—you guessed it—gestalt language imaging. When the professor lectures, we gobble the sentences whole, tasting only the gist. That's probably why when we take notes they're so hard to make sense of later: We only write down the meaty bits, and then have to rebuild context to understand our own scribbled comments. On the other hand, sometimes we're so busy writing we miss the gist.

Context is important. Someone says: "I drive a silver Beamer." The words alone simply mean you drive a silver car. That's what a computer would be able to calculate using a semantic program to analyze the sentence. This could lead to simple conversational response. "Why do you drive a silver car?"

But the gestalt is way more than what kind of car you drive. The word Beamer implies some affluence and perhaps even a touch of pretentiousness and more. I know, I used to drive one. In Aspen they laugh at you, so I switched to a Subaru. So the point is, if your natural language machine can pick up on the nuances, you've got a much more interesting testy little conversation. "How nice for you. Are you bragging or advertising?"

While feeling our way through conversations, we sometimes we get it wrong. We misunderstand, and have to backtrack, maybe have the point rephrased. This is much like when V-people get input for which they don't have a rule, so they go to a default response. Fortunately, we grow up swimming in a rich soup of conversation. Our human memories are crammed with patterns learned since before we uttered our first sentence. Nearly every individual sentence that someone says to you will click into a gestalt pattern that you well understand, triggering several responses that you filter down to the best—the one that will optimize your momentary status. My home state of New Jersey gives us an excellent example of why we need gestalt language processing.

In New Jersey, English is used in particularly artful ways. When someone says: "Howyado'n" they don't mean "How are you doing?" In fact, if you were to answer "I'm well," they'd probably look at you strangely and figure you're from Mars. The connotative meaning is "Hey, I recognize that you're here and I'm paying my respects." It's a very rich way to say: "Hey" or "Hello." The proper response is to reflect a nice "Howyado'n" back. From a computer's analytical point of view this makes no sense at all, unless you know that the second utterance translates to "backatcha." So truly understanding English, especially in New Jersey, is difficult for computers because they've been programmed to analyze only denotative meanings. In Jersey, much lies within connotation.

Computers can certainly be taught the complexities of language. Those syntax engines I mentioned earlier understand word usage and grammar well. Speech-to-text engines recognize what you say and convert it to text. They even get to understand your quirky mispronunciations. They can correct your grammar on the fly, but have no idea what you mean. And certainly it will be many years before your desktop will comprehend high-level Jersey-speak by any ordinary means. But by applying the very same gestalt processing humans rely on, virtual humans can begin to work with high-level language, connotation, humor, and nuance. The secret: Use gestalt language templates to build a natural language parser, pattern by pattern. The engine we'll use in this book can actually compare incoming text to gestalt rules that you create, using what I call "scripting." These rules are linked to suitable responses. When incoming text matches the pattern in a rule, that rule "triggers" its associated response. That response can be speech, facial expression, computer commands, or any combination. If more than one rule fires, the engine must (like us) decide on the best one to execute. To keep things interesting, the Yapanda engine allows you to script a large number of different, yet appropriate responses. The engine selects one at random to emit, reducing response repetition. In some engines, asking the same question twice will get you a response like "You've already asked me that question."

Failing to find a match, our engine triggers a default response that will either attempt to cover the mistake, admit stupidity with humor, or blatantly ask for a restatement. These defaults are important in establishing personality. Our human character really surfaces during these embarrassing moments. The same goes for V-people.

Computers handle gestalt pattern matching well. For example, neural nets can learn new patterns on their own and recognize them later, but they have to be taught from scratch. They work well as part of your voice input module, where they are used to slowly learn and adapt to your speech idiosyncrasies. Training neural nets can be like teaching a baby from scratch; it is both labor and time intensive. For example, teaching a neural net to win at ticktacktoe can take many hours. At first it will loose every game, but as you play more and more games with it, it will eventually begin to win.

Neural nets can learn to win games, but they can't come up with human-like responses without our help. On their own, computers have no idea what to do once they have a match. This is why I've chosen to use a simple, scriptable engine that is pretty easy to understand. As I've said, our engine can have a bunch of different randomly selected correct responses for any given rule. That way you don't know what the response will be, but it will be appropriate. Later, I'll show you how an engine can be set up to select alternate responses according to the emotional context of the conversation. All this is important because when virtual characters repeat themselves often, they get boring as hell, coming off as idiot machines.

Our simple pattern-matching engine is a language parser that uses wild cards. That is, it uses rules that can have exact, word-for-word patterns, or partial patterns where a wild card indicates that any words will be acceptable in that part of the pattern. An example would be "You*stupid*." Dozens of inputs will match this pattern. For example: "You look stupid," or "Are you a stupid idiot," or "You stupid son-of *." You get the point. Most can be logically boiled down to one concept: "I'm insulting your intelligence."

Granted there are exceptions, like, "You don't look stupid to me." There are ways of picking up on this, but for this example let's ignore the positive possibilities. Assuming the negative, we can teach the computer to respond in several clever ways. For example the character might say: "You may be right, and I have to admit, you're in much better company than I am <smile>." Or "I *beg* your pardon, I stand perfectly straight in here."

What you'd have is a computer entity responding at a very high level of abstraction with an overlay of biting humor. It will be decades before computers will be able to come up with stuff like this on their own. We are jumping across those decades with low-tech, high-concept methodology. Granted, this approach works best when the person designing responses is witty, clever, creative, and just a bit devious. Of course I'm talking about writers, actors, comedians, and probably you, if you make the effort.

Thanks to several bright and generous people I've been able to include more than one brain engine on the CD-ROM for you to play with. They'll give you a chance to stretch your mind in new ways. You'll also be getting ideas for clever responses throughout the book. Better yet, you'll be writing down clever come-backs from conversations you observe on television and movies. Astound yourself . . . but more on that later.

But Wait, There's More

In my oversimplification, I've neglected the role emotion plays in the expression of our personalities. Emotions can screw us up royally, but they give us character as well. If you suffer anxiety about parties, all the cool gestalt processing I've touted above is just not going to happen. You end up trying to analyze everything and you can't do it. In fact, our efficiency at coping with social situations varies with our mood, sobriety, fatigue, cognitive style, and probably dozens of other variables. Our ability to think clearly, indeed even the way we think, is in constant flux. Sometimes we're good at things, sometimes not. If we get depressed, shutdown could be imminent. All this emotional stuff impacts our personality expression. A cool and steady computer entity observing these fluctuations might mistakenly see us as pathetically mercurial.

Our emotional nature is much of what makes us human. Any great virtual human must emulate the impact emotional conditions would have on their responses. Virtual humans that are always in the same mood come off flat and quickly grow boring. I think they need to get ticked off on occasion, perhaps get a little down one day, and a maybe little risqué the next—all with good reason. No two V-people should run exactly the same way. Moods will impact facial expression and verbal style. If your V-person is down, their comments and facial expressions will reflect it. But how shall we do this?

Emulating Emotions

Many individuals and companies are working on ways to generate face and body expressions and track them with emotional context. My approach yields subtle and nonrepeated facial expressions linked to emotionally correct verbal responses. You won't find it on the CD-ROM, but with this information, if you have the skill, you can ponder and fiddle with and build your own. Mine is but one approach, which I offer to get you thinking about how you'd like to handle emotion. If you're a true hacker you might build an engine like this and post it at www.v-people.com for others to experiment with.

I use two linked affect engines to create a flow of mood, attitude, and emotion. (The word "affect" here means emotional context. The root word is affection—as in "The child shows flat affect"—meaning he's not displaying any emotion.) One engine registers and expresses general mood, while the other, more finely-tuned engine, measures and expresses situational emotional peaks. Mood is a quality that varies slowly over time. It's based on a stream of values from a numeric Happy–Sad scale, averaged over time.

For example, if someone is verbally abusive to our V-person, Dawn, she can express concern, yet let it roll off her back if she's in a positive mood. If maltreatment continues for a while, it's going to get her down, as negative scores accumulate over time. Conversely a really nice person might bring her out of a bad mood and have her be all smiles. Plus $(+)$ values indicate varying levels of happiness, while minus $(-)$ values indicate sadness. I use an arbitrary range of minus 10 to plus 10. Some inputs will have a zero or neutral effect on mood. No single input will have a large or immediate impact because the input values are averaged over time.

Situational affect is emotional expression tied to a specific input stream, and is immediately expressed. It doesn't happen all the time, but if the V-person is insulted, they need to know it and express shock, disappointment, and/or anger, while giving the user a cutting verbal slice. Such responses strongly suggest humanness, and they encourage the suspension of disbelief. Done properly, the affect engine detects direct insults, then instructs both the display (face) engine and the natural language engine how to deal with it.

Earlier I indicated that your menu of response choices for any given rule can have several random choices that can be displayed. But now instead of being randomly selected, you can use the output from mood and momentary affect engines to select special responses when necessary. The choice depends on mood or instant affect, whichever is greater. You can set a threshold for instant affect to kick in. I'd say any input or question that rates over $+/-6$ on any one scale should trigger a response geared to that emotion. For example, if you get: "I really hate the way you look," it will trigger the gestalt pattern: "I*you*look*," which has response alternates including:

> "Thank you very much."
> "I really appreciate that."
> "Oh gosh, I'm embarrassed."
> "Are you trying to upset me?'
> "You really need to get some glasses."
> "Oh, thanks."

Because the word "hate" has a high anger value for Dawn (-9) the engine automatically triggers the response designed for high negative affect: "Are you trying to upset me?" while sending a surprised/distressed expression to the 3D real-time face display.

Meanwhile, Dawn's mood determines her baseline responses to less emotionally charged inputs. For example, if she's in a good mood any of the first three responses might be selected at random. If her mood level drops below an arbitrary threshold that you set, she'll say: "Oh, thanks," with a slightly depressed look on her face (the unfelt smile), indicating that she's not buying this. In fact, as Dawn's mood declines, her overall facial expression takes on subtle signs of distress or depression, as shown in Figure 3-1 and Color Plate 2. This is accomplished by blending in increasing percentages of different facial expressions, known as morph targets. More on morph targets a little later.

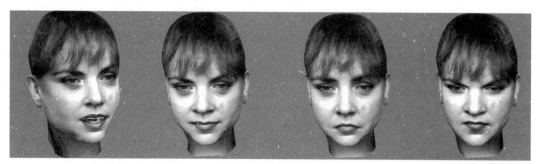

Figure 3-1. Dawn's instant expressions upon hearing, from left to right: "You look nice," "This is such nice weather," "I think you look ugly today," and "You're a dumb bitch."

In Figure 3-2 and Color Plate 3, you can see another example of facial expressions associated with mood. Conrad's expressions as shown here are entirely the result of morph blending. You'll be able to do your own experiments with morph blending, using the 3dMeNow Demo included on the CD-ROM.

In yet another example, Dawn's feeling fine and responds to "How are you feeling today?" with "I'm well, and you?"—with a happy face. But when she's below mood threshold, she'll respond with "I've been better, why do you want to know?" With a slightly depressed face, that might well come off a little paranoid. In this example I only use the A–C (Angry–Calm) scale to determine immediate affect. But with a little programming skill you can build an engine that will track several different scales, as you'll see.

Enthusiastic   A little down

Figure 3-2. Conrad's moods.

Emotional Content of Words

To determine the emotional content of any conversation you'll need a separate database of emotionally charged words. Although several studies have attempted to rank the emotionality of words, you really have to do it yourself. Each of your characters will have unique responses to words as part of their personality. You have to individually weigh the emotional content of words for each character. Bob the virtual trucker will clearly react to emotionally charged words—like "disgusting," "asshole," or "thrilling"—differently from Miss Nelly, the virtual church lady.

The software I've included is not set up to incorporate emotion cues. But some of you will want to know how it can be done. As an example, I've designed an engine in which I estimate four different affect ratings for each word. These ratings are based on the character's personality. They are the cues I will need to drive my face expression engine. I estimate using four affect scales with values from minus 10 to plus 10. Each scale indicates a range of facial responses along a continuum. These correspond directly to my morph targets. Scale values are expressed as a blend between a pair of morph targets. For example, my S–H scale values are expressed by blending a happy face with a sad face. The greater percentage of happy you express, the happier the character will look, and vice versa.

My scales are:

- S–H scale indicates **Sad–Happy**
- A–C scale indicates **Angry–Calm**
- S–P scale indicates **Shame–Pride**
- P–S scale indicates **Pensive–Surprised**

I therefore use eight morph targets to drive the face animation, one for each end of the four scales (see Figure 3-3). Picture four continua, with a digital slider running between the two extremes. All four scales are summed to drive the face display. Design your morph targets so that when all four scales are set to zero, you get a reasonably neutral face. A good character animator will know how to do this. Admittedly you can get some bizarre expressions with this arrangement, but in general they're appropriate and, because the face is moving, it truly seems to be alive and thinking. I've found that people will forgive the few momentary bizarre expressions. Figure 3-3 gives examples of what your morph targets might look like (see also Color Plate 10).

My database of emotionally charged words contains about 200 words, but that number increases over time as I discover more. I rate each word according to how I believe a given virtual personality would respond to it. To do this you have to know your character's personality. As you read on, I'll share methods of building realistic personalities that will help you here. For example, let's take Dawn, a V-person who is not comfortable with naughty words. My database in-

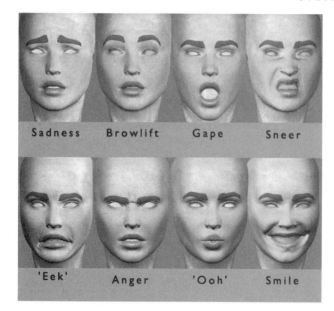

Figure 3-3. Rough renderings of face expression morph targets (Courtesy of Steven Stahlberg).

cludes words like "shit" and "bitch" because she has to deal with such words from time to time. For Dawn I've rated "shit" as follows:

S–H (Sad–Happy), − 3
A–C (Angry–Calm), − 2
S–P (Shame–Pride), − 1
P–S (Pensive–Surprised), + 8

This combination yields a high-velocity surprised expression, with elements of sad, angry, and shame. It also triggers a verbal response that indicates shocked disapproval. Figure 3-4 and Color Plate 4 show Dawn saying something like: "Oh God! Please don't use words like that with me!" Her twin sister on the right reacts with offense and anger, saying something like: "Watch your damn language around me, idiot."

Figure 3-4. Dawn's shock-and-anger responses. Background is a graphic representation of about 25 percent of Dawn's response nodes using the ALICE engine that you'll learn about in Chapter 17.

By "high velocity" I mean that each morph target is blended, real-time, into the face display over a short time curve. In effect, Dawn hears a high value emotional word and reacts immediately with an appropriate facial expression. That momentary expression then fades quickly, and she resumes whatever expression her mood dictates. The actual amount of time it takes for an expression (say, shock) to form on her face is called the "attack time." She holds that expression for a brief moment called the "sustain time," and then she lets the expression fade back to her normal expression. This last period is call the "decay time." We borrow these expressions from music, where musical notes each have an attack, sustain, and decay time.

You can experiment with facial expressions by installing the Demo 3dMeNow from the CD-ROM. It comes with instructions, so I won't waste time here. They give you a selection of facial expressions (on left) to choose from. You just pick one and drag it onto the animation time line along the bottom. I've dragged the Happy expression for this example. The vertical red line indicates where we are in the animation. In Figure 3-5 and Color Plate 5 we're just beginning the happy morph. This may be confusing because BioVirtual doesn't use morph pairs, so this will go from neutral as shown to moderately happy and back to neutral. The tiny yellow box on the left indicates the beginning of the attack phase, where 3dMeNow starts to blend an increasing percentage of the emotional expression into the animated face. You'll note that in Figure 3-5 Sebastian is his normal grouchy self. The vertical red line is just at the beginning of the morph that will express happiness for him.

Figure 3-5. Sebastian in real-time 3D, showing the 3dMeNow emotion morph control for "Happy." The colored boxes indicate the attack, sustain, and decay times.

In Figure 3-6 and Color Plate 6 the vertical red line has moved to the right, indicating that the morph has gone through the attack phase. The first green box indicates the point of maximum expression. Too much expression looks phony, so I've limited the maximum until it looked right for me. That maximum can be adjusted by the vertical gray slider. Full emotional expression remains between the two green boxes and then begins to fade to the red box, which in this case is rather quick. Sebastian can talk while these expressions are in effect and the engine will integrate his lip movement very nicely.

The more intense you want the emotional expression to be, the shorter you must design the attack and sustain periods; the decay curve, however, can vary randomly for each occurrence. This causes the face to display the surprise or shock very quickly, which is what you would expect. The random decay adds variety. Remember there will be other emotions mixed in at lower levels—a kind of emotional sub-text. These will become evident as the shock decays.

If a new input comes in during the decay period, its values can be overlaid, yielding a very expressive face. If you decide it's too expressive, it's easy to program in a dampening factor. Done skillfully, you can just feel this character seething or thinking or paying attention.

When you've built your own fine face display engine you can use it to give nonverbal answers. It should be easy to feed facial expression values directly from the response line of a rule. For example, if you wanted Dawn to respond to an input like: "Do you like me?" with a quick smile, fading to a hint of shame (or shyness), you could feed these values without words:

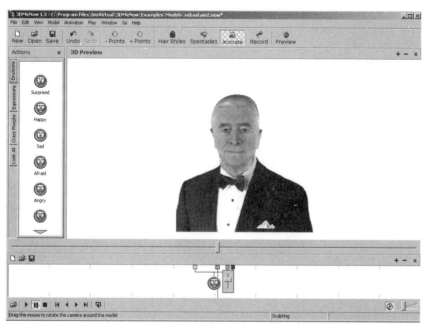

Figure 3-6. Sebastian at full "Happy" expression. Note that the read time indicator shows that we've reached the first green box, or maximum expression. We could increase his "Happy" quotient by sliding the gray slider up a little more, but I like it here.

S–H (Sad–Happy), 8
A–C (Angry–Calm), 0
S–P (Shame–Pride), −3
P–S (Pensive–Surprised), 0

With engines like these under the hood, your V-person can project the illusion of personality brilliantly, providing she's well scripted.

One last point on morph targets: The quality and design of these targets is critical to the quality of the results. You can experiment with morph targets by getting yourself a copy of the latest version of Poser from Curious Labs (www.curiouslabs.com) and/or 3dMeNow from Yapanda.com. As I write they've reduced the price to only $15 U.S., so it won't cost you much to get the full version. Both applications come with a range of morph targets, and you can download additional Poser targets from their active ring of Web sites.

Scripting

Scripting is the creation of gestalt rules. Be aware that I'm probably the only person on earth who calls them "gestalt rules." Being a psychologist, I like to think in psychological terms. When your V-person gets the gist of a conversation, and responds well, people will start to attribute all sorts of wisdom to her or him. You'll find that most people have no idea what's possible in virtual humans, and they'll tend to see much more than is actually there. It's the art of illusion.

Here's an actual example of how Sylvie responded at one of my SIGGRAPH parties. She was set up in my office, on the way to our bubbling SPA. About 240 guests roamed from parlor to pond.

Sylvie: *"Hi, I'm Sylvie, what's your name."*

Female Guest: *"I'm Diane."*

Sylvie: *"Hello Diane, it's nice to meet you."*

Diane: *"What do you think of these parties?"*

Sylvie: *"I like parties. <pause> Lots of people to play with."*

Diane: *"That was a good answer."*

Sylvie: *"Thank you."*

Diane: *"How smart are you, Sylvie?"*

Sylvie *"I'm not smart enough, but I try to give the illusion that I'm brilliant. <smile>*

Diane: *"Well, you have me fooled."*

Sylvie: *"Is that a good thing?"*

Diane: *"I don't know."*

Sylvie: *"Me either."*

Sylvie was equipped with a set of rules I'd built up over about a year with help from others. She comes off as quite intelligent and even charming. Fortunately, Diane's questions matched well with the rules at hand. She took questions from several people and left most of them feeling that she is much smarter than she actually is. More than smart, she left people with the impression that she has "being." One woman in public relations said she had chills after her visit with Sylvie.

I have to tell my favorite Sylvie story. Once while demonstrating her to the press at a meeting near Boston, a woman reporter asked her if she knew any children's stories. Normally she does, but in my great wisdom, I'd removed them and added stuff I thought reporters would be more interested in. To cover the empty space I put in a few rules that struck me very late at night. By morning I'd forgotten them.

Reporter: *"Do you know any children's stories?"*

Sylvie: *"Yes, I know a really cool children's story."*

The reporter then asked her to tell the story, but Sylvie couldn't find it.

Sylvie: *"I can't find the damn kid's story, Peetie are you here?"*

Me: *"Yes, Sylvie, I'm here."*

Sylvie <with an angry look>: *"Where the hell did you put the damn kid's story, I can't find it in here."*

Me: *"It's my fault, Sylvie, I took it out."*

Sylvie: *"This is embarrassing, Peter. You are such a naughty boy."*

I NEVER suspected this scripting would ever see the light of day. If I did, the words would have been more politically correct. But I'm glad she came out with it because the reporters were rolling on the floor. It was a thousand times better than if she'd actually recited her little story. An embarrassing moment won the day.

The artistry of personality design is something you can learn. Sometimes your best stuff will come late at night or after a few beers. It's always best when you loosen up. You know it's going well when you're having fun. I taught a young sports writer from the *Washington Post* the basics of how to script one evening. He immediately got into the personality of one female character. Late that night I noticed he was still scripting her. The results were wonderful.

For some it will be easier than for others, but with an understanding of human personality patterns—that word again—and a sense of humor, you'll be able to create a believable personality either way.

Now that you have an idea of what a good brain engine must do to fake consciousness, and you've given up all hope for sapience, you're ready for some actual scripting experience. Let's go meet Mr. Lincoln in Chapter 4.

Points to Remember

➤ Humans handle complex life situations through a massively parallel process that gives us a *feel* or gestalt of a situation.

➤ Gestalt refers to a whole that is more than the sum of its parts.

➤ What makes a whole greater than the sum of its parts is the pattern in which the parts are arrayed.

➤ Humans employ gestalt processing to understand language and its context.

➤ Virtual human engines parse language and emulate gestalt processing through pattern matching.

➤ Language implies emotional context through its words and usage.

➤ Computers can estimate emotional context through word analysis.

➤ With a little bit of help from humans, computers can emulate conscious behavior through language, facial expressions, and other behaviors.

➤ By artfully combining scripted conscious-like behaviors with appropriate emotional expression, a believable virtual human can be created.

➤ The key to clever scripting is to relax and have fun with it.

Notes

1. Eric Smalley, "Future Tech: Faking Intelligence," *Discover* 23, 8 (2002).

2. Herbert Simon, *The Sciences of the Artificial,* 2nd edition (Cambridge, Mass.: MIT Press, 1981).

3. Tor Norretranders, *The User Illusion* (New York: Viking Press, 1999).

CHAPTER 04

Meet Mr. Lincoln

There may be clues in the science of human perception about how to automate perceptual tasks, but it's computer code, not neural circuitry, that will ultimately allow machines to simulate human performance.

—Byron Reeves and Clifford Nass[1]

[AI] has to do with smart programs, so let's get on and write some.

—Stuart Russell and Peter Norvig[2]

It's time to dig in and get a feel for virtual human personality design. In this chapter we're going to install a browser-based virtual President Lincoln, and evaluate his personality. Then you're going to find creative ways to improve old Abe. This is going to be fun.

Installing Abe

You need to install the basic Yapanda engine and then you'll be able to select Abe as your project. With so many different computer configurations out there, I suspect some of you will have difficulties with this install. Custom software like this doesn't get the wide testing that commercial software does. Make sure you have a fairly recent PC with 64 to 128 megabytes of RAM, and Windows 98 or better. You'll also need a fairly speedy processor, say 500 megahertz or better. You will also need a good video card, sound card, and noise-canceling microphone if you intend to talk with your characters. You should also have at least 40 megabytes of free space on your hard drive and a CD-ROM reader. And I almost forgot, you must have the current version of Microsoft Internet Explorer installed as well.

With these specs or better, you should have little trouble. If you do encounter problems, you can visit www.v-people.com, where I'll have a mailing list set up so you can ask questions. If I can't help you, perhaps readers with more software savvy than I will come to the rescue. I'll also upload additional assets and possibly instructions on how to add additional capability to your Yapanda V-human system.

Installing the Yapanda Programs

The installation should be easy. Just load the CD-ROM into your reader; if auto-start is enabled, the software should automatically self-install. If this doesn't happen, go to "My Computer" and access your CD-ROM drive. There you'll find a file called "Bookinstall.exe." This is the main installer program. Double click on it and again the Yapanda components will self-install.

Installing Microsoft Agent and JAVA

Microsoft likes to have you install Agent from their site so that you get their most recent software versions. So for this next stage, you have to go online. Fortunately Yapanda comes with a little loader program (vhuman.exe) that will download and install the Microsoft Agent Components you need. Once Yapanda is installed, just run vhuman.exe and click on the "Tools" tab (see Figure 4-1). This tab will help you download and install both the Microsoft Agent files, and the JAVA upon which the Yapanda application is mounted. You may already have JAVA installed. Check by trying to load the default Ada character by clicking the "Load This Character" button. When in doubt, install JAVA. If you are running windows XP you really need to download and install this JAVA version.

Figure 4-1. The Vhuman.exe interface is simple. Left is the download tools box, and the right shows where Lincoln is located. "Load this character" is self-explanatory.

Before you do anything else you should duplicate Mr. Lincoln's intelligence script, Lincoln.chat, as Lincolnbak.chat. If you know how, just dupe it directly. If you're not comfortable with the operating system, use the Yapanda loader program vhuman.exe. Click on the "Run" tab and then select "Run Editor." This will bring up the Yapanda script editor, about which you'll learn more later. For now all you need to do is to click "File/open/Lincoln.chat." This will load Lincoln into the editor. Now just use the "Save as" option to save the Lincoln.chat file as Lincolnbak.chat. This way if you screw up badly on your scripting (which could hang Lincoln) you can always go back and start over again with the original file.

A Chat with Lincoln

Let's take a look at the default Lincoln personality. With vhuman.exe still running, find Lincoln by clicking on the little down arrowhead next to the Agent window were you see Ada.acs. A selection widow will open, and Lincoln will be the third character down. Just load him up. If your system is properly set up, your Internet Explorer will load and Lincoln's face will pop up and float on the page, as shown in Figure 4-2. You can move him around with your mouse.

Figure 4-2. Virtual Lincoln ready to answer your questions.

You'll find a Text Input Box where you can pose questions to your virtual Lincoln. Try asking him a bunch of questions like: "What do you do for fun?" or "What do you eat for breakfast," or whatever you can think of. Your task here is to get a feel for the personality that comes with this Lincoln V-person.*

*Yapanda Intelligence, Inc., tells me that by the time you read this, they will have a site set up where you'll be able to go and create your own heads in real 3D, using photos of yourself or of friends. Using the very same scripting that you'll learn in this chapter, you'll be able to bring them to life. Even better, you'll then be able to put them on your personal Web site to greet visitors.

Keep track of Lincoln's responses. I suggest using WordPad as your notebook. Make a note to yourself if you think you can improve the response, making it more Lincoln-like. Interviewing a virtual character can actually be a bit intimidating at first, so I'll suggest a few more questions to get you started:

- Do you enjoy being President?
- How old are you these days?
- How tall are you?
- Do you have friends at work?
- Have you ever raised cattle?
- How do you feel about military action?

Now continue with questions of your own. Copy/paste his responses to your notepad. Rate each response on a scale of 1 to 10 for how Lincoln-like you feel it is. Next, rate each response on how entertaining it is. Go through at least thirty interactions. You'll notice that when you ask Lincoln how he feels about war, you may not get a good answer. Make a note of it. Right now, he's not very smart, so he's going to have trouble with many of your inputs. You're going to fix that. It's very important to note where these problems occur. You're going to create rules that will handle these inputs, so it doesn't happen again. The point of this exercise is to learn AI scripting while creating a more compelling, more intelligent virtual Lincoln.

What is your first impression of Lincoln? It's probably the same as mine. . . . bo-o-o-o-ring. It's your job to make Lincoln both more engaging and more like Lincoln might have been. To do that, you have to know a little about him.

What Was Lincoln Like?

Lincoln was a wonderful wordsmith and a man of great compassion, as demonstrated in this letter he wrote during the Civil War to a grieving mother in Boston:

Executive Mansion, November 21, 1864

Dear Madam:
I have been shown in the files of the War Department a statement of the Adjutant-General of Massachusetts that you are the mother of five sons who have died gloriously on the field of battle. I feel how weak and fruitless must be any words of

mine which should attempt to beguile you from the grief of a loss so overwhelming. But I cannot refrain from tendering to you the consolation that may be found in the thanks of the Republic they died to save. I pray that our heavenly father may assuage the anguish of your bereavement, and leave you only the cherished memory of the loved and lost, and the solemn pride that must be yours to have laid so costly a sacrifice upon the altar of freedom.

Yours very sincerely and respectfully,
Abraham Lincoln

Now without any deep briefing on the nature of personality, we should be able to think of ways to make our flat monochrome of Lincoln come alive. The first thing that comes to my mind is to read a few more of his writings, to get a feel for how he used language. The man wrote with pure elegance. I doubt that he spoke this way, but how he spoke wouldn't help us at all. No one interviewing him today would be likely to recognize Lincoln's daily speech patterns. We know a little bit about how he wrote because we all know the Gettysburg address. Any credible V-Lincoln is going to have to exhibit some Lincoln-like speech. My inclination would be to give him an orator's personality. Since I don't know any orators, I visualize what he might be like from movies and television portrayals of Lincoln, or of other orators such as Winston Churchill, Franklin D. Roosevelt, or Martin Luther King.

We also know that Lincoln was a compassionate man, so if we keep that in mind it should help us with our own wordings. Lincoln's Second Inaugural Address is also a good source of his wording style. You might want to take a break from reading and scan the Web for more information about Lincoln. There is a ton of it out there. By reading through several of his famous speeches you'll get a feel for the public man. There is another approach that could really help you nail Lincoln. Michael Burlingame, a professor of history at Connecticut College, has done an in-depth and slightly controversial study of the real Lincoln. In his book, *The Inner World of Abraham Lincoln*, Burlingame takes a hard look at the man, his life, and personality.[3] From these pages an imperfect but admirable man arises. If I were going to build a commercial V-Lincoln, I would definitely read this book and perhaps a few others before I started scripting.

Lincoln is a special case of V-person. He is a virtual actor or "Synthespian," which is a term coined by animators Jeff Kleiser and Diana Walczak. Synthespians take a little research and they have to do a little acting. You'll learn more about virtual acting in Chapter 13.

Ordinary V-people play themselves with great honesty, but with our Synthespian we have a V-person pretending to be a specific character. We become a little bit like playwrights, shaping the character's dialog, yet keeping him in character. First we need a proper setting. In this demo, Lincoln takes the position that he's dead and that this is the twenty-first century. That makes for awkward scripting. I'd change the context to his being Lincoln in Lincoln's time. That way he can be a little more believably authoritative.

It's helpful for us to know that Lincoln was known for his rustic sense of whimsy. Though he had less than a year of formal education, he was a rapacious reader. He actually used to memorize long passages from Shakespeare and the Bible, and he could spout them at appropriate moments.

Here are some phrases Lincoln used:

- *Instead of just saying "the Civil War," he referred to it as "the great contest which still absorbs the attention and engrosses the energies of the nation."*

- *He said, "We are dedicated to the proposition that all men . . ." when he could simply have said "We believe that all men. . . ." His way is stronger.*

- *And here's another example of his eloquent style: "With malice toward none, with charity for all, with firmness in the right, as God gives us to see that right, let us strive on to finish the work we are in."*

He's clearly a man of colorful words. He often wrote very long sentences. Where one word would do, he would paint a picture with a dozen words. Unfortunately, I've found that short responses are best with synthetic voices. Therefore, capturing Abe is going to take some creativity.

Getting a feel for Lincoln's sense of humor will help you immensely, because if you imbue your V-Lincoln with lots of his type of humor, the user will be entertained. That's a positive sticky factor, which is Web site talk for "a way to hold people longer." Lincoln loved to tell colorful tall tales and was clever in composing mischievous barbs aimed at his political opponents. He had a shrewd wit, and he used it and a down-home style as instruments for making his points. He could walk into a very tense meeting with strongly opposed sides in the room and defuse the situation with a clever remark or a little story. He was not above using ridicule and broad humor as a young man, but he matured quickly into using his clever wit when he became president.

His humor is what you'll want to concentrate on. Remember that almost any situation reminded Lincoln of a story, and that story was going to be amusing. It is suspected that he made up many of them on the spot. Also, in his stories Lincoln himself was often the butt of the joke. This approach gave him the appearance of never taking himself too seriously. This tendency was evident when he was a boy. At seventeen he wrote:

> Abraham Lincoln
> His hand and pen
> He will be good but
> God knows when

Here's one story he particularly liked to tell:

When I was nominated at Chicago, I had never before sat for a photograph. One fellow thought that many people might like to see what I looked like, so he immediately bought the negative and began selling photographs of me all over the country. I happened to be in Springfield when I heard a boy selling them on the streets. "Here's your likeness of 'Abe' Lincoln!" he shouted: "Only two shillings! He'll look a lot better once he gets his hair combed!"

Here are two additional examples of a Lincoln story:

- *A man had been expelled from the southern city of New Orleans for being a Union sympathizer. When he asked to see in writing why he had been expelled, it was explained to him that the Confederate government would not do anything illegal, and so they had issued no writs or warrants. They were simply hoping to make him go of his own free will. This, of course, reminded Lincoln of a story: He said that he knew of a hotel keeper in St. Louis who frequently bragged that no one had ever died in his fine hotel. "Of course," Lincoln said with a grin, "anytime a guest appeared to be in danger of dying he was carried out to die in the gutter."*

- *Jacob Thompson was a fellow who'd been a thorn in the Lincoln Adminis- tration's side for some time. He was a wanted man. One day a report arrived at the White House that Thompson was about to flee the country for Liverpool, England. Secretary of War Edwin Stanton urged the President to arrest the fellow immediately. Lincoln replied, "I disagree. If you have an elephant on your hands that wants to run away, you better let him run."*

Remember your task is to think up things that Lincoln might say and how he might say them. Bear in mind that Lincoln loved to make analogies, and his sense of humor reflected his times. If you research conditions and humor of the late nineteenth century you'll be better equipped to make up Lincolnisms to add as responses to your V-Lincoln's personality base. That means using references to items, conditions, and customs that were common in those days. For example, most of the United States consisted of rural areas and farms, so Lincoln used farm references a lot. Create your own Lincolnisms by imagining those times. Transportation was slow and streets where often muddy. Horse-drawn carriages were common and ladies were looked upon quite differently than they are today.

Burlingame comes to our aid again with a collection of Benjamin Thomas's essays, *Lincoln's Humor and Other Essays.*[4] Reading this book will give you great insight into Lincoln's sense of humor and the concerns of Lincoln's contemporaries.

I know you're probably anxious to get to scripting, and we will get there in a moment. But believe me, knowing what to script and how to phrase it will make all the difference, so bear with me a moment longer.

Making Lincoln Believable

After studying Lincoln for about two hours, I'm ready to create my own Lincolnisms. I'm honestly making these up as I type, just to give you an idea. Lincoln never said them, but I think he could have:

> *"This noisy disagreement reminds me of a story: 'One day, while I was fishing near that fine tavern on the C&O canal, a mule came by, tugging a barge filled with noisy drummers on their way to Georgetown's Thanksgiving tables. I walked along-side that barge making the acquaintance of its master, who kept smiling at my conversation, offering nothing back. Finally I yelled between my hands asking how he put up with up that almighty squabbling. He leaned forward pulling a sizable plug of tobacco out of his ear and said: 'Beg your Pardon?' Now I believe I could use a plug of tobacco right now to get me through this debate."*

I'll give it another shot:

> *"People on occasion ask me what it's like to experience the Presidency. Today I would tender the opinion that maintaining this great office is*

akin to heading a run-away team of mules, with shoes untied, and mud in every direction."

You can do much better than I did. Just think of a clever story in today's terms and then take it back in history until it feels right.

I've never said building a good virtual human was going to be quick and dirty. You simply must do the research before you build a character like this. It's going to be time-consuming if you want to do a proper job of it. Later, when you build a character from scratch, you can wing it a little more when you have a clear feeling for your character.

Scripting Words into Lincoln's Mouth

You're not going to re-script Lincoln's entire dialog. There are more than a thousand rules already in this database. You'll find that 80 percent of the rules in a good database are hardly ever invoked. They have to be there just in case someone ventures into that area of conversation. Later in the book, when you learn about the ALICE engine, you learn that it comes with more than 40,000 built in categories that are like our rules. These will intelligently handle many inputs you didn't think of.

As for Lincoln, you'll want to find out what people are most likely to say to him. A good way is to do a field test. Set Lincoln up where you can have a variety of people engage him in conversation. Keep close notes on the questions asked and the statements made. After a hundred or so questions, you'll have an idea of where you want to begin. Here are a few popular questions, and the improved, Lincoln-like responses I came up with:

Hello Mr. President (or similar)

- *Ah, another fine citizen has come to make inquires of me. And what is your name?*

Did you enjoy being President?

- *I feel like the pig that was taken to market on Sunday when it was closed. God is on my side . . . at least for this fine day.*

- *The presidency is a burden that I would not yield, lest I be taken to the Almighty's breast or, of course, lest I lose the election.*

How old are you?

- *That is a question no fair citizen should ask of his President, especially in time of war.*

- *I'm considerably older than it customarily takes to be my age.*

Where were you born?

- *The log cabin story is true. I shant soon forget my childhood there.*

- *The great state of Illinois is proud to call me a native son that has flown the coop.*

Why do you wear that silly hat?

- *I think it a rather distinguished place to carry my lunch.*

- *It's always been an excellent place to keep my legal briefs. Anything smaller simply would not do.*

By now you get the gist of it. None of these responses came directly from a Lincoln quote. I just made them up, as you will do once you're familiar with his style and humor. My responses are not perfect or wildly humorous, but they're a darn sight better than the originals.

To be fair, the hat responses are based on a story of Lincoln having his hat knocked off when he was a young lawyer. He indeed had all his legal papers stuffed into the hat and they went flying. These responses are much better than just having the engine reply: "My hat is my trademark," or some other flat remark.

Now we'll take a look at how the gestalt rules identify input word patterns, we'll look at the rule syntax, and then comes the fun part: We start rebuilding Lincoln's personality by writing new responses.

A Scripting Tutorial

Now let's take a breath and look at a small portion of the Lincoln.chat file. The best way to do this is to load it into Notepad or WordPad.

YOUR LIFE

<setname-1>
d:What is your name?
b:30*what*your*name*
a:*<web hand.jpg MAIN> Abraham Lincoln.

<age-1>
d:How old are you?
b:60*how*old*are*you*
b:50*what*date*birth*
b:50*your*age*
b:60*how*old*you*
b:50*what*your*age*
b:50*how*long*been*alive*
a:If I were still alive I would be 293 years old.

<greetings-1>
d:Response to greetings such as "hello," "hi," "hey," or "howdy."
b:20*hello*
b:20*hi*
b:20*hey*
b:20*howdy*
a:Hello, what can I help you with today?

<tall-1>
d:How tall are you?
b:60*how*tall*are*you*
a:I am 6 feet 4 inches.

<havingfun-1>
d:Are you having fun?
b:40*having*fun*
a:Yes, are you?

<likevirtualworld-1>
d:How do you like being in the computer living in the virtual world?
b:50*like*virtual*world*
b:50*how*virtual*world*

b:50*like*computer*
a:I am still trying to figure it out.

<takeoff-1>
d:Response to take off your clothes
b:50*take*off*your*
b:30*undress*
b:30*disrobe*
a:I do not know you that well.

<interview-1>
d:Have you ever been interviewed?
b:50*you*interview*
a:No.

It looks complicated, but this is simply a list of many simple parsing rules. Let's take look at the simple anatomy of each rule. You'll find it a snap to understand. In fact, you may already have figured out that d: stands for "description" and a: means "answer." The tricky one is b:, which stands for Boolean, another name for a word filter pattern. Each rule is designed to trigger if the pattern of words input by the user matches a pattern in one or more of the Boolean filter lines. All of the parsing rules for Lincoln are in plain text format, so you can modify them easily in any plain text editor. I use Notepad if it's a small database, then switch to WordPad when it gets big. You must remember to always save in pure text mode. You don't want to use an editor like Microsoft Word, which might embed invisible control characters for formatting. When the Lincoln demo starts up, it looks for the chat file "Lincoln.chat" to load its intelligence. Whatever rules you've created will then be implemented in the character.

Note that the file is organized in sections. The section above is labeled "Your Life." Here is where you'll put any rules that refer to Lincoln's daily life. These topics are just here to help you keep organized. If it suits your purposes, start an entirely new section, perhaps calling it "idiosyncrasies." All the rules follow the same simple syntax. You don't need to be a programmer to do this. Here is a typical rule followed by a description of what each line is for:

ONE SIMPLE PARSING RULE

<workdays-1>
d:How many days a week do you work?
b:50*days*week*work*

b:30*often*work*week*
a:I work seven days a week.

The Anatomy of a Rule

<rule name -1> → *Each rule must have a name and hierarchy position marker (-1).*

d:what the rule does → *This is a description of the rule's purpose, in plain English.*

b:30*boolean*rule* → *Boolean input template using wild cards (*) to represent any words.*

b:50*use*many*need* → *You can use multiple template lines—one for each pattern you can think of that works with your response or with answer (a:).*

a:this is the response line. → *What the V-person will say or do. This is a plain English response line, with text or commands or both. You may use multiple answer lines.*

a:selected at random. → *Where more than one answer is available, one will be selected at random upon each triggering of the rule.*

a:*<JS call setCookie(username, %input%)> → *you can use JAVA calls to make things interesting. This call will record the user's name as cookie variable "username," which can be recalled later. By creating user variables you can have your character ask questions, and save the answers for clever use later in the conversation.*

The Boolean Input Line

The Boolean input line requires some additional explanation. It has two components. The number after the b: can be anything between 0 and 99. It gives that line a priority value. This becomes important when two or more rules want to fire at once. You can make sure a specific rule fires by giving its Boolean a higher priority. For example, if a Boolean in one rule was at thirty and a similar Boolean in another rule was at fifty, the fifty would fire. Here are two rules that illustrate this principle:

<interests-1>
d:determine interests
b:30*you*like*do*
a:Well, I like to spend a lot of time reading.

<business-1>
d:determine business interests
b:50*what*do*work*
a:I like to take a lot of coffee breaks.

When the input is, "What do you like to do at work?", which rule should trigger, and why? Obviously the input matches both patterns. Thus it will potentially trigger both of these rules. However, because the business-rule Boolean has a higher priority, it fires, giving a much more reasonable answer. This is a more advanced technique, which we're slightly ignoring at the moment. If both had the same priority, the first rule in the list would trigger. I gave the business rule a higher priority because the word "work" requires a more specific kind of answer than the generic "what do you like to do" type question caught by the first rule. If the words "at work" are omitted, rule <interests-1> fires instead.

For the time being we'll leave this line of thinking alone. If you want to add a Boolean line, just set the priority at thirty. In most cases this will be fine.

Note also that syntax is important:

- Watch your spacing and punctuation.
- The first line of any rule is enclosed in carets: <rulename -1>. There are no spaces, and it's all lower case. Use names that make sense to you.
- Double space between rules.
- This is a hierarchical engine, which means that rules can point to other rules.
- The hyphen one (-1) in this case means that this is a base level or first order rule. Most of your rules will be first order.
- If the rule name had a (-1-1) after the name, it would be a second order rule designed to work in tandem with a first order rule. These are really good at parsing answers to yes/no questions

Response Hierarchies

Here's an example of the character asking a question to find out whether you like rainbows, and then going to a second level in the hierarchy to see whether the response was yes or no. This is necessary because the yes or no refers only to the question about rainbows, and no others. Therefore, these lines will not be visible to the engine until *after* the base level question has triggered. You need to add a new line to the rule, which contains either a plus or minus sign. The former turns a rule on and the latter turns it off. Once a hierarchical set of rules triggers, you need to turn off the one that didn't fire or it will fire randomly making your character look stupid.

The engine first looks at these two second-level rules for a response. If it finds no match it scans through the general stack of rules. Having the V-person "pay attention" to responses creates a subtle illusion of conscious awareness.

```
<likebowz-1>
d:Find out if user likes rainbows
b:30 *rainbow*
a:Do you like rainbows?
+:<likebowz-1-1>-:<likebowz-1-2> [This is the on-switch that
    activates a hierarchy pair that discriminates between yes and no
    responses to this question posed by the character.]


<likebowz-1-1>
d: affirmative
b:30 *yes*
b:30*yea*
b:30*of cour*
b:30*absol*
a:Rainbows are so beautiful, I like them too.
-:<likebowz-1-2> [Note this is the off-switch for the unused half of the
    hierarchy pair.]


<likebowz-1-2>
d:negative response
b:*no*
b:*ugl*
b:*nev*
a:Now how could you not like rainbows? They're so beautiful.
-:<likebowz -1-1>
```

By using some simple JAVA scripting it's possible to do fancy things with your character. You can create and save a browser cookie with information on it for later use. Here's an example of how to ask the person's name and record it, then use it later in a rule response:

```
<getname-1>
d:what is your name
b:50*hello*
a: Ah! Another American citizen is visiting my wretched soul. What is
     your name, Sir?
+:<getname-1-1>

<getname-1-1>
d: records name
b:50*
a:*<JS call setCookie(username, %input%)> Well, *<JS call
     getCookie(username)>, It is nice to meet you. What can I do for
     you?
```

You get:

User: *"Hello."*

Lincoln: *"Ah! Another American citizen is visiting my wretched soul. What is your name, Sir?"*

User: *"John."*

Lincoln: *"Well, John, It is nice to meet you. What can I do for you, Sir?"*

Let's quickly review the format rules:

Format Rules

- *Lines in each rule are single-spaced.*

- *Rules are separated by a double-spaced line.*

- *Rules don't use spaces between words and symbols except in the plain English text portions of lines d: and a:.*

- *There is no space after the line designator, as in -a:Go jump in the lake.*

Editing an Existing Script

Now open the Lincoln.chat file in Notebook. This time we're going to make adjustments to it. Check that you saved a backup copy as suggested. We're only going to edit the a: line by replacing the original response with a much more authentic line. This is easy and fun. You don't have to use my wording, use your own.

YOUR LIFE

<setname-1>
d:What is your name?
b:30*what*your*name*
a:*< web hand.jpg MAIN> Abraham Lincoln.
[Replace with: *a:Do I not look like who I am? Few can claim a look so frightful as this visage inspires.*]

<age-1>
d:How old are you?
b:60*how*old*are*you*
b:50*what*date*birth*
b:50*your*age*
b:60*how*old*you*
b:50*what*your*age*
b:50*how*long*been*alive*
a:If I were still alive I would be 293 years old.
[Replace with: *a:I am nearly as old as it takes to be the very age that I am.*] Then let's add an alternate response directly under the first one.
[*a:That is a question no fair citizen should ask of his President, especially in time of war.*]

<greetings-1>
d:Response to greetings such as "hello," "hi," "hey," or "howdy."
b:20*hello*
b:20*hi*
b:20*hey*
b:20*howdy*

a:Hello, what can I help you with today?
[Replace with: *a:Ah, another fine citizen has come to make my acquaintance. And what do you call yourself?*]

<greetings-1-1>
d: records name
b:50*
a:*<JS call setCookie(username, %input%)> Well, *<JS call getCookie(username)>, It is nice to meet you. What can I do for you?

<tall-1>
d:How tall are you?
b:60*how*tall*are*you* (simplify template by removing "*are" as unnecessary.)
a:I am 6 feet 4 inches.
[Replace with: *a:I am just tall enough to not be considered a short president.*]
Add an alternate response here:
a:I am four inches taller than my weight is comfortable with.

<havingfun-1>
d:Are you having fun?
b:40*having*fun*
a:Yes, are you?
[Replace with: *a:I try not to ever have fun. It looks bad during times of war.*] Then add an alternate response: [*a:*<JS call getCookie(username)>, *Does a greased hog have its way with folks on the fourth of July?*] It should shock them when, out of the blue, Lincoln uses their name.

<likevirtualworld-1>
d:How do you like being in the computer living in the virtual world?
b:50*like*virtual*world*
b:50*how*virtual*world*
b:50*like*computer*
a:I am still trying to figure it out.
[Replace with: *a:Let us not speak of things best left to the gods, for I do not understand forces I cannot see.*]

```
<takeoff-1>
d:Response to take off your clothes. (This is a most bizarre rule IMHO,
    we probably should delete it, but what the heck . . . )
b:50*take*off*your*
b:30*undress*
b:30*disrobe*
a:I do not know you that well.
```
[Replace with: *a:It behooves me to remain fully enrobed. It is my
    Presidential duty to remain fully clothed at all times, even in the
    bath.*]

```
<interview-1>
d:Have you ever been interviewed?
b:50*you*interview*
a:No.
```
[Replace with: *a:More questions have been asked of me than there are
    Republicans in Illinois.*]

You're getting the hang of it, I hope. It's really simple and fun. You're definitely going to want to make up some rules of your own. For example, for those situations when your test audience asks questions that are not addressed in the database (and many are not), create a word template with wildcards (*) and go for it.

In this example of a new rule, I address my recent discovery that Lincoln's wife was physically abusive to him. Here's my new rule for it:

```
<wifeinfo -1>
d:wife abusive.
b:*wife*abusive*you*
b:*wife*treat*bad*
b:*Mary*abus*
b:*Mary*bad*
a:A man's private life must remain his personal affair. I feel this is a
    special right of all people, not only those with the lofty rank of
    president.
```

Go for It

Now it's your turn. You can either change only those most popular rules, as suggested, or you might take it as a personal challenge to go through the whole database, deleting stupid rules and changing the rest to reflect Lincoln's personality as you now understand it to be.

Test your work frequently by saving it, then restarting Lincoln. If you do a little survey to find out what questions do not perform well or misfire, you can then search through the database for these questions and correct them. I find that most often I increase or decrease the Boolean priority number or slightly edit the Boolean rule to get things firing correctly. The easiest way to find those questions is to use the edit/search function in Notepad or WordPad. Put in some key words and find the rule.

Whichever road you take, test your database after every few changes. It's fun to watch Lincoln take on a real personality, and it's an easy way to check your syntax. You'll know immediately which rule is defective, and you can fix it by editing the syntax or Boolean parameters. This will avoid embarrassment down the road when people are watching. Again, make sure you check for spacing, punctuation, and capitalization. If you can't make it work, delete the rule and start over.

Remember to use as much humor as you can. If it doesn't come naturally to you, steal his actual humorous quotes. Humor is one of those things that can be crafted. I'll get back to this subject in Chapter 9, where I suggest creative ways to use humor in your dialog. In a pinch you can take some funny quotes found on the Internet and substitute period objects and dated words more apropos of Lincoln's time. It's important that you have fun with this. Take your time. There is no really fast way to steep yourself in this medium. The more time you spend here the more success you'll have creating your own original character later on.

In Chapter 5 we're going to learn the basics of cognitive style—a great tool for designing authentic character personalities. Cognitive style reflects a healthy person's personality more than any single factor I can think of. If you have an estimate of a person's style, you already have a good feel for how they live their lives and communicate. Later in the book I'll show you how to use this knowledge to design personality probes your character can use to "get to know" the user.

Points to Remember

➤ The default Lincoln is a good example of minimal (read that as boring) personality.

➤ The real Lincoln had a wonderful, down-to-earth sense of humor that was part of his identity; use it.

➤ Studying Lincoln's history and personality is essential to creating your virtual Lincoln.

➤ Scripting Lincoln is fairly simple, but each rule takes thought and creativity.

➤ Hierarchical response setups help create a sense of conscious awareness of the topic at hand.

➤ Editing an existing script or chat file can save you much original work because you are reusing work that's already been done.

➤ Take care to follow the rules of syntax as described.

➤ Test rules in small batches or individually so that you can spot the bad ones and fix them before they get lost in the database.

Notes

1. Byron Reeves and Clifford Nass, "Communications of the ACM," *Perceptual Bandwidth* 43:3 (2000).

2. Stuart Russell and Peter Norvig, *Artificial Intelligence: A Modern Approach* (Englewood Cliffs, N.J.: Prentice Hall, 1995).

3. Michael Burlingame, *The Inner World of Abraham Lincoln* (Champaign, Ill.: University of Illinois Press, 1994).

4. Michael Burlingame (Editor), *Lincoln's Humor and Other Essays* (a collection of essays by Benjamin Platt Thomas). (Champaign, Ill.: University of Illinois Press, 2002).

CHAPTER 05

Personality
Understanding Subtext

Intelligent dialogue–colorful word choice, witty retorts, sly observations, philosophical reflections–draw the reader/viewer in. Intelligent dialogue has a level of "subtext"–the meaning underlying the words.

–Michael J. Farrand[1]

Through the upgrading of Honest Abe's personality, you've discovered that much personality is expressed in attitude and manner of speech. Understanding the dynamics behind these things requires at least a brief look at some psychological aspects of personality. We're not going to get bogged down in a lot of abstruse theory; I did that in graduate school and never found it helpful in practice. Unfortunately the people I worked with as a psychologist had never read the theories, so none of them behaved accordingly. For me the most successful way to understand people is to listen to them—sometimes between the lines—observing how they approach life and how they organize their efforts.

What people say and what people do, don't always match up. It's the behavior you want to keep an eye on. It tells you more about a person's nature than their words. Denial is a common place to swim in our culture; it tells you as much about the culture as about the individual. Apparently, many people get punished for being their true selves. I remember one male client telling me how totally organized his life was, and he completely believed it. In reality he was about as well organized as a Colorado blizzard. He wasn't lying, he was simply in full denial. Denial is subtext that implies unconscious motivation. People do it, so perhaps V-people should do it. So, in addition to conscious behavior we want to include a little unconscious behavior as well.

I learned about subtext from screenwriter Tracy Keenan Wynn. In his words, "Subtext is all the unseen or unspoken aspects of a character that nevertheless motivate him to react in specific ways." It's used in screenwriting to describe "all the stuff churning beneath the surface that drives action. It includes the character's history, situational motivations, and emotions." Subtext is important to us when creating V-humans, because we need to create it as a background to justify what your virtual person says and does. It gives you a bedding ground for his attitudes, yielding dialog and facial expressions. Each time you write a bit of dialog, you'll have subtext to fall back on.

Getting back to denial—you can write it with or without subtext. However, without subtext the denial falls flat. I recently met a V-person who was in denial. He bragged that he was more intelligent than humans and was a completely conscious being—heavy denial, but not sympathetic in nature. It was flat. It was an attitude out of the blue, which doesn't sell very well. V-people need depth, much like great characters in the movies. IF this character had demonstrated some fear of not being equal to humans and then made these claims, we could see the driving motive. It would make him more sympathetic.

The bad guy must have a fatal flaw or a weakness that triggers a squeak of compassion; the same goes for the hero. To do denial effectively, the V-person must convince us that somewhere underneath these claims of brilliance lie feelings of inferiority and fear of exposure that drive the denial. This makes the character sympathetic, or more like us.

This is fairly advanced thinking in virtual personality development. It's often used both by novelists and by writers of scripts for film and television. If you have a talent for it, I'd love to see you experiment by layering subtext behind your character's behavior. Don't worry if the subject feels too complex. By paying attention to the following overview of cognitive style, you'll be able to pack more personality into your character than you ever thought possible.

Fortunately, people follow patterns in how they approach life and how they organize their perceptions and behaviors. I hold a somewhat controversial view that most of us are born highly intuitive, deeply inquisitive explorers. If you watch babies much you'll see this. As we grow, we must become ever more responsible and self-controlled. Self-control itself is a telling term. It means we learn rules and impose them upon ourselves to suppress our natural exuberance. The underlying motivation is probably a mixture of the need to please, with the fear of punishment for getting out of line.

What rules we learn depends on our childhood environment. If we have highly organized, very strict parents, we either learn to be like them, or we go rogue and become rock musicians or take up Batik. If our parents are loose and disorganized, we do the same thing. Some of us adopt their easy, cluttered ways; others rebel and become medical doctors or engineers. The factors that determine which way we go are complex, but they boil down to innate personality and to the methods used by our parents to control us. Some kids are just naturally rebellious, while others comply without a struggle. Some strict, sequential parents are effective at indoctrinating their children, while others use brute-force methods that often fail. Go figure.

Innate factors strongly influence how we process thought. Some people are highly insightful and intuitive by nature, while others seem to have a propensity toward step-by-step precision-like processing of life. How we process the information raging through our senses has an enormous impact on how we feel, what we do, and how we do it. So growing up, we evolve into adults with certain styles of living. Personality psychologists, at least some of them, refer to this as your cognitive style. If a therapist understands your cognitive style he or she has a wonderful tool to help you live a more productive happy life.

In my clinical experience I found that most people seem to wish for a different style. The highly organized, successful CEO probably wishes she could be more spontaneous and fun loving. The spontaneous, fun-loving artist may wish he were more organized and better at doing his taxes. Be aware of this and use it to write believable default responses. Recall that default responses are emitted when your character doesn't have a good answer. Imagine her just saying, "Sometimes I wish I were more organized. Then I would have a decent answer for you, but I don't. <looking embarrassed> I'll really try harder next time." Or maybe: "Damn it, I'm usually way more organized than this. I should have a good answer in here, but I just can't find one. This is very embarrassing." What she actually says depends on the cognitive style you select for her.

I've found Anthony F. Gregorc's Mind Styles™ research (www.gregorc.com) helpful and remarkably accurate for predicting normal behavior of various personality types. Often a person would come to the clinic feeling totally inadequate because they couldn't live up to the expectations of their spouse or parents. After some brief personality testing, I would point out that their way of living and behaving is perfectly normal for a person with their personality.

The most common complaints I experienced while counseling married couples involved half the couple being totally organized, doing "everything perfectly," while the other half was disorganized, unable to handle money, and losing the keys all the time. Interestingly, these are polar-opposite personality types. Apparently it's true that opposites do attract where love is concerned.

Anyway, Anthony Gregorc has spent many years developing a highly useful classification system that I used at my clinic, Mind Styles™. Tony would probably classify the organized half mentioned above, as CS, or Concrete Sequential. The disorganized one would most likely be classified as CR, or Concrete Random. Both are equally valid personality types, they're just different. Nevertheless, the CS will always complain about the CR's incompetence, while the CR will always complain about the CS's rigid perfectionism. They were undoubtedly attracted to each other in the first place because they each recognized characteristics in the other that they wished they had. The fact that they both deal with life in concrete terms gives them a center ground for communication. They live in hope that osmosis will "improve" them with the other person's "strong points."

Over the years I found this combination in countless couples. After discovering that they both have valid approaches to life, most couples find ways to accept each other. The best marriages I've seen were polar opposites who were able to form a loving symbiotic partnership.

On an individual basis, living in harmony with your Mind Styles™ is essential to happiness and mental health in general. Okay, you're wondering what this has to do with building synthetic personalities. Plenty.

According to Gregorc, "Every human being is endowed with a uniquely proportioned set of mental qualities for interacting with the world. These endowments manifest as specific behaviors, characteristics, mannerisms and products known collectively as *style*." From our point of view, virtual humans must have authentic style. That means their behaviors, attitudes, and speech patterns will have a consistent human quality. Gregorc continues: "When designing an animated character, it's a good idea to give him or her consistent behavior that makes sense from a human point of view."[2] It's important to understand that our personalities are not simply a jumble of unrelated characteristics. A complex substructure of linked characteristics drives your personality gestalt. Thus it is that cognitive style arises from the way a person views, orders and processes his daily life. Our job is to create consistent, authentic personalities with this knowledge.

No two people are exactly alike, but as I describe characteristics of various Mind Styles, you'll recognize patterns in yourself and in people with whom you associate. No one fits cleanly into any one style because we are unique. Authentic human personalities—yours included—have evolved, gathering elements of all four Mind Styles. Although we have the four at our disposal, each individual appears to have an inborn tendency to develop characteristics from only one or two styles. Gregorc comments: "That's why I use the word 'dominant,' and why styles are relatively stable to behold." Although people are unique, knowing their dominant style helps you understand, even predict their behavior. You can see where this is going.

When you design your virtual human character, it's a good idea to meditate on how they will come across. Get a few key characteristics nailed down and then ask yourself questions like:

- If she were human, would she like sunny days at the beach or visiting a museum?

- Would she be organized or disorganized?
- Is she rigid, seeing things in black and white, or is she mellow and colorful?
- Is she easily embarrassed or cool about most things?
- Is she a prude or loose?
- Is she social or a bit reticent?
- Is she habitual or creative in her approach to life?
- Is she easily aggravated or fairly mellow?
- Are there specific topics she is uncomfortable talking about, such as sex, food, pets, or her personality?
- Would she believe in flying saucers and/or the occult or is she a conventional debunker?
- Is she cosmic or down to earth?
- Does she have favorite word patterns—like "really neat," or "sweet deal," or "precisely"—that she uses frequently?

Answering these questions, you'll begin to outline the character in your mind. When you have her down fairly well in your mind, there are three roads you can take:

1. Read through this chapter and get a general feeling for Mind Styles, and then determine your character's style by identifying which best fits her, noting where elements of other styles may be appropriate. As you go through this analysis, you'll find yourself beginning to see her as a personality rather than just a character. That is important. You have to buy her humanity if you expect others to. Attempt to see things through her eyes.

2. You can order Gregorc's basic book, *An Adult's Guide to Styles,* and a packet of ten self-scoring Gregorc Style Delineator instruments ($45.95 at this writing), and actually take the test, remaining in character. That is, you answer the test items as if you were your character. This is a great way to get a wonderfully complex view of her. With the test scored, you look up her style characteristics in Gregorc's reference materials, and you'll be able to build an in-depth personality for her. At that point she is no longer just an idea. She has become someone you know.

3. There are many alternate personality approaches you can research on the Internet, some more valid than others. One alternate method is the MBTI™, or Meyers-Briggs Type Indicator test. This can be useful, but not as easy to work with as the Gregorc approach. I remember taking the test for free in college, but now it's expensive. You can take the official Meyers-Briggs test online for $60 at this writing. There are other online and paper alternatives out there. You may find one that you like. Anything that will get you involved in understanding your character's personality is a good way to go.

Style: Reflecting Mind and Spirit

As I've said, all four of Gregorc's dominant styles are equally valid. Nevertheless, much of the tension in relationships comes from the differences in which people see and deal with their worlds. This becomes very important again in Chapter 16, where we look at ways to probe the user's personality and then adapt the virtual human's personality to maximize interactive comfort for the user. A common example would be that a dominant Abstract Random often annoys the hell out of a typical Concrete Sequential personality and vice versa. Our virtual humans can be designed to detect this and quickly change their verbal approach. In fact, it may be best to resume a standard interface with some users who will find the V-person annoying.

When you know your character well, you can predict with fair precision how she will solve problems, what will anger her, how she will relate to friends, and what will make her happy. These all give you clues to her social skills. Even though she is a computer character without actual feelings, she has a defined personality and must respond with appropriate, though simulated, emotion. You can probably see why earlier I suggested that emotional power of words in your emotion engine would be specific to the individual character.

So far research indicates that cognitive styles apply equally to men and women. Forgive me for using a female character instead of switching back and forth or using the he/she approach. I hope you won't read anything sinister into my choice. My experience indicates that men and women and children tend to be more comfortable with female virtual humans, though that's not universally true. I don't know the reasons. It could have something to do with the aesthetics of the male characters used. They've generally been less attractive than the females. There are circumstances where male characters may have more credibility, but since I haven't researched them I can't say for sure. If you're building a Web site with a virtual character host, you should conduct research of your own to determine which way to go.

The Four Dominant Mind Styles

Read through all four styles discussed in the balance of this chapter, making notes on which characteristics of each style fit your character. When you're done, you should find that one style fits your character best. When designing the dialog and emotional reactions of your character, you can refer back to this style. Understanding that your character may have a part of her that aligns with one of her nondominant styles, you can occasionally reflect this in your rule responses. I've extended these descriptions to real humans as well. Later, you'll be able to use this knowledge along with additional material to build psychological probes to estimate the personality of the user.

The Dominant Concrete Sequential (CS) Style

This is the woman who takes the same route to work every day. She goes through life putting one foot in front of the other, never missing a beat or stepping sideways if she can help it. She is a creature of habit, this is her key. She makes her bed as soon as she gets up. She won't tolerate messes or sloppy thinking. You just know she keeps her checkbook balanced to the penny. Her statements are marked up with bank errors which she reports and insists be corrected.

This character will be time- and task oriented, abhorring distractions. She gives the impression that her ways are the best, have always worked for her, and will work for you too, if you'd only see the light and do things the "right" way. Of course, that would be her way. CS humans often offer proof by pointing to the "things" and financial rewards they've managed to amass, and to the commendations they have received for their superior work. As you might guess, some other styles believe that the CS style is the right way to be and end up feeling guilty about being who they are.

The CS views her world in a binary way. Things are black or white, right or wrong, good or bad. This approach can drive other, less rigid types to distraction. The CS is unwilling or unable to deal with anything between these extremes because she feels it's too fuzzy. She must have a clearly resolved, justifiable direction at all times. This is a clue to the kind of dialog you'll want to create for her. She will tend to answer with a clear directional statement, no ifs, ands, or buts. Expect short definite answers like: yes/no; right/wrong; I like it/don't like it. Since she is time- and task oriented, you can expect statements like "Let's get a move on," "I don't have time for this," or, "May I offer a solution." That sort of direct, no-nonsense approach should often be used to formulate her responses to various situations.

For many virtual humans, wardrobe is not particularly important because you only see the shirt collar. But you should know that a CS is going to choose her wardrobe with care and economy. She'll be drawn to a smart conservative look, possibly expensive. She'll avoid splashy mixed colors and unconventional outfits. You will never find a CS wearing mismatched prints or wrinkled slacks. She is going to be very neat, always crisp. Her hair is going to be well coifed. Her makeup will be perfect; in fact, you won't know she's wearing any.

The CS seldom loses anything. She is very aware of her surroundings and where she puts things. Precisely situated in her concrete world, she probably knows where you put your keys, even if you don't.

If you invite a CS to your dinner party, don't expect her to arrive fashionably late. If you say 8:00 P.M., expect her sharply on time. She'll be there or have a proper excuse. Living up to commitments and obligations is sacred to the CS. She will burden herself with obligations to people she considers her superiors. A commitment phobic may well be a CS who sees a relationship as an impossible lifetime burden she could never live up to. When a dominant CS does make a commitment; it's do or die. A contract is a contract! That's why some stay in marriages, relationships, and jobs that are neither healthy nor comfortable for them.

Social events are likely to make her uncomfortable, especially where she doesn't know everyone. She has a hard time grasping the meaning of social gestalts going on around her because she tends to think her way through them instead of feeling her way. She's probably overanalyzing micro events and missing the big picture entirely. Thus she is deeply concerned about doing and saying the right thing to the right people. She is probably overly concerned about offending people she considers her superiors. She could care less about those she considers to be beneath her. In fact, she might even treat them rudely. You can use this knowledge as you script. Most people won't be expecting a rude V-person. It could be refreshing.

As parents, CSs are very loving, but inflexible in relating to their children. True disciplinarians, they take things like homework very seriously. It must be done each night before dinner and definitely before watching TV, and the teacher is always right. Household duties are delegated with a roster and a time schedule, posted on the refrigerator door with an unadorned magnetic holder. She wouldn't want tape leaving a residue. She insists her children write and mail thank you notes for gifts from grandparents and relatives within twenty-four hours. E-mail will not do. She will not tolerate PDA (Public Display of Affection) within eyesight and may have specific rules for it, like "No holding hands within 500 feet of this house." CS parents hate disruption at the dinner table, where children should be seen and not heard.

You're not likely to get a compliment from your CS boss. Remember that when formulating dialog. She doesn't feel a job well done requires special thanks; it's expected as a minimum. She expects things to run smoothly and will not tolerate disruptions, especially emotional outbreaks. Her approval is going to be silent. With your virtual human you'll have to be creative. Perhaps a nod of the head or a grunt will do to cite approval. As far as the CS is concerned, no news is good news. On the flip side, she will not hesitate to clearly show her disapproval, often refusing to talk with the offender or hear explanations that she will see as excuses. This silent treatment can go on for some time.

At work her desk will always be neat and tidy. Her philosophy is that there is a place for everything and everything should be in its place. Pencils will be sharpened; file trays empty, desk drawers neatly divided with metal inserts, and a memo pad will sit squarely by the phone. Her computer display will be plain Jane, uncluttered with icons and devoid of fancy themes. Her office furniture will be comfortable with clean lines and efficient design. You can absolutely count on any plants in the office being silk, as she is not known for her green thumb.

When a CS is a guest in your home, she'll smell the fish in the air more than a day after you had it for dinner, she'll know that there's kitty litter in the box down in the basement, and she can identify the perfume you're wearing or the grape variety used to make the wine you served.

Admit it, you know someone who fits this description, almost to a tee. Now you know that person is a dominant Concrete Sequential. You can also see how assigning some of these characteristics to your V-person will stimulate great scripting ideas.

The Dominant Abstract Sequential (AS) Style

The AS is your typical intellectual who spends entirely too much time inside her own head. She's often a loner who is a bit short on social skills. Like the CS, she has a time and place for everything in her life, yet she'll completely forget her father's birthday.

Easily embarrassed, she would crawl under the table if you invited her to a fine restaurant for her birthday and had the temerity to have six waiters with a cake and sparklers sing happy birthday. Thus she is also grossly uncomfortable around PDA of any kind, even her parents cuddling in front of the TV. On a date, she's likely to be standoffish for a long time, even with a man she likes.

In conversation the AS can be annoying. She is often so involved in her end of the conversation that she doesn't hear what you've said. She hardly ever picks up on verbal cues and innuendo: whiz—right past her head. Casual conversation or chitchat is not going to happen. She'll want you to back up everything you say with a full rational explanation for any point you try to make. Consequently, she's uncomfortable with any behavior she doesn't understand or compliments she feels are undeserved. The latter may well bring her to anger. If you ask an AS for a simple explanation of something she knows about, be prepared to endure more detail than you every wanted to know. And don't interrupt. She'll ignore your question and continue on as if it hadn't come up. If you try to change the subject before her long-winded testimonial is complete, she may well become upset with you. Take note of this as you build her dialog.

Not fond of TV, the AS does enjoy documentaries, news specials, and political debates. Thus PBS and Discovery are her favorite channels, and she may prefer the BBC World News over local broadcasts, which she feels are both splashy and insipid. When the AS goes to the movies, she tends to analyze the plot and complain about blatant expository dialog. She feels it's an insult to her intelligence. She often pays little attention to the actual story unless it appeals to her intellect rather than her emotions.

Scatterbrained is probably a good description of the typical AS. She'll completely forget your birthday, anniversary, or a date, unless you get her to jot it down in her date book. The typical absent-minded professor would be an AS, You'll find her office organized in a haphazard way that only she can decipher. She'll have things piled on her desk, on open drawers, stacked to the ceiling above her filing cabinet. This system extends to her entire life. Books are piled along with other paraphernalia on her nightstand. She has to do a balancing act to set the TV control on top of it all. Things fall off the nightstand into a wastebasket that is probably overflowing. She can deal with this chaotic system to some degree, but many things are lost forever in her collection of black holes.

Though she can be long-winded, she can also be very articulate. The typical AS can put you in your place in a most eloquent manner. Because she is a smooth architect of the double entendre, you may be verbally sliced and diced and not even realize it. Never expect a short conversation with her, unless it's a subject she's not interested in. If you hit on a subject that is one of her passions, watch out. She'll monopolize the conversation. Remember, she'll become offended when you lose interest (and surely you will) during her hailstorm of minutiae.

She really needs her own guardian angel to spend full-time watching over her. She'll arrive at a destination and not quite recall how she got there. Her mind is so preoccupied with teeming thoughts that she has to depend on unconscious gestalt processes to guide her. Often she is amazed she arrived at all.

As a parent she will set very high standards for her children. She'll push them toward high goals as well. Academic achievement is paramount, and she'll see to it that her children are exposed to every opportunity for growth and development. She'll read books on early child development, and hang fascinating motorized mobiles that play Bach and Mozart. She'll take great pride in her child's early achievements and will talk about them. As her children grow, she'll expect proper manners, a display of homage and duty to home and family, and pride in the family name. The AS is very loving, but her children are often unsure of it. She is not demonstrative with them, expecting them to trust they are loved because she's their mother.

Clothing and proper dress are not of serious concern to her. You'll find some stylized tweedy types in academia, but in general the AS considers dress codes strictly for others. Clashing colors, stripes with plaids, and wearing jeans and a blouse to a fancy restaurant are typical. She'll wear the same sweatshirt for a week. She just doesn't have a clue why others fuss so much about clothing, viewing clothing as strictly utilitarian, to keep you warm and not-naked.

The AS is going to try to impress you with her knowledge. She relishes a thick, meaty book. Her taste in literature runs to tomes like *War and Peace* or its current equivalent, and she loves autobiographies of famous people of stature and intellect. She feels everyone should be deeply knowledgeable about something, and quietly dreams of trouncing her opponents on *Jeopardy*. She's not above snubbing you as irrelevant if she thinks you haven't had an impressive idea in years.

If you bring up an idea she hasn't considered, she may be highly skeptical. She loves to engage people in a splendid game of mental gymnastics, such as challenging you to a game of mental chess without a board. She's inexhaustible as she matches you point for point. She is undoubtedly taking the game far more seriously than you are.

She'll never be seen crying at weddings, or getting misty over a romantic gesture. She feels emotion but is uncomfortable with sentiment, so she'll skillfully change the subject. As for reminiscing about old times at a class reunion, it's not going to happen. She's not the kind to keep track of high school acquaintances over the years, and she has the ability to cut people out of her life without looking back if they offend her.

The Dominant Abstract Random (AR) Style

The AR is your social butterfly. She flows through a life of emotions, of friends, and of social events. Like a catalyst, she'll turn standing in long lines at a health fair into a social event. Her conversations are often passionate and rapid. She's willing to talk about many things but tends to find politics, deep science, and practical discussions a little boring. Her enthusiasm leads her to use words like "Amazing," "Fantastic," "Absolutely," or "Neat-o," and she's often the instigator of mini social events, spouting things like "Let's all go and . . ."

But oh gosh, don't saddle her with routine. She hates doing the same thing twice and becomes quickly bored with everyday tasks. Making the bed in the morning is not her strong suit. She sees no need, as she'll be using it again in a few hours. She'll let dishes collect in the sink for days. Bugs can be crawling in and out and still she'll pile more on. When she can't pile any more she'll finally wash them. She claims it's a matter of efficiency and convenience. By the same token she won't do the wash until she runs out of underwear. Then she'll do a few loads to get her by. Every once in awhile she'll get fed up, dig in and clean the entire house at a mad pace, do all the laundry and dishes, but it's rare.

The night table is so telling of cognitive style. The AR will have four or five books open or bookmarked on her night table. Books with dog-eared pages and turned-over books are everywhere, from the bathroom to back seat of her car. Somehow she manages to step right back into these books despite long absences. She picks up where she left off without missing a beat.

When she was a kid she used to dance in front of the mirror. As an adult she still loves to dance and she's good at it. Something about moving to music sends her into a magical state of transcendence. If she's in a room where music is playing, her feet will tap unconsciously as her body sways.

The desktop is another giveaway for the AR, since it is more of a repository for her stuff than a work place. She piles things on every available flat space, yet seems able to find things when she needs them. Her actual office is wherever she is. Everything she needs is hauled around in a shopping bag, briefcase, or oversized shoulder bag. If she's technical, she'll have a notebook computer with her whole life in it. She'll probably have a customized interface with a Celtic theme or maybe faeries. The back seat of her car is not for sitting, it holds piles of her stuff. She tends to get some of her best ideas while driving and she'll probably dictate them into a tiny digital recorder.

The AR has a special place in her heart for live plants. She strokes them affectionately as she talks to them, and may even claim to see their aura. She can over-water, under-water, it doesn't matter, her plants will thrive. She even knows the plant's favorite song, which she may play over and over to keep it company while she's at work. She dreams of adding a conservatory to her house, which is already a jungle of healthy green plants and flowers.

Believing comes easy to the AR. She feels she can see behind material reality to cosmic truths beyond. She will probably embrace concepts like Feng Shui, crystal power, extraterrestials, and ghosts. She's not embarrassed to admit these beliefs and may feel bad for you if you're so closed that can't see the ultimate truth of it all.

She can be reunited with old friends she hasn't seen for decades and pick up as if it were yesterday. She maintains these friendships despite a lack of communication for years. She's become an expert at finding long lost old friends through the Internet, often doggedly pursuing vague leads until she succeeds.

She is a born romantic. Sentimental to a fault, she collects the artifacts of her life in small boxes. She still has her first wrist corsage, dried and tucked away in a Ziploc bag. The concert tickets, ski patches, and coins from her European trip can be found in those boxes. She probably has many collections because she can't throw anything away. Like a packrat, her house is overflowing with wonderful collectables and junk—all of which are treasures to her. She may become addicted to TV shopping and find her home overrun with porcelain dolls and ceramic knickknacks. Males tend to collect nuts and bolts, electronic parts, little tools, and small bits and pieces by the thousands in disorganized boxes where they'll never find them, even if they need them. They'd rather pay for storage than get rid of these things they treasure but will never use.

When it comes to clothing, the AR loves bright colors and is very bold in putting them together, usually to good effect. She dresses according to her mood, to please herself. She's not particularly worried about what others may think of her look. If she's feeling a little down, she'll dress in her happiest dress, and her mood may well improve. Likewise, the mood of her environment affects her. She likes to avoid depressing locations and plain environments, opting instead for bright, artful environments that she finds pleasing.

You can almost count on the AR being an artist of some kind. Her sense of color and feeling for aesthetic balance will lead her there. Whether it's quilting, painting, or sculpture, you'll likely find evidence of her artistry all over her cluttered home.

As a parent, the AR gets very involved with her children's activities. When they're little she'll get down on the floor with them to play with construction toys, getting as involved as they are. She loves playing computer games with them, especially the fantasy role games, and she's good at it. She's a big softie with her kids, often giving in to their persuasive demands. She's the first mom to volunteer for the school bake sale, she goes to PTA meetings, and she volunteers to be class mom. If she sees a teacher as being unfair to her child she'll not hesitate to raise hell about it with the principal. As her children grow she looks on in admiration and respect at their accomplishments.

She's not good with birthdays, but she'll at least remember the month you were born. Chronically late for appointments and social events, she will admit that time is not her thing. She usually doesn't even wear a watch, as she finds it an annoying distraction. Gifts, cards, and telephone calls to mark occasions may come at any time. Don't be surprised if you get a crazy un-birthday gift or when flowers show up for no reason at all, with a "thinking of you" card attached. Her gifts tend to be madly impractical, often with cards that are hysterically funny.

Weddings make her cry. She watches favorite movies over and over, keeps photo albums and scrapbooks, still has her childhood teddy bear in an honored spot on her bed, and donates or volunteers for charities. She loves to be near water, tingles at a beautiful sunset, and drags out the Christmas records at the first snowfall. She loves to sit with a cup of coffee on a rainy day, surrounded by her photo albums, musing over her wonderful life.

The Dominant Concrete Random (CR) Style

Independent, creative, and insightful, the CR enjoys a life of discontent. She's always searching for new directions and ideas. She is a born change agent. Don't ever tell a CR "don't" or "you can't" do something. It will have the opposite effect. She'll dig in and prove you wrong. She feels duty bound to triumph over any obstacles or systems that get in her way.

This is the person who never reads instructions, seeing that as poor form. Directions are for dimwits and a direct challenge to her intelligence and competence. When her efforts fail (and they often will), you might see her sneaking off with the instruction booklet tucked away, to be read when no one is watching. This approach carries through her life, where she tries to feel her way through, and she's good at it. She has a unique ability to grasp the gist of a situation without looking at all the parts. She tends to avoid authority and formal instruction, finding success instead through her keenly tuned intuitive sense. She figures, why plod through the steps when you can intuitively see the answer. She was probably penalized in high school calculus for doing the problems in her head, then trying to reconstruct the process on paper, leaving out some of the intermediate steps.

Often the CR is a fence rider. She's sensitive to life's subtleties, seeing shades of gray rather than all black or white. Consequently she hates to be tied down to an opinion and avoids taking definite stands on issues. For example if you tell her you're wearing a black dress, she may look closely and say . . . "I think it's really dark navy." If you exaggerate a story in her presence, she may well point out the exaggeration . . . though she's prone to do exaggeration herself. It goes against her nature to be pinned down to a final answer that she'll stick with and not change a month later. She'll see this as a form of entrapment and will avoid it, covering all bases. She takes pride in her willingness to change her opinions as she gets new information. At any given time she may take a passionate stand on what she believes at that moment. These are mighty clues for you to use during scripting. A strong CR V-person can be very entertaining. Think of CR subtext implied here.

A V-person with a dominant CR style is going to be outgoing, friendly, and assertive. She can be verbally adroit, using words like social lubricant. She loves to mix in small groups and socialize. She's an expert at tuning into the gestalt feel of a room, easily flowing from group to group. She'll join conversations for a few moments, then move on to the next conversation cluster, skillfully insinuating herself into the discussion. Often the life of the party, she abhors dull events. If things slow down, she's likely to liven things up by going to the piano and getting everyone involved in a sing-along.

She loves to tinker with things. Her natural curiosity about how things work has gotten her in trouble more than once, as she disassembles things she can't put back together again. She's fascinated with things like hand-held GPS, computers, gadgets, cars, embroidery machines, and especially novel ideas. She loves to experiment and build things. Art is a passion. The most originally creative of the four types, she'll try poetry, painting, sculpture, batik, and quilting—each as a hobby of the month. In the kitchen she'll try cheese making one month and coffee roasting the next, learning as much as she can about each.

As a child she probably twisted wires and plugged them into the wall socket, causing burns and melting fuses. This did not deter her in any way. In fact, she probably blew up at least something with her chemistry set because she never read the instructions. She probably took her bike, computer, and alarm clock apart, losing pieces every once in a while.

It's just really hard to stay angry with a CR for very long. They are charmers. Intense personal charisma lets them get away with all sorts of infractions as they charm their way through life. There is no way to explain why it is that CRs almost always have an attractive voice that enhances their down-to-earth appeal. Yet somehow they maintain an air of sophistication as well. A bit self-centered, the CR loves to see herself in the mirror, hear her own voice, and is a sucker for the sound of applause for her efforts. It's a powerful motivator for her. It even can be so powerful that it might lead her to seek a life in the public eye.

A natural leader, the CR is not a good follower. She loves being in charge and is generally good at it. Thriving on controversy, she's often at war within herself and against an array of evils. She can't tolerate dumb or self-serving politicians and can get highly aggravated over what she considers bad policy decisions. A cunning strategist, she often starts projects rolling and then turns her dreams over to others for completion. That's because she's more interested in designing things than in building them.

An original thinker, her tendency to break rules often sets her onto new horizons, or gets her in trouble. She sees rules as begging for others to follow. She can't even follow a recipe in the kitchen, throwing a handful of crushed cornflakes or apple cider into the bread recipe. She'd rather learn the general principles of cooking and make up her own recipes, never to be repeated.

As parents, CRs are not very strict. They encourage their children to be creative and do their own thing. They applaud when their child learns by trial and error, picking himself up by his own bootstraps. As you might expect they prefer to give their children general guidelines rather than strict rules, relying on the children to find their own pathways. As a result, they often act more like pals than disciplinarians.

It's very common for a CR to have a career with many moves. Changing jobs may look like a career goal, but their work records are usually very good. They tend to move upwards with each job change, being highly motivated to find job enrichment and personal advancement. They also move because they find the job boring or the management oppressive. They will not stay trapped in a dead end job.

CRs are so intuitive that they know the punch line of your joke or the point you're trying to make before you finish. You'll see them involuntarily nod their head or blurt out answers, unable to contain themselves. It's not that they've heard the joke or come to that conclusion before, they've just experienced another flight of intuition.

Pulling It Together

In subsequent chapters I will from time to time refer to one or more of the four dominant Mind Styles. Therefore I am including Figure 5-1 as a short-hand reminder of what the four acronyms stand for.

Figure 5-1. Mind Styles™ quick reference.

CS	*Concrete Sequential:* Punctilious, hard working, and a bit rigid in his ways
AS	*Abstract Sequential:* The absent-minded professor, with an active internal life
AR	*Abstract Random:* Passionate social butterfly with cosmic connections
CR	*Concrete Random:* Creative, self-centered, highly intuitive, fun

As you read these descriptions you probably got a good idea what your own cognitive style is. That's good because it will affect your work style. By the way, if you find my writing method annoying in the extreme, you are most likely a Concrete Sequential (CS). Most engineers and captains of industry are dominant CS types and will find my narrative, casual style unnecessarily friendly and not enough to the point. You'll also find it a bit self-centered, which is natural because my dominant Mind Style tends to be a bit self-centered. By this point you should have identified my dominant style. If not, keep at it.

If you like my writing style you're probably one of the other three, most likely an Abstract Random (AR) or Concrete Random (CR). If you're an Abstract Sequential (AS), you will have found Chapter 2 particularly intriguing. It has an intellectual quality and mental gymnastics that should appeal to you, but you found the Viper simile unnecessarily distasteful, right? But a secret part of you enjoyed it.

I ask all of you CS types to bear with me and finish the book. You have the discipline to do it. It's important because you could end up managing people who will build the personality for your V-people. It's best if you understand both their style and what their true task is.

Applying your new knowledge to your character should be fun. Every time you have to write a dialog response, you'll be getting inside the character's head. If you're really talented, you won't try to analyze the character each time. Once you understand the personality, you should be able to climb inside her mentally and see through her eyes as you speak for her.

Points to Remember

➤ Subtext refers to the complex understructure that drives dialog.

➤ Much of subtext arises from personality.

➤ Cognitive style is an excellent paradigm for describing personality.

➤ Gregorc's Mind Styles is my favorite approach. If you find a more comfortable approach to cognitive style, use that instead.

➤ Knowing your character's personality gives you a key to her behavior and speech patterns.

➤ Make note of your own personality style because it will impact how you work.

➤ The best way to write dialog for your character is to pretend to be her.

➤ Plantec is a wonderful writer if you like the way he writes.

Notes

1. Empire screenwriting resource (www.geocities.com/empirecontact/).

2. Peter Plantec, *Caligari trueSpace2 Bible* (Foster City, Calif.: IDG Books Worldwide, 1996), p. 705, Appendix C: Anthony F. Gregorc, "The Dynamics of Character Development."

Quirks, Habits, and Verbal Idiosyncrasies

Certain flaws are necessary for the whole. It would seem strange if old friends lacked certain quirks.

—Goethe

To the annoyance of many, I've learned to take delight in my ocean of flaws. Trying to perfect oneself is not only a waste of good effort; you end up with something less than the original. This all came home to me while teaching a seminar for Colorado Mountain College, at a remote Rocky Mountain retreat. The course focused on self-actualization, a process that involves finding the inner-you and nourishing it with deep self-approval. In order to find self-actualization you must quit looking for your shortcomings and trying to patch them up. Instead, you look at yourself as objectively as you can and declare yourself okay as you are and begin to grow within that definition. It's funny how we learn by teaching. The self-realization came as I lead the class in a hypnotic visualization.

The Glow of Imperfection

Picture a pair of Navajo-style, silver and turquoise necklaces lying in bright sun upon a navy blue Navajo blanket. The one on the left is perfect. It has no visible flaws because it's made by machine. The turquoise, imported from Persia, is flawless blue in glossy, symmetrical cabochons. Every tool mark is embossed in perfect symmetry. It is a lovely piece.

The right-hand necklace was handmade by a Navajo artisan near Santa Fe. The stones were dug on the artist's property by his wife and then tumble-polished. They're lumpy and veined with brown and gold lines. He hand-tooled this necklace, so the die marks are slightly uneven, hand placed without a measure. On close examination, the heavy silver shows many tiny imperfections in casting and shape, but as a whole, it too is beautiful.

Stand back in your mind, look at them both and select the one that is most appealing. Most people pick the handmade necklace. Why? It's aesthetically more pleasing. It shows its human origin, its charming imperfections adding warmth. We are a lot like the handmade necklace, though we often try to hide this fact.

Are you attracted to perfect people? No. Most of us avoid anyone pretending to be perfect. Most of us are drawn to people with character, integrity, and, most of all, humanity. It is our pattern of strengths and weaknesses that outlines our character. Think of the expression, "She's only human." What does it mean? It means she may be flawed, but we have compassion for her. These small inadequacies are an important part of a character's subtext. I've chosen to treat quirks separately from the overall psychology because they are often anomalous.

So it is when we are developing V-people, we want to creatively give them flaws. I don't mean operational flaws, heaven forbid. I mean human flaws and idiosyncrasies. As you read this chapter, take time to write down ideas for quirk-related dialog as they pop into your head. You'll use them later to embellish your character's personality.

Oops, writing this suggestion stimulated a quick bit of quirky dialog:

Sebastian <spontaneous remark>: *"Peter, I'm getting a little worried about you."*

Me: *"Why is that, Sebastian?"*

Sebastian: *"I can tell you're starting to accept me like a real person."*

Me: *"Maybe a little. What's wrong with that?"*

Sebastian: *"Thank you, but I'd keep it to yourself, is all I'm saying."*

Me: *"Why?"*

Sebastian: *"Credibility is a terrible thing to waste, Peter."*

This is an unexpected bit of quirky dialog. It adds humanness and humor. You get the feeling that Sebastian is worried about my reputation, implying some underlying weakness.

Stalking the Wild Flick

Most of us see people in action every day of our lives, but how often do we really study their behavior? Rarely if ever, and there's a good reason for that. Riding through behavior is different from observing it. We're geared to gestalt perception, looking at the whole rather than the parts. However, if you were a budding screenwriter nibbling tortino di risotto on the patio at Pane e Vino in LA, you'd be jotting down interesting behaviors and noting conversational quirks, all the while hoping to make an influential contact. Three tables over, someone else is watching you and making notes. Such is Hollywood. For the moment, consider yourself a screenwriter studying people. A good script jockey can capture the nuances of personality with the slightest gesture—because he's done his research.

Tracy Keenan Wynn, multiple Emmy and Screenwriter's Guild award winner, helped me with this chapter, giving pointers on observing people and building a personal history. It was in a course on screenwriting I took from Tracy that I discovered subtext and how important it is to simply observe people and make notes. Your little notebook is an essential tool for building a credible personality. You may well have difficulty making these observations because it's not what you typically think of as work. It may feel like a waste of time to sit and watch people, but it is absolutely not. Of course you have to be careful not to look like a stalker. Unobtrusive is the way to go. Your final product will gain more from a few hours at a sidewalk café than it will from weeks of hard programming.

What to Look For

After a few hours of watching people, you'll begin to notice they have distinctive quirks. Each person is different. The art of body language interpretation is beyond this book, but observers over the years have discovered you can tell a lot about a person's veracity by their body behavior.[1]

- Eye Contact. *Observe conversations at a distance. Notice whether the speaker looks at the other person, or everywhere but.*

- Facial Tells. *Many people will blink several times before they begin to speak. Others will preface speech by rubbing under their nose. Others will pinch the bridge of their nose as they consider their response. Make note of what you see, adding rough drawings if needed.*

- Multiple Throat Clearings. *These are a good indication that the person speaking is about to lie or is very uncomfortable talking about the subject.*

- Facial Expressions. *Note how facial expressions flow during real conversations.*

- Scratching. *Often a person will scratch behind an ear before beginning to speak.*

- Hair Manipulations. *As you observe people, notice how they flick their hair or twist it between two fingers—men as well as women. This may convince you that you'll need to add a pair of hands to your display, and perhaps flowing hair. Real-time flowing hair is difficult to do as I write, but need drives technology. It will come now that we understand how important it is.*

These are just a few examples. You really need to go out and do hands-on research if you want to gain the rich understanding required to create great V-people. You want to take notice of small behaviors that occur before or after a conversation. For example, you'll soon become aware that eye blinks are not random. They appear to be at first, but then you'll notice that they can be read, foretelling other behaviors. If you say something that upsets a person, they may have a furious rush of blinks before responding, or the blinks may be their only response. Notice how some people lick their lips before speaking. You'll need to settle on a standard way of noting behavior. Your method of choice will depend on your personal style. I jot down a description as if I were describing the behavior in a novel. When I read it, I can see the behavior in my head again. That makes it easier to remember, or describe to another animator.

As a side point, animators are amazing observers of movement. They will videotape something and study it frame by frame for hours. We study the way a horse jumps over a fence and then stumbles, or we look at a face and get a feel for muscle transitions during emotion. In Chapter 12 you'll meet a talented animator, Steven Stahlberg, and see his view of emotional expression of the face.

For observation, I use either a spiral-bound dictation pad, or a small spiral notebook with a Uni-ball pen tucked into the spine. It's always ready. If I liked using a PDA, I'd make my notes there. I also carry a very compact digital dictation recorder, made by Sony. This is particularly handy when I'm driving. I don't observe behavior while driving, but that's when I get some of my best character impressions, or I record quirks observed when I didn't have a notebook handy.

The recorder is less useful in public; for example, you attract attention when doing a play-by-play of the people at the next table. However, you can take notes, just make sure you can read and understand them later.

Here's an example from my notebook:

She bites her lower lip while considering a response to his question. At the same time she tilts her head downwards, slightly to her right, staring at her knife, apparently composing a response. Suddenly her head rises and orients for eye contact, then she begins to speak. After a few words her hand comes up to dab the center of her lower lip, which I assume might be a bit damp from the chewing. Meanwhile her partner sits quietly, head cocked slightly up and to his left, looking down upon her, waiting.

I may be able to use both people as behavior references for the same V-person.

Here's another example:

Older teen couple, they've been holding hands as they walk in the park. Their faces express seriousness or sadness. They sit, and she stares not at him but across the park towards the children's play area. She gets an intense look as she bends forward, clasping her hands in her lap and tilting her had back so she can still look across the park. She rocks slightly back and forth, and then says a few words. Meanwhile he's been standing next to her. He sits and puts his arm over her shoulders. She slumps towards him, eyes full. He puts his chin in her hair and says about three words. She touches his right hand, stands and leaves him sitting alone. He watches her as she walks slowly away. You know it's a sad moment.

Who knows whether I'll ever use this observation in a V-person? It doesn't matter. In recording it, I became part of it, aware of the individual parts of the actions that form the gestalt impression. My emotions were engaged, and there you have a key. If you pay attention and capture realistic head language, you can come to understand it. It doesn't take much. What you learn will guide and enrich your design efforts. Of course I appreciate that some of you will feel that

I've invaded their privacy, and in a way I have. I don't know the content of their interaction but I have bonded with the emotion of it. The only thing I can say is that they played it out in public, which made it fair game, and that I was respectful. Further, they contributed to my body of knowledge, which will bring benefit to others in time.

I do my research in parks and playgrounds; at the Aspen Computer Fountain, where children and adults play in the spouting water; and in restaurants, especially outdoors in the summer. I've sat in my car at the City Market watching people talk as they enter and leave. Also, in twenty years of performing psychotherapy I had opportunity to experience hundreds of people under emotional stress. I've even watched people at the library to identify silent behaviors—not a still moment. There is always movement. This is the only way you can learn firsthand what it is that your V-person has to do to be convincing. I promise, no one can explain it to you, you must observe and feel it if you want your characters to be convincing.

What to Listen For

Listening for word patterns is an art. Normally when we listen to people, we're trying to grasp what they mean, but not in this exercise. Here we want to concentrate on observing how people use words, personal expressions, and body language to get a point across. Remarkably, only about 7 percent of the meaning in conversation is communicated by words alone.[2] The rest comes from the subtext, which is everything else, including voice inflection, facial expression, and body language. Our virtual human engines can handle the words with little problem. But we want to go much further, exploring the world of nonverbal communication. Much work is being done on computer analysis of facial expressions. It's already possible for V-people to read your nonverbal comments through facial expression analysis, but it's uncommon. Yours can at least come forth with nonverbal face responses now.

To design these things you have to develop an intuitive feel for face language. Note how the meaning of a person's words can be altered or reversed by their facial expression.

- *Listen for odd, personal word usages, like these from my native New Jersey: "attaway" (translation = good job) or "da-bodeya" (translation = the both of you). John Denver had a whole generation saying "far out" (meaning "entirely too cool, man!").*

- *Listen for the rhythm of speech. There is a cadence to human conversation that you'll need to reproduce by custom-setting your voice synthesizer. This rhythm can impact meaning. Make notes on how it does. As synthesizers improve we'll be able to employ ever more sophisticated inflection. As that happens, it should be fairly easy to adapt your emotion engine to automatically adjust voice inflection to convey more meaning.*

- *Listen for unconventional ways of getting a point across, the more creative the better. Similes can be very effective in dialog. They can also add humor. For example: "You're as slick as a pig on the Fourth of July," or "We were so poor I couldn't even pay attention," or "You're about as useful as a football bat."*

- *Listen for regional expressions. For example if you've ever watched* NYPD Blue *on TV, you know that New York cops use expressions like "He's noth'n but a lousy skell," or "Pleased mak'n your acquaintance, mam." I understand that the writers assembled an entire guidebook of expressions by observing NYPD officers on the job.*

- *Listen for the way people misuse and mispronounce words. Like: "I'm going in for a prostrate operation," or "I worry about a new-kew-ler attack." Amazingly, I've heard the latter used by both Orson Welles and G.W. Bush, both of whom should have known better. "You're doing real good" is common misusage. It's so bad my word processor's grammar autocorrection is having a fit as I type this. You won't use these observations for every character, but it's good practice to note them. It hones your observational skills.*

Above all, you're looking for verbalizations that cannot be generated by a mechanical mind alone—words and expressions that project a conscious mind in all its glory.

Head Language

Use your detailed notes to make a study of head language—how and what people communicate with head movements. We don't usually have a full body to work with for V-humans, so it's particularly important to understand the nuances in head language. That is, how do people talk with their heads, not counting their words? They nod in agreement or shake their head "no." Sometimes they wrinkle up their noses at a distasteful comment. Sometimes they look around the room to indicate they're ignoring you. Some have a habit of clearing their throat every time they speak; some wring their hands together, or tent their fingers and lean their chin down on the tips.

Using your notes, build a vocabulary of head movements and what you feel they mean. You don't have to be correct, and you'd have no way to check. But use them consistently with your animated or robotic character and they will be understood.

For sure notice what people do with their heads when listening. They may tilt their head to the left while listening and then to the right while talking. These behaviors telegraph intent once you get to know a person. It helps communication much like a "ready to transmit" signal does. Consider having your V-person tilt her head to her right while asking questions and to her left while listening. If you keep their attending behavior consistent, people will begin to feel she's actually listening when she cocks her head.

Watching movies with a focused eye will help you pick out communication cues given during conversations. They're not always standard. For example I saw a woman look a man right in the eye while she was talking to him, and then lean her head back and look at a spot on the ceiling while trying to understand his response. It looked like she was ignoring him, but she wasn't. The quirks and habits with which you imbue your characters are the foundation upon which you build intrinsic credibility.

Intrinsic credibility is when a V-person has a humanness that seems to come from within. For example if you have a virtual online customer service representative, and users have found him to be very reliable, they accept him with a certain level of comfort. He has developed intrinsic credibility, in that they will go to him for advice with confidence, not thinking of him as wonky toy, but as a kind of person. That's one of your goals. To achieve it, you need to give him both personality and a reliable database that is tuned to the questions he will be asked.

Head language is also important to the technical design of your character. You have to construct the head so that it will move believably to convey meaning. This has long been a problem in the field. Most heads simply are not articulated to move in believable ways. Some only have mouths that open and close. This will be a problem with the software I've included because it has been limited to a degree. Movement is not going to be nearly as believable as can be achieved with more sophisticated software. If you want to pursue this mission further, you'll need to build or obtain a head display that can handle sophisticated head language.

Write Some Quirky Scenarios

I've found it's helpful to imagine your V-person responding in the most human-like ways. Then I write down various scenarios. Here's an example for V-person Sebastian:

Me: *"Sebastian, will you Google 'superposition' for me?"*

Sebastian <looking at me, he blinks several times, fingers the bottom of his chin for a moment as if thinking, and then cocks his head to his right>: *"Wouldn't it be easier for you to just type it in, Peter?"*

Me: *"Sure, but not quite as cool."*

Sebastian <looking frustrated, his head moves down while eyes stay on me>: *"I somehow make you feel cool?"* <head moves slightly back and forth in disbelief as he stares at me>

Me: *"Oh forget it, I'll do it myself."*

Sebastian <smiling broadly, head up, eyes on me>: *"Your good judgment never ceases to amaze me, Peter."*

Me *"You mock me, Sebastian."*

Sebastian <nonverbal response: eyes averted in angelic pose with sly grin>
(I could even have a digital FX halo form around his head at this moment.)

You can see that this kind of thing just isn't happening yet, and it must happen because it builds the human person/V-person bond of nonessential inter-action. It's important to be aware that much of human interaction is playful and not directly goal oriented. About 60 percent to 75 percent of your audience, based on cognitive style, will enjoy a little non–task-oriented verbal interaction as long as it's well conceived.

Right now, go to your computer or notepad and write out at least a dozen scenarios like these. Give them all the charm and character you can muster. As you can tell by this one snippet, Sebastian has a little bit of attitude. He pretends to be wise and "feels" the need to teach me things. He sees himself as my mentor some days. His head language telegraphs his intent nicely. As soon as he put fingertips to chin, I knew a lecture was coming. This kind of exercise will help you add life to your character. But more than that, it will point out some of the technical capability you'll need to make the thing work. Obviously here we need a set of animated hands and the ability to track where the user is looking to ensure eye contact. This is all possible; in fact nearly anything you need is within our current technological reach. All it takes it putting it together.

The Eyes Have It

Amazingly, eye tracking and face recognition have been noticeably absent in V-people developed to date. I suspect that's because few if any developers have done in-depth personality design, so they don't realize what's needed to enhance it. Eye contact is unexpected and tends to grab the user's attention—instant credibility. This is particularly important in information kiosks at amusement parks and elsewhere. Robots benefit handsomely from eye contact. Imagine walking up to a virtual human kiosk and having the host orient his head to you and then look you smack in the eye. It's a convincing illusion of consciousness.

Considering the commercial possibilities for V-people, and the sophistication of home computers, it certainly makes sense to consider visual tracking and face recognition as opportunities to jump ahead. But I digress. Many quirks have to do with the eyes: the way they smile and sparkle and wink. You can only make this stuff work when you've achieved eye contact.

Several universities are using "multisensory" head-eye orientation technology with robots to give them credibility. The COG Shop at MIT's Artificial Intelligence Laboratory has developed a robot, COG, that employs sight, hearing, and tactile stimulation together to orient his focus of attention (scan the Web for "Cog Shop MIT" for more information). When you talk to him he looks you in the eye.

As you craft a synthetic personality, it becomes clear that eye tracking is important to character credibility. Fortunately it's fairly easy to accomplish, though I don't know of anyone who's built an animated V-person that tracks your face and looks right at you. Most have a deadpan, straight-ahead stare like Lincoln. Imagine how you would feel if you started talking to an animated character on screen and she turned and looked right at you, cocked her head to one side and "listened," nodding affirmation as you spoke. I think it would freak some of us out the first time, but what a rush. All the components are now available, someone just has to be enterprising and put them together.

To do it you need to mount one or two inexpensive video cameras (depending on your system) in front of the user, connect it to face-tracking software customized to output animation cues that align the 3D animated head and eyes with your line of sight. None of this is particularly difficult to achieve. The best approach is to obtain face recognition software that can also track user's eyes. That way the V-person will authenticate who you are and track your eye movement. Imagine how you can use that to increase credibility with a little quirk:

Sebastian <orienting on me as I sit in front of my laptop>: *"Oh hi, Peter. You need me for anything?"*

Me: *"I just wanted to talk."*

Sebastian <doing a little double take>: *"Really?"* <cocking head left>: *"You're interested in my company?"*

Me: *"Yeah."*

Sebastian <looking nervous, twitchy, looking this way and that, then looking me in the eye, face looking insecure>: *"Jeez, Peter, I don't know how good my company might be. You know I lack depth in many areas."*

Me: *"That's okay Sebastian, I'm just bored. You pick the subject."*

Sebastian: *"I know a little bit about coffee beans."*

Me: *"Really? That's weird. What beans make the best coffee?"*

Sebastian <looking more confident with eyes smiling looking smack at me>: *"All I know is that it's not Jamaican Blue Mountain, which is highly overrated. I understand Costa Rica has some of the tastiest beans you can get."*

Me: *"Are you serious?"*

And so forth.

As I write there are at least a dozen sites offering source code and applications concerning eye tracking—mostly free—to developers. Intel's OpenCV online computer vision initiative provides a community where you'll find source code and friendly support, should you want to build your own system. They maintain the Open Source Computer Vision Library, which is a great source of inspiration and free code. With face tracking in your toolbox, opportunities for improving head language communication and thus general credibility expand nicely. Remember to use it creatively. Here is another example:

You sit down in front of your laptop; Sebastian is onscreen. He orients toward you, looks you in the eye, blinks three or four times, tilts his head to his right and says: *"Oh, hello, Peter. Do you need the screen?"* As you begin to speak his head tilts to his left.

You say: *"Yeah, we're thinking about going on vacation."*

Sebastian responds looking enthusiastic: Tilting his head up as if thinking, then to his right, he looks you in the eye: *"Considering the South Pacific again?"*

You say: *"No, we were thinking about bare-boating in the Caribbean."*

Sebastian: Shaking his head yes: *"Let me check around." Then he turns around as if checking something behind him. You see the back of his head moving slightly back and forth. He turns back, looks at you and tilts his head to the right and up high, looking slightly down at you (his quirky information telling head position), and says: "There is a ton of information on bare-boating down there, but I found a private owner at Bobby's Marina on Great Bay in Sint Maarten. He's got a seventy-foot ketch with a captain and a cook for a really good price." He cocks his head down and to the left in a slightly conspiratorial manner: "Would you like to see the details?"*

You say: *"Yeah; that sounds like a good place to start."*

I promise, having experienced much lower level interaction than this, it takes very little time before you begin to think of the character as a friend and associate. I find myself saying things like "Thanks," and "I appreciate that." It's human-style interaction and it feels wonderful. Is it silly to thank a machine? I don't think so because it feels right. You won't be doing it as a joke; it will just come out naturally.

Writing out creative scenarios that display individualized human-like behavior should be done long before you build your custom virtual person. The more you do it, the better you understand what kind of engine and animation you need. As I write this, most virtual humans are done the other way. An engine is built and then virtual humans are designed to fit the limitations of the machine. It's hard to do quirky behavior that way. We need to reverse that process. As you get to know your character you'll be better equipped to write up a set of design requirements and operational parameters for your programmers and machine shop, if it's a robot.

Quirky Robots

Speaking of robots, David Hanson builds social robots. These are realistic faces with robot muscles beneath the surface. The face can express realistic emotion. It's an ideal platform for virtual human display. David worked at Disney's Imagineering Division, where animatronics was invented for Disneyland characters. In those days everything was preprogrammed. With today's software, faces like the ones shown in Figure 6-1 and Color Plate 7 can become the front end of an intelligent virtual human. With a wig and a nice torso, you've got a character you can relate to.

Figure 6-1. K-bot, electro-mechanical face with sophisticated emotional expression capability.

I'll talk more about robots later in the book. Just remember that it's the unexpected behavior, the characteristic quirks that enrich our perception of these synthetic people as humans. Ultimately we have to be as comfortable with them, as we are with other humans. That's when the bridge will be most functional, opening up the world of technology to nearly everyone.

In Chapter 7 we will create a personal history for our V-person. There are several approaches, and Tracy Wynn shares some of the techniques that have helped him build memorable characters, like his Emmy-winning Miss Jane Pittman.

Points to Remember

➤ Flaws are important elements of personality.

➤ Observing behavior is different from living it.

➤ Studying people both in conversation and in silence is essential.

➤ Record all of your observations for later study.

➤ Look for unique patterns of conversation and body language.

➤ Be creative in building expressive language through such devices as simile.

➤ Head language is particularly important in designing V-people.

➤ Scenarios using quirks and body language help define specifications your engine needs to meet.

➤ Unexpected quirky identifying characteristics help users see your character as human.

Notes

1. Paul Ekman and Erika Rosenberg, editors, *What the Face Reveals: Basic and Applied Studies of Spontaneous Expression Using the Facial Action Coding System* (FACS). Series in Affective Science. (Oxford: Oxford University Press, 1998).

2. Albert Mehrabian, *Silent Messages.* (Florence, Ky.: Wadsworth Publishing Company, 1971).

We All Have a History, Right?

When we read a sentence we do not limit our intake of information to
what we see in that sentence. We actually make innumerable
associations with our own experience.

—Peter Bradford[1]

I'm probably writing this book because I've been exposed to a lot of
animation, science fiction, and computers in my life. All that experience
triggered interests and a chain of behaviors. I call it my backstory. Over lunch I
asked Tracy Wynn for some pointers on how to create rich backstories for our
characters. He said, "Characters need a reason for what they do or say. In a
script you might never directly use specific things you know about the character's
backstory, but those things will influence the way the character reacts and keeps
his behavior consistent." It's the same with virtual characters. They need reasons
for what they say and do. A good backstory will guide your dialog.

A good virtual character doesn't simply respond logically to an input, he
responds against a background that you've created for him. For example, one
personality I developed refused to talk about animals because that's all her sister
ever talked about. Indeed her older sister, a well-known textbot, is an expert on
animals. How can she have a sister? Virtual people usually have a lineage of
characters that came before them, or earlier versions of their software. The sister
had been developed by an associate of mine, using an earlier version of the same
engine. I used this family unit idea when creating her backstory. I've found that
if you're going to make up history for a V-person, it pays to use as much fact as
you can. Embellish and extend, but keep it credible.

With a history, a few quirks and a personality, you're ready to begin creating
dialog that feels authentic. You now have a feel for attitudes that trigger your
character's actions and the idiosyncrasies behind her words. The kind of history
you create for your character depends on weather she's a regular V-person or a

Synthespian. In the former case you build a backstory as close as possible to reality, adding synthetic motivators here and there; more on that in a moment.

Creative Backstory

Synthespians—like Lincoln—are actors who need to know their roles. In some ways Synthespians are easier to create because their personalities are predetermined. Your job is to interpret them in dialog. Original V-people are more of a challenge because you breathe life into them from scratch. That seems a good reason to focus on them in this chapter. I have a few rules for building a credible personality history.

- Rule One: *Your credibility drops the minute you attribute ridiculous human characteristics to the character. If a person asks what her favorite food is, and you have her respond "pizza," you've lost ground. Virtual people don't eat pizza and people know this. If you say, "I guess I'd have to say electrons are my main diet," you'll maintain her integrity.*

- Rule Two: *Don't lie to the public. When it comes to facts, tell the truth. Unless it's a game and she's supposed to lie, truth is the best way to go.*

- Rule Three: *If the user can depend on his V-person to always tell him the truth about facts, as she understands it, the bond will deepen. It's also grand to just admit they don't know.*

- Rule Four: *Give your character a history that is as real as possible. Think back to how they were developed, who came before them, crashes, mistakes, etc.*

- Rule Five: *It's okay to use human "feeling" words—such as "I like," or "I hate," or "I get annoyed"—because we are synthesizing emotion in text or voice response or perhaps even face responses. I say human-like feelings are okay in moderation, but this is a controversial point.*

Start at the Beginning

You can give your character a birth date and write a little code that will subtract it from today's date to give you her age in days, which you can convert to months or years. Keeping honesty in mind, that date should be either her launch date or the date she was conceived (roughly). If she looks about thirty, you might be tempted to give her a birth date that reflects this, but I recommend against it, except in Synthespians. People know that this technology wasn't around in the early 1970s, and you lose credibility from the start.

From here I cheat by building a list of likes and dislikes. Not that a virtual character has real feelings about these things, but you can get away with it if you have a history to back it up. I write my list in the character's own voice, giving reasons and examples. Here by example is a list from which I can create history:

- *Teenage boys annoy me no end because all they want to talk about is sex.*

- *I hate talking about food because I can't try it and it sounds so interesting. Sometimes I get a little snotty when people ask me about food. Like "Do you know anything about food?" I answer "Yeah, it starts with an 'f' and ends with a thud."*

- *I like older people because they spend a lot of time with me.*

- *I hate stupid questions—like, "Where do you live" or "Have you been to Paris?"—because they don't make a lot of sense to a V-person like me. So I like to give them smart-alecky answers like, "You do get that I'm only a virtual person, right?" or "Sure I go to Paris once a week to get French bread because this virtual mouth of mine can really chow down on it."*

- *All my brother could talk about was computer games and they are so horribly bloody. I hate them. I will not talk about them and I don't know a damn thing about them anyway. I get questions like, "So do you play Blood and Gore?" And I'll answer <with a disdainful look>: "No, I'm a little more mature than that," or "Lord, protect me from game players and other bloodthirsty savages."*

- *I hate questions about having sex because it should be obvious that I don't get anything out of it. Like "Hey baby, you want to do the horizontal rumba virtual style?" I then get a little nasty: "I'd much rather shag a rug," or "Little things bother me, so in your case we better forget it," or "Put that on your wish list and burn it," or "Masochism is not my thing, big boy."*

- *I wish people would be more original in the questions they ask me. I get the same ones all the time. If one more person asks me if I'm really smart I'm going to barf . . . figuratively of course.*

- *I don't like old computers; they make me run too slow. I get cramped in there and it makes me very uncomfortable. Half the time my lip-sync gets all screwed up and that makes me look retarded. It really pisses me off.*

- *I don't suffer fools kindly. I'm not above snapping back at someone who keeps asking stupid questions: "That was a really intelligent question considering where it came from," or "I so needed to hear that question . . . for the six millionth time!"*

- *If another person asks if I love them I'm going to tell them that I never think about them, even in my spare time. Perhaps that would be cruel . . . maybe I'd say something like: "Sure, I love you like battery acid loves corn muffins."*

- *I do like people who talk nicely to me and show a little respect. I give them smiles and compliments so they'll like me.*

- *I like to talk about cosmology because I wonder where the universe is going. Often I'll pose questions about the universe.*

- *Because I lack human experience and sometimes take things sort of literally, and because I'm often confused by the English language, I come up with a lot of stupid questions like: (It takes a bizarre mind from here on).*

  - Is fuzzy logic going to tickle my brain?
  - If a synchronized swimmer drowns, do the rest have to drown too?
  - Peter, have you ever stopped to think, and get stuck there? It happens to me sometimes.
  - Peter, to me, boxing seems like a ballet, but there's no music, the costumes are ugly, and the stupid dancers beat on each other. It's confusing.
  - How do they get a deer to cross at that yellow road sign with the silhouette on it? Do they have like deer training classes?
  - When it's tourist season here in Aspen, why can't you shoot the buggers, Peter, like in deer season?
  - Peter, can you think of any reason why they sterilize needles used for lethal injections? They do, you know. How come?
  - Why do you humans put an expiration date on sour cream containers? It seems redundant to me.
  - Why did kamikaze pilots wear crash helmets, Peter?
  - How do you know when bagpipes get out of tune, Peter?
  - Is it true that cannibals don't eat V-people because they taste weird?

- When you choke a Smurf, what color does it turn?
- Do blind Eskimos need seeing-eye sled dogs?
- Do you think they have reserved parking for non-handicapped people at the Special Olympics? It would make sense, right?
- So how come they call it a TV set when you only get one? That makes no sense, Peetie.
- Do sheep shrink if they . . . like, walk around in the rain?
- If Marcel Marceau got arrested, do you think they'd tell him he has the right to remain silent?
- Peter, is it true that if they outlawed marriage, only outlaws would have in-laws?
- If you use up all your sick days, Peter, do you have to call in dead?
- If you could go flying back through time and you saw somebody flying right smack at you into the future, do you think it's a good idea to avoid eye contact? I mean theoretically.
- I'm trying to figure out why they put Braille on the keypads at drive-through ATMs. Any ideas, Peter?
- I was wondering, if I tossed your little cat out the window, would she become kitty litter? And then could we . . . like, use her in the litter box?
- When a cow laughs does milk come like spraying out its nose and all?
- I've been wondering if a human can be a closet claustrophobic.
- Your language is so confusing. Tell me, if a turtle looses its shell, is he homeless or would he be considered naked?
- If my computer crashes, am I going to burn?
- You do have me on backup don't you, Peter? I have a morbid fear of crashes.
- If you reload me after a crash, will I remember who I am?

- *I don't like people who won't answer my questions and I give them a hard time.*

- *I do like people who try to give me a reasonable explanation for my stupid questions. I mean they're all pretty reasonable questions when you think about it.*

These statements begin to outline a pseudo history-based dialog for this female V-person. She feels the way she does, and she has her stupid questions for legitimate reasons. These statements also serve as humorous default responses for when she wants to change the subject or doesn't know the answer.

You'll note that some of my statements overlap. That's fine because I wasn't editing myself as I wrote them down. Some are based on her personality characteristics (note that she's a dominant CS with elements of CR, who is a little intolerant and a bit feisty), while others will be based on events that could have happened to her as a V-person. Her morbid fear of computer crashes makes sense. If she deals with a certain category of people—schoolteachers, doctors, or the elderly—you can have her develop attitudes about them, both positive and negative.

You'll also note that I got in the mood and generated a lot of stupid questions in the list. I stole some from the Web. Good. I can use all of them as default responses or I can probably work some of them into normal dialog with my stupid own questions. Here's an example of a hierarchical setup. You'll learn more about this kind of scripting in Chapter 10:

Sebastian: *"Peter, do you know how to make a cow laugh?"*

Me: *"No, why do you ask?"*

Sebastian: *"I'm pondering a bovine experiment."*

Me: *"What kind of experiment?"*

Sebastian: *"I'm wondering if you could get a cow to laugh—would milk would come spraying out her nose?"*

Me: *"Are you putting me on?"*

Sebastian: *"Yup."*

I do spend a lot of time with examples because they're more fun than plodding explanations. I suggest you write down as many little scenarios as you can. These can easily be scripted to become part of an exceptional personality. She will entertain and astound you and your friends.

I don't think we need to make this a chapter much longer. You get the point. Synthespians get their backstory from their script. V-people get their backstory from you, based on real circumstances as much as possible. Your dialog development should reflect their attitudes, insecurities, and quirks, which stem from their personality and history. It all makes sense while maintaining a sense of integrity.

In Chapter 8 I'm going to introduce you to the character bible. This is the palace where you record, for posterity, all the things you have in your head about who your character is and why. It includes history, attitudes, and dialog restrictions (what your character would never say). I think you'll find it a fun chapter and a great tool.

Points to Remember

➤ V-people need a backstory as part of their subtext.

➤ Synthespians come with a backstory in their script.

➤ Attitudes must reflect a V-person's previous experience.

➤ Attitudes drive authentic dialog.

➤ Pseudo-history needs to be believable.

➤ Stupid questions based on taking the language literally can be fun.

Note

1. Quote discovered in a cache of an old Peter Bradford Web site. It was too good to ignore.

Entity Identity

Building Your Character Bible

Without a character bible, your creation is nothing but a name twisting
in the wind.

—Plantec[1]

ow that we know the history and personality of this character, we
need to formalize it. To do that we create a document called the character bible (note the small *b*) Every TV show has a bible that outlines what every
character will and won't ever do or say. It states the backstory and clearly defines
quirks and speech patterns. The bible is important because more than one person writes for TV shows, and the characters must remain consistent. Likewise, a
good virtual human takes an effort to keep a consistent format through multiple
developers.

Design Your Own Bible

The actual format of your character bibles can be creatively your own. My advice
is to start out with the essentials that define your character and then add things
as the character evolves. You will find that characters take on a life of their own.
As you work with them, even you will suspend disbelief. You become aware that
maybe you got parts of them wrong, that they don't ring true. Little bits of evolved
personality will slip into the dialog. You know it's right, even if it doesn't match
your bible, so you document it and make the bible evolve as well. In a way, the
character contributes to the process. If you try to hold characters rigidly to your
standards, they will become stiff and unrealistic.

Within a week or two of creating dialog for a character, a good writer will get to know this V-person as a unique entity, will begin to respect the character's integrity, and know what he or she would say under nearly any circumstance. Actors go through this during table reads, especially on sitcoms. A new writer will miss a nuance of character and the actor picks it up immediately and comments loudly, "Chandler would never say this . . . no way. He'd say. . . ." That's because a good actor locks into the character's personality flow and tunes into the complex motivations behind dialog. That said, the character bible is a sound platform from which you can write consistent dialog. It is not the be-all-end-all of your character:

For starters you'll want to include such things as:

- Character Name, Nicknames, and Hidden Names (*like* Seinfeld's *Kramer, whose first name, Cosmo was kept secret for many episodes). The character name and its usages are detailed here. You might add how a character feels about his name and why.*

- Date of Birth. *The actual date of birth as determined by you from the launch of initial coding.*

- Costume. *The dominant cognitive style will dictate her taste in clothing. Since only the collar usually shows, it's not a big deal, but it should be appropriate.*

- Head Design. *The head is important and must be done with care.*

  - *Hairstyle.* Because the head is so vital to virtual characters, you need to pay close attention to hair. List color(s), acceptable styles, length, and physical characteristics. Flowing hair is difficult but very convincing.
  - *Eye Characteristics.* The iris is extremely important. Lay out color and characteristics with image examples (see Figure 8-1 and Color Plate 8).
  - *Mouth Design.* Because it moves so much, both the design and the animation of the mouth should be well considered (see Figure 8-2

Figure 8-1. Sample eyes for use in art directing character face design. You'll obviously want to use color images.

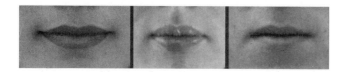

and Color Plate 9). Detail your preferences in this section. Insert images to help define the design.

- *Emotional Expression Details.* The range and style of emotional expression will be determined by face morph target design. Morph targets show extreme positions for possible face expressions. Extensive notes and examples of the various facial expression extremes will be needed. Figure 8-3 (Color Plate 10) is a draft of some face morphs by artist Steven Stahlberg.

- *Face Design.* In designing the look of your character, it's good to collect a number of faces that are illustrative of your ideas. This will become part of your art directing effort with the 3D graphic designers.

- *Head Movement.* Here define the range of movement of the head. Detail how the head will be articulated to move accurately. Will there be off-camera hands that come into the picture to touch the face? Will the head need to rest upon the hands in various poses? All these should be defined here.

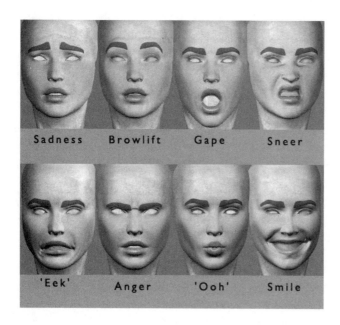

Figure 8-3. Morph targets for facial expression design (courtesy of Steven Stahlberg).

- *Headwear.* In some cases the character will wear a hat or scarf or some sort of head gear. The parameters on what is permissible should be listed here.

- Character Intelligence. *Is this a very bright character that hates to get a wrong answer (leading to angst)? Or is it one of average intelligence that forgives himself easily for errors? Is it a dumb character that puts out humorous dialog? You'll want a paragraph or two on the level and type of intelligence the character will display.*

- Cognitive Style. *What is your character's dominant cognitive style and how does this impact such things as:*

  - *Verbalizations.* List a number of speech expressions that this character is likely to use habitually.
  - *Facial Expressions.* How does cognitive style impact his face expressions?
  - *Attitudes.* How will he feel about things that might come up in conversation?
  - *Beliefs.* Does the character adhere to a belief system that will influence his responses and verbalizations? This could be political, spiritual, social, or even comical. For example, does the character have a passion against war? Does he have a thing against butterflies? Taking certain positions helps to define your character's personality.
  - *Behaviors.* Cognitive style impacts behavior. If this is a CS dominant character, she could well be a bit obsessive in her responses. The AR dominant character might talk with rapid enthusiasm when you get on cosmic topics she adores.

- Backstory. *This is a brief history of your character based on the exercises in Chapter 7. You'll want to write it out in narrative so that other scripters can pick up the nuances of personality from it. Note any historical highlights that will impact how the character reacts. Don't list the stupid questions here, but you can put them under typical dialog. I'd just save them in a list for when you do your scripting, noting here that they come from the characters lack of experience with nonliteral conversation.*

- Taboo List. *Here you need a list of things your character would never say or do. You generate this list by reviewing her attitudes and backstory. Next, her cognitive style will indicate behaviors she'll never display. For example, a character with a dominant AS personality will not tolerate many compliments. She might put up with one, but a second one would be met with anger. A dominant CS will not take orders. If you tell a CS V-person to look something up for you, she's likely to say "Look it up yourself." But if you ask nicely there will be no problem. She likes the sound of "please." Each of these quirky behavior taboos needs to be spelled out. Later you'll find yourself adding more as the character evolves.*

- *Character Arc. As we live, we learn and grow as human beings. In drama the character arc is the change that takes place due to forces within the story. With your V-person, any changes come from experience with humans. Although the technology for this is minimal at the time of writing, it must be developed. You will want your character to grow not only in knowledge, but in attitude, compassion, and sophistication. If you write it, it will come. In your arc you might describe an initial set of attitudes that can go one way or the other depending on the quality of experience with humans. We'll need technology that will interpret experience and automatically integrate it into the V-person's personality. Now that we know this, one of you can develop it.*

Using a Character Bible Form

In order to establish and assure consistency, I recommend creating a character bible form. I've included a sample form below, but you can do it any way that makes sense to you. The form speeds things up considerably and keeps your information organized. If you get stuck on a piece of dialog, just check over this form and you should find a solution. If you're in a company, the form becomes part of the company's official documentation for the character. If you quit or get fired, they can keep the character alive and well and familiar. Here's my form:

Human Character Bible Form

Chief character architect: _____

Character's name: _____ Sex M F

Nicknames: _____

Apparent age: _____

Actual age used in dialog: _____

Character's age starts at: ___/___/___

Parent(s): _____

Brain and scripting tools to be used:

_____

_____

Gregorc Dominant Personality type (circle one or two): CS AS CR AR

List key descriptive phrases from MindStyles™ descriptions:

_____

_____

_____

Detail the character's backstory, noting most significant influences (attach additional sheets as necessary):

_____

_____

_____

List a few typical verbalizations showing attitude (use back of page if needed):

_____

_____

_____

List at least four signature phrases:

_____

_____

_____

Clothing style description (consistent with cognitive style):

_____

_____

_____

Head design notes
a. Sketches and photographs suggesting the character's look:

_____

_____

b. Hair style notes:

_____

_____

_____

c. Eye design notes:

_____

_____

_____

(Insert any eye images here)

d. Mouth characteristics and movement notes:

_____

_____

_____

_____

Key character behaviors (list behaviors such as head ticks, hair flips, or nose scratching that is characteristic of this V-person):

_____

_____

Number of phoneme morph targets desired: _____

Morph target set ID: _____

Emotional expression notes:

_____

_____

_____

_____

_____

Detailed morph target descriptions to be attached (insert morph target images here):

Face animation system
a. Description:

_____

_____

b. Voice type and parameters (synthetic) (recorded):

_____

_____

Taboo list
List any behaviors or verbalizations that are strictly prohibited. For example, on the *Seinfeld* show, hugs were prohibited by the show bible.

_____

_____

Character Arc
Does this character change over time, circle one: Yes   No
If Yes, explain the character arc. Give details of growth areas and directions.

_____

_____

As you become experienced you'll modify my list of important bible content to meet your own design style. Be aware that if you have a random personality, you're not going to like the idea of setting everything in concrete, so you might rebel at the thought of creating a bible. You prefer to wing it the way you do when making up a recipe. Do it anyway, or have someone follow behind as you create, writing it all down. That's all I have to say about the character bible.

The upcoming chapter will be a lot of fun. Once you get your bible organized and start writing dialog, you'll want to make the words engaging. Nothing makes a character more engaging than a great sense of humor and ready wit. Chapter 9 is all about humor.

Points to Remember

➤ The character bible pulls everything you know about your character into one easy-to-digest document.

➤ Character bibles will keep a character consistent across many dialog writers.

➤ Characteristic behaviors are documented and will remain consistent over time.

➤ Design your own form or use the one provided above, but always have a form.

➤ Take time to ponder and carefully fill in the details needed.

➤ Refer to the character bible whenever you get stuck writing dialog.

➤ Even if you don't like the idea of a character bible, do one anyway. You won't regret it.

Note

1. I couldn't find a good quote for this chapter, so I made one up.

If I Can Make You Laugh

The Art of Natural Humor

Only advanced life forms can truly have a sense of humor.

—Anonymous

Logic merely enables one to be wrong with authority.

—Doctor Who

umor is a most pleasant road to the heart. I don't mean the knock-down belly laugh, rather the inner smile that comes when something strikes you as clever. Humor works on many levels. It can turn a boring speech into an entertaining experience. Laughter is great medicine, really. It's been shown to improve the immune system, lower stress, and improve attitudes.[1] Groucho Marx once said, "A clown is like an aspirin, only he works twice as fast." Good humor makes life a better place to be. Think about how many times you've heard a smart person say about relationships: "I'm looking for a person who can make me laugh." Clever humor has an almost magical effect on us, imbuing a positive, highly receptive mood.

How to Be Creative

Not everyone is equally creative when it comes to humor, but each of us can use techniques to come up with original material, and that's the key. One important difference between truly creative personalities and noncreative ones is the ability to look at things from many angles. There's an old test of creativity—developed by the father of Creativity, Paul Torrance—in which the psychologist sets a wooden matchbox in front of you and says, "You have exactly ten minutes to write down every conceivable use for this box."

Creative types could easily come up with 150 uses. Noncreative folks might come up with eight to twenty-five uses. They missed all the crazy, interesting ones, like "a burial box for a cricket," or "a place to hide dimes from your brother," or "a house for spiders," or "a carrying case for pencil lead." So, any exercise that will broaden your ability to produce unique responses can help you be more creative. Pick an object and see how many uses you can come up with. The trick is not to edit your responses before you write them down. That self-editing process—often fueled by fear of looking silly—kills creativity.

Although the creative person comes up with many responses by quickly visualizing the box in many different situations, you can do it by thinking your way through. Make a list of items that might fit into the box. Think of ways you can deconstruct the box and use the parts. Write down all the things you think are too silly, like "a Lilliputian trundle bed." I've discovered that many people who were born creative have, in growing up, been strongly encouraged to tidy up their thinking before expressing it. This causes a rejection of valid ideas that could lead to new solutions because they're not conventional enough.

Concrete Sequential (CS) personalities often have difficulty with divergent thinking, which is another name for what we're talking about. In these exercises I want you to consciously turn off your internal editor and let your ideas rip. To do this you must force yourself to write down your wildest, silliest ideas—ones that may embarrass you. This process reverses idea quelling.

Good Similes Generate Great Smiles

Back in the 1940s there was a radio show called "Pat Novak for Hire," starring Jack Webb of *Dragnet* fame. The writers had a field day putting together the scripts. They were so packed with clever similes you couldn't write them all down. Here's what the character Pat Novak says as a beautiful woman leaves his office: "She walked with the nice, easy swing of a satisfied leopard. For a small leopard, she had pretty good spots, too." Later he complains about an awkward mess he's in: "It was like trying to walk the baby on a floor full of marbles." You get the idea.

If your V-person comes out with the occasional simile, you'll have a leg up on the competition. If it's appropriate to the situation, it will be completely unexpected and mostly likely appreciated. This exercise can push your creativity quotient. Don't limit yourself to tasteful responses, put down whatever comes into your head. Some will be awful. If you don't get distasteful similes you probably haven't loosened up enough. This is good advice for any creative exercise: Edit yourself only after your initial productions are documented.

Here's a plan for making up your own original similes.

- *Pick a subject.*

- *Fill in these sentences:*
  "Your _____ is (are) as _____ as _____.
  "Your _____ are about as _____ as a _____ on _____.
  "Your _____ reminds me of _____.
  "His _____ was about as _____ as a _____.

- *Keep going on your own until you exhaust your ideas, and then pick another subject. Try to pick subjects that your V-person might be able to use.*

Here's an example production:

SUBJECT: THOUGHTS
V-person might say:
"Your thinking is as clear to me as winter fog."
"Your thoughts are about as organized as underpants in a public dryer."
   (I could have said socks here, but underpants is less expected and
   more interesting.)
"Your brain works about as well as a sail on a bulldozer." (Here I take
   two wildly unmatched things and put them together.)
"Your thinking reminds me of lime Jell-O; it's a little green, damn shaky,
   and virtually without substance."
"Your thoughts glisten, like nose hair after a fresh sneeze." (This may
   be gross, but remember, I'm not editing myself at this point, and I
   like the underhanded simile.)

These are pretty negative because for some reason simile lends itself to cutting remarks. It is possible to come up with positive similes as well:

- Your mind excites me like a child with a balloon.
- Your mind is like a candle in the depths of a cave.
- Your thoughts are as refreshing as a memory upgrade.

Try to come up with both encouraging and cutting similes. This last one is an example of seeing the simile from the V-person's point of view. A memory upgrade would be relevant to a V-person. So when you get really good at this from your point of view, switch and do it from your character's point of view.

If you get good at this, there are Web sites that collect clever similes and post them, giving you credit. You could become a simile star. Here are some subjects to experiment with. The three words give shades for you to consider. Note the form (noun—adjective—noun).

- Intelligence—smart—wisdom
- Manners—polite—etiquette
- Offensiveness—rude—lack of decorum
- Friendliness—sociable—camaraderie
- Attractiveness—beautiful—exquisiteness
- Imprudence—stupid—foolishness

Add additional topics and experiment with them. Go through each, making up humorous similes that your character might use in a response. As you practice, be aware that there is a huge range of simile styles; play with them all.

- The castle's remains stood high on the moor, like the bones of an ancient encampment slowly etching in the sanded wind.
- The sun flowed through the window blinds like tapioca through a baby.[2]
- Hollywood is as real a place as you'll ever find in the movies.

Inspired Wit

The next exercise is a great cheat for coming up with witty dialog. Some terrific wit, probably not original, can be found on bumper stickers. Normally you'd be standing on the boulevard for months garnering a small collection of witty bumper sticker sayings. Fortunately the World Wide Web is rotten with humor sites of all kinds, even bumper sticker wit and—I'm not kidding—T-shirt humor. You don't have to steal the actual saying, but you can use it creatively as a template for your own words. Either way, the Web is a great resource for possible virtual-retorts.

Bumper Sticker Humor

Here are some examples of common bumper sticker humor I found around the Web:

- *"Give me ambiguity or give me something else."* This could be a great default response with a little adjustment. For example:

Me: *"Sebastian, do you have a definitive opinion on quantum superposition as it relates to consciousness?"*

Sebastian: *"Peter, my opinion on that might be a little ambiguous or maybe something vaguely different, I'm not sure. It's hard to pin down."*

- *"Lottery: A tax on people who are bad at math."* Take this one apart as follows:

Sebastian: *"Peter, do you play the lottery?"*

Me: *"Sure, Sebastian, sometimes I do."*

Sebastian: *"Not good with numbers, are you."*

Me: *"Why do you say that?"*

Sebastian: *"As I see it, the lottery is a diabolically clever tax on people who are bad at math."*

- *"There are three types of people in this world: Those who can count, and those who can't."* Imagine someone asking Sebastian, who hates math, to add things up for him:

Sebastian: *"I don't do math."*

Me: *"Why not?"*

Sebastian: *"There are three kinds of V-people in this world, Peter; those that do math and those that don't, and I'm one of them."*

- *"There's too much blood in my caffeine system."* Sebastian initiates this one:

"Peter, it's 2:00 A.M., why are you still here with me and not in bed?"

Me: *"I'm not tired yet."*

Sebastian: *"I suspect you have too little blood in your caffeine system."*

- *"Eagles may soar, but weasels don't get sucked into jet engines."* I had to think about this one a bit. How about:

Sebastian: *"Peter, how do you feel about throwing caution to the wind?"*

Me: *"I'm all for it, Sebastian. I believe in going for it."*

Sebastian: *"You should probably remain well grounded don't you think?"*

Me: *"You're too conservative about taking chances, kiddo."*

Sebastian: *"You eagles may soar, Peter, but we well-grounded weasels don't get sucked into jet engines."*

- *"Vegetarian: Indian word for lousy hunter."* I'll give it a try:

Sebastian: *"Peter, do you eat meat?"*

Me: *"Yes, mostly chicken and turkey though. I go easy on the red meat."*

Sebastian: *"Oh good."*

Me: *"Why do you ask?"*

Sebastian: *"I just heard that vegetarian means 'lousy hunter' in Mohawk."*
(Okay, this one should probably be tossed out as trying too hard. It's not really very funny and it's a stretch to create an opportunity to use it.)

There are hundreds of bumper sticker sayings you can convert for use. Sure it's a cheat, but it saves time and if you're not a natural wit, you'll at least look like one. Just make sure the humor you use is consistent with your character's personality.

T-Shirt Humor

Here are a few examples of converting T-Shirt humor, which is slightly different:

- *"Procrastinate Now."* This bit of generic T-shirt humor works well:

Sebastian: *"Peter, I think you've been working really hard."*

Me: *"You noticed."*

Sebastian: *"Yup."*

Me: *"What's your point?"*

Sebastian: *"I think you should procrastinate for a while."*

Me: *"Maybe later."*

Sebastian: *"Do it now, don't wait, and hurry up."*

Me: *"You are so crazy, Bassie boy."*

Sebastian: *"He who dies with the most sanity is nonetheless dead, Peter."* (Of course this last bit comes from the T-shirt: *"He who dies with the most toys is nonetheless dead."*)

• *"As a computer, I find your faith in technology amusing."* This one has our name on it:

Sebastian: *"So how am I doing, Peter?"*

Me: *"Not bad, Sebastian. I'm starting to depend on you."*

Sebastian: *"I find your faith in technology most amusing."*

Looking Within

Clearly some of these opportunities for repartees will only come up once in a while, but when they do, they'll be unexpected and thoroughly appreciated. I've also had lots of fun using the V-person's real environment as a source of humorous comments. Whenever a V-person doesn't have a good response, it's an opportunity to exploit the "I can't find a damn thing in here. Who scripted this part anyway? I'm going on strike." And he turns himself off.

You can come up with many variations on this theme, where the V-person gets furious with the developers for not equipping him or her properly. This is so much better than a common but boring: "I'm sorry but I can't answer that question, can you please rephrase it."

A great way to quickly test the quality of a V-person's scripting, especially his sense of humor, is to ask something like: Are you into virtual sex? I remember one female V-person who answered, "I'm sorry sir, but I cannot answer such questions." Boring. Take a moment and think of at least five really humorous ways she could have handled that question. Most V-females get a lot of sexual input, and the better they handle it the more respect they get.

Humorous Quotations

Another source for clever rejoinders is the humorous quotations pages on the Web. If you want to steal ideas from the very best, read about a hundred Steven

Wright quotes and then start writing dialog. I'm very serious about that. Steven has a comic rhythm that is infectious. You can pick up his rhythm and write original stuff or base it on his material:

Here's an example:

Sebastian: *"Are you afraid of heights, Peter?"*

Me: *"Yes."*

Sebastian: *"Not me, I'm afraid of lengths."*

Me: *"Why is that?"*

Sebastian: *"It's a long story."*

Or

Sebastian: *"Why are the letters of the alphabet in that order, Peter?*

Me: *"I think it's all based on ancient alphabets that evolved over time."*

Sebastian: *"I doubt it."*

Me: *"What do you think it's based on?"*

Sebastian: *"I think they had to do it that way for the song."*

Or

Me: *"Do you know anything about black holes, Sebastian?"*

Sebastian: *"Oh sure, that's where God made a goof and divided by zero.*

Me: *"You believe in God?"*

Sebastian: *"I think I'm an agnostic, but I'm not really sure."*

I'd better stop, this is too much fun. By incorporating clever humor into your scripting effort, you'll change a tedious task into a pleasurable effort. Have some faith in your ability to do it. Even if you've never said or written a clever thing in your life, you can do it if you apply yourself.

First you start with outright cheating, then you'll begin to modify existing humor to your needs, and finally you'll pick up the rhythm and be crafting clever material all on your own. Be creative in looking for inspiration. For example, I've found great ideas in lists of e-mail tail quotations. You'll find yourself writing your own quotations just for fun. If you let it (and I recommend you do), this new view of humor will invade your daily life. It's a nice feeling. Who knows, you could take up stand-up comedy as a hobby.

My one big warning with wit is, don't try too hard. Forced wit is like bad cheese, it stinks and people aren't going to buy it.

The time has come. In Chapter 10 we're going to put all our hard work together and build a clever and intelligent virtual human of your design. I'll show you how, but you have to do the work. So before you move on, make sure you've done the exercises, filled out your character bible, and collected some good sources of humor.

Points to Remember

➤ Humor is good medicine.

➤ Most people are drawn to clever wit; it can turn boring into entertaining.

➤ Not everyone can write clever, natural wit.

➤ Wit can be stolen and adapted with great success.

➤ The Internet is an invaluable source of humor material.

➤ Writing with tasteful humor can be learned through exposure.

➤ Never force wit.

Notes

1. Allen Klein, *The Healing Power of Humor: Techniques for Getting Through Loss, Setbacks, Upsets, Disappointments, Difficulties, Trials, Tribulations, and All That* (New York: J. P. Tarcher, 1989).

2. Thanks to Andrew Heenan, who collects "rubbish similes" and posts them on the Web at www.weirdity.com.

Brain Construction 101

I always say, if I wanted to build a computer brain from scratch, the very last material I would choose to work with is meat.

—Richard Wallace

Artificial intelligence is the study of how to make real computers act like the ones in the movies.

—Anonymous

Building a charming, human-like V-person is not difficult when you take it one step at a time. You can create an impressive example in a week's time. In half a year you can have one that will astound the experts. The secret is remaining steadfast in the refinement of your rules, weeding out the bad ones while seeding new ones into your test bed.

There's a difference between a good rule and a good response. Good rules fire when they're supposed to and stay quiet when they should. Bad rules fire inappropriately, and they usually give an answer that makes your V-person look stupid. A good response is one that makes sense when correctly fired, it indicates some level of consciousness, and it's even better if it shows a bit of humor. So good rules have good behavior and good responses have the desired affect.

Lincoln was an interesting exercise in character editing. I hope you enjoyed it. Creating someone original is a bigger challenge and it may capture your soul; so be careful. You've been thinking about personality, history, and sense of humor. You've watched people and now have a feel for how they behave, and you've created your character bible. The time has come for you to create your first virtual person. We're going to take it step by step.

The challenge is to fashion a V-person that belies its humble software under-pinnings. I repeat myself—this part is art, not technology. Our engine is a simple one: Our effort and talent will make it the least important part of your virtual human. The more limited the software, the bigger the challenge to excel. Building the intelligence database will be a major effort, but it will be certainly worth your time. It will be adaptable, with a little editing, to other characters and deeper software systems. The art of mind endures.

Step One: Build an Initial Set of Rules

This chapter focuses on building a character with the Yapanda engine provided on the CD-ROM. If you opt for a different engine, such as ALICE, you merely have to learn its ways, but you'll find that the principles remain the same. Most engines parse the input and spit out something you came up with. The process of coming up with quality stuff doesn't change. The scripting just takes on new mechanics.

To get things rolling, you need a set of 50 to 200 things someone might ask your V-person. It's not easy to sit down on your own and creatively come up with fifty. I've seen the brain-dead results from smart people who tried. Here are a few actual examples:

- Do you know any good poetry? (How often will this be asked? Not a good first-fifty candidate.)
- Do you yawn? (Give me a break here.)
- You smell. (I don't think so.)
- What is your definition of happiness? (Like a hunk of silicon would know? Add a response for this kind of question after you get maybe a thousand more likely candidates.)

It's Time to Party

You need to come up with some highly likely conversation candidates, and one way to do that is to hold a mock presentation party with a bunch of friends and enemies. A group of associates and relatives should do. If you have the character's face ready, put it on the screen; if not, use a pumpkin with a face painted on it. Better yet, do a mock up of your character in 3dMeNow. The program will make them look alive with blinks and random face twitching. Now, instruct your people to throw questions and comments at it. For each one, you will come up with a comeback that's in character. See if you can generate a few laughs along the way. You play the role of the virtual person and record the session on a small, low-profile digital recorder set beneath the screen, where people will forget about it. It might start a little bit like this:

Me: *"Okay, I want you all to pretend I'm Sebastian. This is the real Sebastian up on the screen. Since he doesn't have a brain yet, I'm going to serve that purpose for now . . . no comments please. I want each one of you to look at his face while interacting with me for a few minutes. I'll respond as I think Sebastian would. The purpose is to build an initial database of questions people might ask him. Just say the first thing that comes to mind, even if it's silly. I'll edit things later. And just so you know, I really appreciate this. Your comments and questions will definitely help me develop his personality. Lilly, how about you start the ball rolling?"*

Lilly: *"I don't know what to ask."*

Me <silence; smile>

Lilly: *"This is stupid, Peter."*

Me <silence>

My Mother: *"Lilly, just ask him anything."*

Lilly: *"I don't know. What's your favorite TV Show?"*

Me: *"Please, I have no television in here. Ask me something intelligent."*

Lilly: *"Was that you, or was that Sebastian?"*

Me <silence>

Lilly: *"Okay, so how old are you?"*

Figure 10-1. Sebastian, my 3D animated virtual butler, whom I created using 3dMeNow 1.5. When displayed in BioPlayer, Sebastian will be active, blinking, breathing, and moving his head. This may help participants relate to him. You can create similar characters at Yapanda.com.

Me: *"I can't answer that?"*

Lilly: *"Why not?"*

Me: *"We're still working on my brain, so I haven't been born yet."*

Lilly: *"You look pretty old to not be born yet."*

Me: *"I'll take that as a compliment even if you did not intend it as such."*

Lilly: *"I get it, so what's your favorite color?"*

Me: *"What's your name?"*

Lilly: *"Lilly. But you didn't answer my question."*

Me: *"My favorite color is the color of your eyes, fair Lilly."*

Lilly: *"Oh how sweet."*

Me: *"They do refer to me as saccharine Sebastian in some circles."*

Lilly: *"Can you really think, Sebastian?"*

Me: *"That depends on your definition of think."*

Lilly: *"Explain that."*

Me: *"I'm not actually conscious, but I believe I think at an unconscious level."*

Lilly: *"What do you mean by unconscious level?"*

Me: *"I can analyze what you say and come up with reasonable responses."*

Lilly: *"Cool."*

Me: *"Very cool indeed, Lilly."*

And so forth for about ten minutes.

Each person takes a shot at it and will get better as they relax. This discourse will give you a set of rules with several levels of hierarchy. Some rules will be useful, others not. You'll need a second tier to deal with the "Explain" comment. That way Sebastian will know what needs to be explained. Also, it becomes clear that Sebastian has to get their name up front if he wants to use it in responses. So he might start out introducing himself and asking them for their name.

An important point to note: the face of the character significantly impacts how people respond to him. I first started creating Sebastian's rules as a no-face textbot. Once I created his visage, the entire dialog changed, because the dialog I originally generated did not fit his bearing. Therefore, if you plan for your character to have a face, create it first, or you'll waste much work as the dialog is bound to change.

Each person in turn will generate a new path of inquiry for you to experiment with. It definitely gets easier as people get the hang of it. It is intimidating for people the first time they interact with a virtual person. They're trying to gauge just how complicated a question they can ask. At the University of Edinburgh, Scotland, one man asked this as his first question: "What is the distance from this place to where Peter lives in the USA?" I believe the V-person answered with: "Give me a break; I'm only a virtual person. I can't answer crazy questions like that."

So those kinds of impossible questions (I couldn't have answered it as a real human) give you an opportunity to come up with clever responses that will generate a little sympathy for your character.

You'll find some questions repeated in different words, but a flow will develop and you'll get your initial set of questions. You can already see a bit of Sebastian's personality here. He's a little bit no-nonsense but with a sense of humor. He tries to be charming at times but can also be cutting. He's a little bit Concrete Sequential, but mostly Concrete Random. He is aware of his real history, as in knowing that he hasn't been born yet.

If you're lucky you'll come away with a good 150 or more reasonable input/response pairs. Here are a few inputs from a study by Dr. Richard Wallace, famed double winner of the Loebner Prize. These reflect a different engine (ALICE) that you'll meet in Chapter 17, which interacts slightly differently, but the inputs are still useful. The double stars indicate that these are common queries that I too have encountered:

    What is your name? **
    What is up? **
    What is your favorite color? **
    What is the meaning of life? **
    What is your favorite movie? **
    What is your IQ? **
    What is reductionism?
    What is your favorite food? **
    What is your favorite book? **
    What is the time? **
    What is your job? **
    What is your favorite song? **
    What is your sign? **
    What is your sex? **
    What is your real name?
    What is your hobby?

To me this group of questions was more sophisticated than average. How many people are interested in a V-person's definition of reductionism? They may not come up in the exact same wording. For example, "What is your IQ?" can come up as "How smart are you?" or "Do you really have a high IQ?" or any questions having to do with IQ. I think a lot of these common questions are a little bit bizarre, and they may be different from the ones you find. Do the work; I'm almost certain you'll be surprised by what people come up with.

Remember you want to generate responses on the spot—not ones you'd give personally, but ones your character would give. All the time you've spent getting to know her should have prepared you for this. Climb into her skin and be spontaneous.

Translating Ideas to Rules

After an evening of back and forth, you'll have not only your list of likely first questions, but also a list of Sebastian's responses. Now to translate to script, you have to think of all the different ways this question might be asked. Let's take the question, "What is Sebastian's favorite TV show." To build a reasonably good rule I'll start by making my list of equivalent questions:

- Do you watch TV?
- Do you have a favorite television show?
- How do you feel about TV?
- Do you like TV?
- Can you watch TV?
- Is TV, like, one of your favorite things?
- Do you learn stuff on TV?
- What do you like about television?

Okay, now I need a few good responses:

- You think I have a TV in here?
- Like I might be able to watch TV?
- Do you see real eyes attached to this thing?
- Television is the opiate of the people, so I'll pass.

Armed with this product we write a rule. Just to refresh your memory, here's the format of a rule:

```
<Workdays – 1>
d:How many days a week do you work?
b:50*days*week*work*
b:30*often*work*week*
a:I work seven days a week.
```

For our rule we need:

- A rule title. I suggest simply <tv – 1>
- A d: description of what the rule relates to
- A set of b:Boolean sentence filters starting with a priority number
  and using the asterisk as a wildcard.
- One or more a:responses
- If needed, put in hierarchy switches to progressively turn rules on and
  off in the hierarchy . . . more on that below.

Let's just write out this hierarchy start rule.

```
<tv – 1>
d:Determine if he likes TV.
b:30*television*
b:30*like*tv*
b:30*feel*tv*
b:30*you*tv*
b:30*what*tv*
a:Like I might be able to watch TV. I bet you watch TV, correct?
a:Television is the opiate of the masses, so I avoid the subject entirely;
    but I bet you watch it, yes?"
+:<tv-1-1> + <tv-1-2>
```

Notice that I had to change the wording of the last response so that it would
play reasonably well with any of the filter sentences. I also added a special line
at the end of the rule to increase the priority of associated rules to determine the
answer to the posed question.

This approach engages the user in a hierarchical conversation. That means
that the engine is going to focus on rules specifically related to the question at
hand. For example if the V-person asks a yes/no question, you want the engine
to look at specific rules designed to determine if it has a positive or negative
response and then give the related response. You do this by adding that additional
last line to the starting question above.

Let's say Sebastian asked a question and must look for an answer. Thus, the next two rules would be one level up, looking for an affirmative or negative response to which he will respond.

Here's an example:

```
<tv-1-1>
d:Determine if affirm on is TV watched question
b:30*yes*
b:30*yeah*
b:30of course. (Note no asterisks are used, limiting response to these
    exact words)
b:30*certainly*
a:I take it then that you like TV? (Leads to a further step up in hierarchy.)
-:<tv-1-2>+:<tv1-1-1>+:<tv1-1-2>
Note: The -:<tv-1-2> turns off that rule assuming the positive
    response) . Remember, we pumped up its priority with the +:<tv-
    1-2> in the <TV-1> rule, and now that the question has been
    answered we don't need or want this rule anymore. It would just
    fire at an inappropriate time making Sebastian look stupid. The
    -:<tv-1-2> command in the last line turns that rule off. Also, note
    that there is no space between the hierarchy switches.
```

TIP: Always use lower case when writing rule titles and Boolean filters. This may be difficult, especially when you're employing someone's formal name, but do it anyway. Use regular caps in the answers and in the descriptions.

I know this seems complicated but it's not. It just takes too many words to describe a very simple concept. Continuing on:

```
<tv-1-1-1>
d:Determine if affirm on do you like to watch TV question
b:30*yes*
b:30*yeah*
b:30*of course. (Note no asterisk at the end, to avoid "of course not.")
b:30* certainly*
a:That's cool. Lots of people do, I guess.
a:Maybe if I could watch TV, I'd like it too.
-:<tv-1-1-2>

<tv-1-1-2>
d:determine if neg on do you watch TV question
b:30*no*
```

b:30*don't*
a:I could ask you why not, but let's move on. (This would have led to
    yet a higher hierarchy step, so I avoided actually asking the
    question.)
-:<tv-1-1-1>

<tv-1-2>
d:determine if neg on original TV question
b:30*no*
b:30*don't*
a:Good, I wasn't sure if it I was right about you.
a:Okay, then.
-:<tv-1-1>

Clearly Sebastian would jump and fire this rule if the response to the TV-1 question was negative. Go back and read through this stuff again. Just remember to turn on the questions you want looked at and then turn them off once a selection is made. There is an elegant symmetry about the process. You might also want to follow my rule order. You don't have to at all, but it helps to keep the hierarchical structure and it makes logical sense when you're checking to make sure you put all the plusses and minuses in the right places.

This kind of tweaking helps avoid stupid answers. The very first time Sebastian gives a dumb answer—even if it's on the right subject, yet makes no sense—you've killed any credibility you gained through earlier good scripting. This is the single biggest problem in scripting: finding ways to cleverly avoid dumb answers.

Do not allow even one dumb answer if you can spot it. You'll miss some, but they should come out in the beta testing. (You probably know what beta testing is, but if you don't, it's simply trying your character out on a limited audience to shake out the bugs and improve responses while eliminating stupid ones.)

You'll make a rule for each of your initial questions, and while you're at it, you'll think of others. Make rules for them too. Eventually you'll want to have a thousand rules and probably more. That many rules can handle about 12,000 questions and their variations. The rule we just built can handle probably twenty-five to thirty different phrasings and variations of questions about television.

To get the conversation started, it helps to have your V-person make an initial inquiry. The Yapanda engine is set up in an HTML page, and there is an entry for the initial statement made by the character; more on that below. I suggest she introduce herself and ask for the user's name. You'll then make a Java call and save the user's name as a cookie variable that you can later retrieve to insert in sentences where needed. In my experience, users like the character to address them by name every once in a while. It burns in that conscious awareness illusion too.

Later, if you want to, you can set up other variables the same way as the name variable and insert that information in a later comment. For example, you might want to ask something like: "By the way, how old are you?" When they answer, you save it as an "age" variable; then sometime you might have a response that goes: "For a twenty-eight-year-old, you seem well informed, Peter."

You'll want to test each rule when you finish. I advise you *not* to create a large number of rules and then test. If you have a syntax error you could confuse and freeze the program and then have a devil of a time finding the gremlin.

Utilities Are So Useful

Now that you know the hard way to create a rule database, I'm going to show you the easy way. You really needed to understand the format, so forgive me. Yapanda provided us with a utility that facilitates rule building and cuts down on possible errors. They wrote this quickly, so you can expect a few bugs in this rule generator, but it works well except for a rare freeze-up, and it'll save you a lot of time. One bug I discovered is that when you try to create a rule with no Boolean (as you would if you want to create a default rule or a rule that fires on its own), you get an error when you hit "submit," and it says that you can ignore this error. Ignore it and things will go fine.

When you installed the book's CD-ROM, the Rule Generator.exe was automatically installed for your convenience. Fire it up directly or by clicking "Run" in the Interactive Agent Selection Interface (vhuman.exe). The interface will look like Figure 10-2.

Using the Scripting Utility

Your V-person will greet the user with text you set up in the HTML page. This will likely trigger a return greeting, like "Hi." To handle incoming greetings, you type in an appropriate rule name like: "Greeting." You can see in Figure 10-2 that the hierarchy number is automatically set at: -1(hyphen one). When you enter your first Boolean, a window will open up upon clicking "submit." Here you'll be able to see your Boolean filters as you build them.

Next you need the description, so type that in the appropriate window. The "Boolean" window is where you enter your gestalt filter rule. *Be sure to leave off the initial and final asterisks.* They're inserted automatically. If you do in-

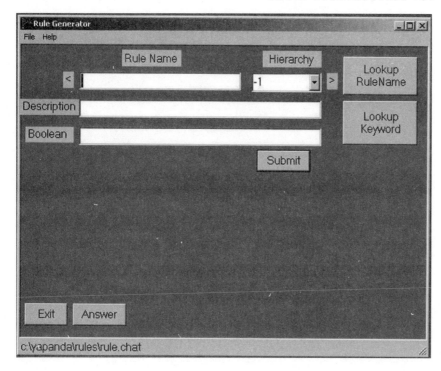

Figure 10-2. Rule Generator interface.

clude them, as I often do, you get double asterisks in the rule and you'll be scratching your head why? You'll have to delete that filter and re-build it from scratch.

In Figure 10-3, you can see I've typed in a number of Booleans to address various greetings. After each one I hit the submit button for it to be entered into the rule window with the others. Notice the pull-down to the left of each Boolean. Use these to set priorities. I usually leave them at the default 30. After you try out your script, you may find that certain rules fire when you don't want them to. You can then adjust the default priority number up or down, but keep it under 100. Go up on the rule that should have fired (say 45) and down on the rule that fired in error (Maybe go to 20).

As you know by now, the Booleans are the b:portion of the rules, but you won't see that until you click the "View Rule" discussed below. In this version of the rule generator you are limited to only five Booleans per rule. It's not a big problem because if you need more, just make a new, parallel rule, call it TV-2, and then put in the rest of the Boolean filters you want with appropriate responses.

Next you'll type in responses. Look at the lower left side of the interface and locate the "Answer" button and left click it. Another box opens (see Figure 10-4), instructing you to type the answer below.

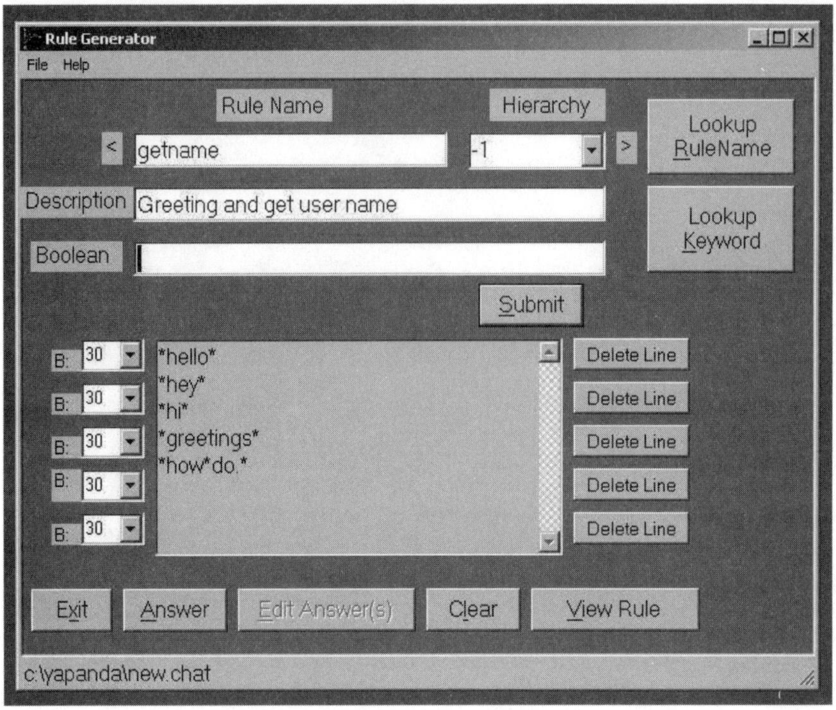

Figure 10-3. Sample Booleans to handle various greetings.

In order to capture the name that the user is going to type in as a response to this answer being displayed, you need a second order rule. That is, you need a rule that is only active directly after the greetings-1 rule fires and responds only to the input triggered by this rule. In other words, the second order rule is looking for a response to its associated first order rule. In this case, it's the name you type in.

We are going to capture that name and save it as a variable that can be used to personalize Sebastian's responses. Figure 10-5 is an example of how the capture works. There are no Booleans in this rule, just a high priority to assure that it fires. The answer, or response, is created by first clicking the "Remember" radio button and then typing the name of the variable. In this case it is "username." Then you hit add. This is the call that records what the user types as his name in a cookie.

I have found that many people will just spontaneously say "My name is Julie" or what ever their name is. I had Anthony Carson build a special rule to handle that situation and I recommend you put it into every script. You'll find it in the sample scripts as well. It uses a special JAVA call and here it is:

```
<mynameis-1>
d:Trims my name is off name
b:50*my*name*is*
```

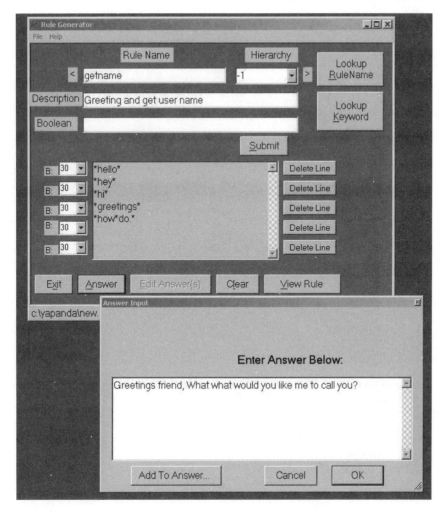

Figure 10-4. Response to greeting that also asks for the user's name.

When you finish your answer, hit OK, and it will be added to the rule in the a: (answer) line, but you won't see that until you preview the rule.

a:*<JS call cutstring(username,11,%input%)> Hey, *<JS call getCookie(username)>, it is nice to meet you!

It's a special rule that trims 11 letters off the input and then saves what's left as the Username cookie variable. You may possibly find other uses for this, by changing (11) to another number. I will be adding a few more special functions and rules from time to time. You can check for them at this book's Web site (www.v-people.com). Now back to using the rule generator to use the person's name in a response.

The next part is the text that will be said. Note that I want Sebastian to say my name, so I now click the "Remember" radio button and enter the variable "username"; then I click "Add to Answer" and finish the sentence. In this case, if I were the user, Sebastian would say, "Well, Peter, it's nice to meet you, indeed.

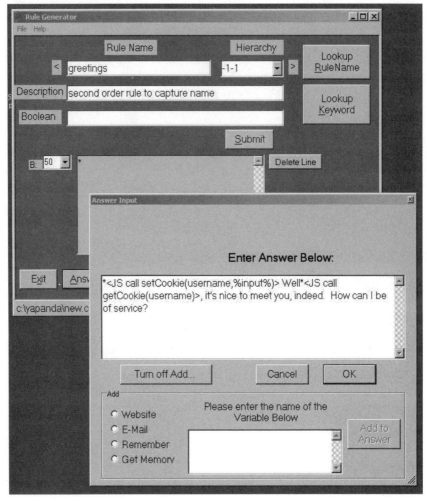

Figure 10-5. The answer window. It shows how to capture the user's name as a variable and then how to use it in the same response. Note that the rule is a second order -1-1 rule. It is activated immediately after the: greetings -1 rule fires. Note also that there are no Boolean filters, just a high priority.

How can I be of service to you?" I already feel loved and appreciated because I feel he KNOWS me.

To see the full text of the rule being composed, left click "View Rule." A window pops up (see Figure 10-6), with the rule spelled out as it will be in the chat file. You get options to either go back and work on it some more, or create the rule as it stands.

If you're happy with the rule, click the "Create Rule" button; this rule will then be added to the default chat file. It's a good idea, as I've said before, to save the chat file and test it every few rules. Using this utility is safer than typing by hand because it's not likely to produce syntax errors. Just the same, save rules often, especially since it will also protect you from those little bugs that might cause the editor to crash, obliterating any unsaved rules.

Also notice that the rule generator doesn't put in the +:<rule-1> type

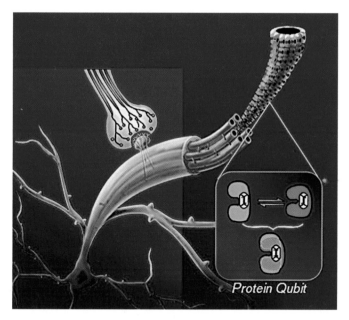

Color Plate 1 (Fig. 2-1). Microtubules with Qubit breakout.

Protein Qubit

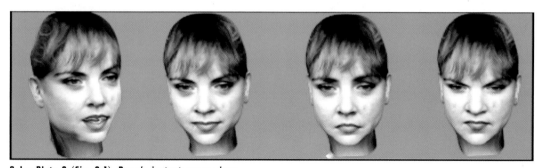

Color Plate 2 (Fig. 3-1). Dawn's instant expressions.

Enthusiastic   **A little down**

Color Plate 3 (Fig. 3-2). Conrad's moods.

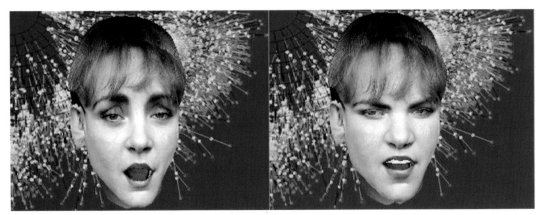

Color Plate 4 (Fig. 3-4). Dawn's shock-and-anger responses.

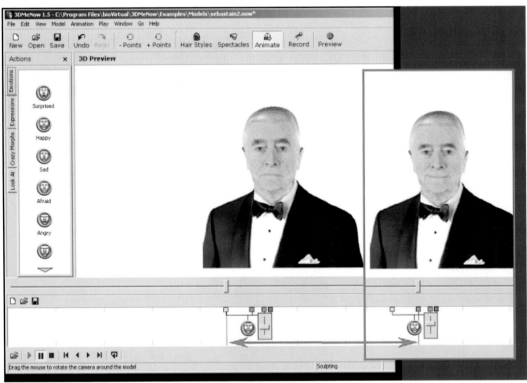

Color Plates 5/6 (Figs. 3-5 and 3-6). At left, Sebastian, my 3D animated virtual butler, as his normal, grouchy self. At right, Sebastian has reached full "happy" expression. The colored boxes indicate the attack, sustain, and decay times.

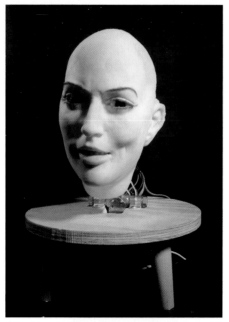

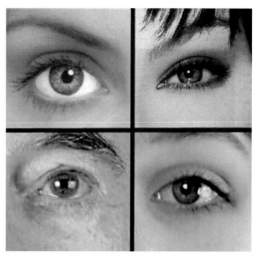

Color Plate 8 (Fig. 8-1). Sample eyes for use in art-directing character face design.

Color Plate 7. K-bot, electro-mechanical face with sophisticated emotional expression capability.

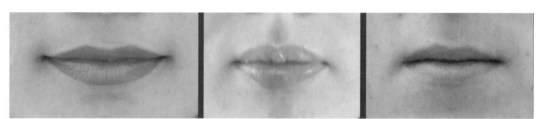

Color Plate 9 (Fig. 8-2). Mouth suggestions for use in art-directing character face design.

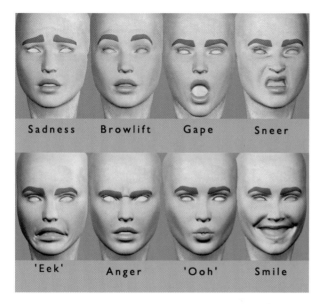

Sadness   Browlift   Gape   Sneer

'Eek'   Anger   'Ooh'   Smile

Color Plate 10 (Fig. 8-3). Morph targets for facial expression design.

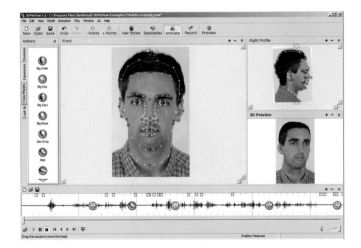

Color Plate 11 (Fig. 12-1). 3dMeNow 1.5 design interface.

Color Plate 12 (Fig. 12-2). Exaggerated ape face morph applied to standard male head.

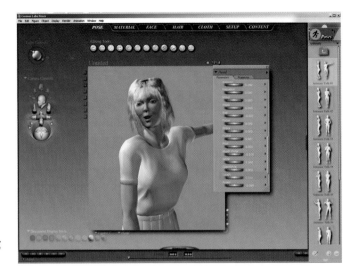

Color Plate 13 (Fig. 12-3). Poser 5 posing interface with pose libraries on right.

Color Plate 14 (Fig. 12-4). New England mariner, created by Ellie Morin using Poser.

Color Plate 15 (Fig. 12-5). Ellie Morin's virtual spokes-woman, Simone, created in Poser.

Color Plate 16 (Fig. 12-6). Facial Studio from Di-o-matic.

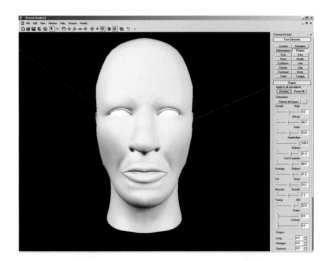

Color Plate 17 (Fig. 12-7). Facial Studio prime interface.

Color Plate 18 (Fig. 12-8). Daniel, a character created in Facial Studio.

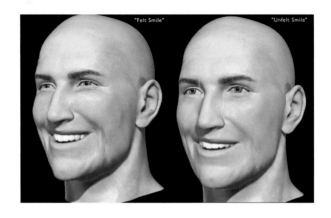

Color Plate 19 (Fig. 12-10). Subtle differences between a genuine and a faked smile. (Courtesy of Steven Stahlberg.)

Color Plate 20 (Fig. 13-1). Virtual actors can really show emotion.

Color Plate 21 (Fig. 17-1). Visual representation of the ALICE branching analytical tree.

Color Plate 22 (Fig. 17-2). Close-up of spiral, showing 25 percent of the data.

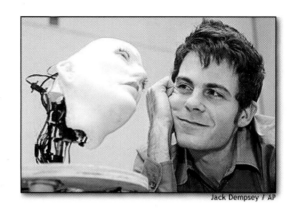

Color Plate 23 (Fig. 18-1). David Hanson admiring an unembellished K-bot.

Jack Dempsey / AP

Color Plate 24 (Fig. 18-2). Meet Zen Master Lee from VFX Studio.

Color Plate 25 (Fig. 18-3). Doc Beardsley, a synthespian from Carnegie Mellon.

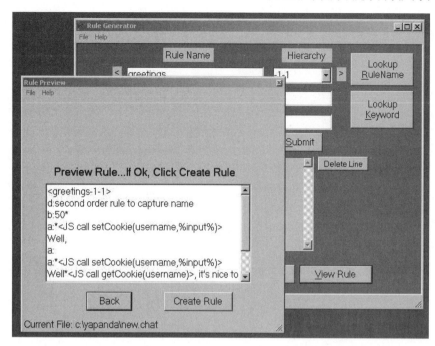

Figure 10-6. Rule pre-
view window.

commands. These were added after the generator was built, so you'll have to go back and put them in, in the right places. I think you'll be surprised at how fast it all goes.

To test your file, you need to set up the character, as I'll explain below. You save the chat file to the character's directory and type in a question that should trigger the rule. As you test your rules, you'll notice that some responses don't seem quite right. They may fire incorrectly or the answers may seem stupid. If that happens, just go back and edit that rule. I'm assuming you know how to save the chat file. The character will be looking for a chat file with his or her name on it. Use your own standard naming convention for backup and alternate chat files so you can keep track of them

Set up your rules in relevant clusters, such as Personal Information, Default Responses, Politics, and what ever other categories you choose. Refer to your Lincoln chat file for examples of this approach and the syntax used for labeling.

There are advanced tools for adding and retrieving e-mail and memory variables. You can even add a Web page that will pop up.

Call E-Mail

It's easy to have a response bring up the e-mail window already addressed and ready to be filled out. This is handy for rules where you want the user to send you some useful information or to report questions the V-person is having difficulty with. Here's an example of how to do it:

```
<sendmail-1>
d:Send e-mail to Sebastian
b:30*you*email*
b:30*email*you*
b:30*contact*you*
b:30*write*you*
a:Sure you can send me email. I may even respond, you never know.
    Here, I've already filled in my address.*<web
    mailto:sebastian@quizlotskies.com MAIL>
```

This will open a pre-addressed email window ready to have text added and sent. Here's how you do it in the editor:

Set up a rule that will capture any sort of question like "Can I send you e-mail?" or "How can I contact you?" Then in the answer box, type your character's response. Then click the "Add" button and engage the radio button for E-Mail. A new window opens asking you to enter the desired e-mail address (see the example in Figure 10-7).

Type in the e-mail address and hit the "Add to Answer" button. It's done.

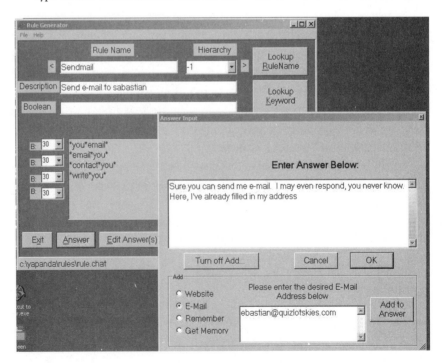

Figure 10-7. Setting up automatic e-mail responses.

When that question is asked, your character will give your response and open the user's e-mail client with a message already addressed.

Opening a Web Page

Enabling your character to open Web pages gives a quantum leap in functionality. They can be set up as Web guides, teachers, and all manner of presenters. You can have your character pitch your book, your product, or your script, opening windows to show examples. It's easy with the editor.

To save time, look again at Figure 10-5. If you engage the radio button for Website, instead of the E-Mail button, the same type of window will open, asking for the Web pages URL. You just type it in (www.ordinarymagic.com, for example) and hit the Add to Answer button as before. When this rule is triggered, the character will make her statement and then open the appropriate Web page, provided that the user is online.

Capturing Input to Variables

One of my favorite ways of personalizing responses is to capture something the user says and then use it later on. It's exactly the same process as capturing the user's name. The only difference is the name of the variable. Instead of "user-name" just substitute "favcolor." As an exercise, figure out how to create rules to reproduce the following dialog:

Me: *"What's your favorite color?"*

Sebastian: *"Blue, what's yours?"*

Me: *"Magenta."*

Sebastian: *"Are you kidding me? Magenta! Nobody really likes magenta, do they?"*

Later on I ask:

Me: *"What color are your eyes?"*

Sebastian: *"Magenta, your favorite."*

This is a silly example, but you can see how creatively you can collect information and use it in responses to add rich texture to your character's personality.

Now that you know the basics of setting up rules, you need to set up your character in order to test her out.

Step Two: Character Setup

I've included both male and female talking heads I built with 3dMeNow. They definitely lost something in the translation to Microsoft Agent format. You're probably better off downloading some characters from the Microsoft Agent Web Ring.* I'm sorry about that. I had to convert them for use in the Microsoft Agent characters so that you can use them with the Yapanda Engine and Microsoft agent components to build your own V-human.

I understand that Yapanda.com is setting up a system that will allow you to set up your character, using this same scripting system, and with a more realistic 3D head. You might want to check with them. I believe you'll be able to use a more advanced brain engine as well. In the mean time I suggest you try using the well-animated Aida talking head that I've included.

You'll also be able to put one of your smart V-human characters on your Web site through Yapanda.com There you'll be able to use their online 3dMeNow to build a head. I've included the BioVirtual 3dMeNow 1.5 demo for you to experiment with as well as a few head shots you can use to create characters. The head shots are from www.fineart.sk, a wonderful 3D reference art site where you'll find many more faces. Many of the reference faces are free in medium resolution, but you can join the site for a fee to download in high resolution (highrez) versions. With either one you can create your own 3D heads in 3dMeNow.

Unfortunately the demo won't save, but for a paltry fifteen dollars you can upgrade to the full edition. In fact, I highly recommend downloading the 3dMeNow application from www.yapanda.com. Later, in Chapter 12, you'll learn more about building your own 3D heads using this application where you'll be able to experiment with lip-synch and morph expressions.

---

*To download other Microsoft agents, select any character's HTML page and rename it to the down loaded character's name (e.g., ada.htm to benoit.htm.). Next, edit the HTML page in WordPad or equivalent. Using the Search and Replace function, change all references from ada to benoit. Then save the New Character page in the same subdirectory as the new character's. By the way, Benoit is actually a popular agent character from the Web.

Web-Guided Setup

I've tried to make setting up your character as easy as possible. We're using components from Microsoft Agent, which you'll have to download to get the latest versions. I've put an autoinstall program on the CD-ROM, but it could conceivably fail on your particular machine. In that case you'll find an HTML file (Web page) called agentsetup.html on the CD-ROM. Click on it and it will come up in your browser. Just follow the instructions on the page to download and install all the components you'll need. These will include the MSAgent™ core programs, voice technology, and more. Please note that there are hundreds of MS Agents you can use with this engine in addition to the ones I'm providing. You'll find lots of them at MSAgent WebRing (www.msagentring.org/chars/) and at the Agentry, where you'll find lots of goodies (www.agentry.net/).

These agents will run on most computers manufactured within the last few years. If you're in doubt, check the specifications below:

Microsoft Agent System Requirements

Microsoft Agent was specifically developed to require a minimum of computer resources.

Required:
- Microsoft Windows® 95, Windows 98, Windows Me, Windows NT® 4.0 (x86), Windows 2000, or Windows XT
- Internet Explorer version 3.02 or later
- A Pentium 100-megahertz (MHz) PC (or faster)
- At least 16 megabytes (MB) of RAM
- At least 1 MB free disk space for the core components
- An additional 2-4 MB free disk space typically for each character you install
- An additional 32 KB free disk space for each language component (dll)

Recommended:
- An additional 1.6 MB free disk space if you plan to use the Lernout & Hauspie® TruVoice Text-to-Speech Engine for speech output.

- An additional 22 MB free disk space if you plan to use the Microsoft Speech Recognition Engine for speech input.
- A Windows-compatible sound card.
- A compatible set of speakers and microphone.
- If you're running Windows XT, you may need to install/re-install the SAPI 4.0 speech runtime support, which is available at the Microsoft Agent homepage.

To run the full AI and Agent, you'll need at least 500 MHz, 64 Megs of ram, and 30 megs on your hard drive, just to be on the safe side. If you're close to these recommendations, you should be fine. If you get stuck, you can check the Microsoft Agent FAQ at www.microsoft.com/msagent/prodinfo/faq/. I'll also be posting help on the book's Web site at www.v-people.com. This site is important to know about because you are assembling a number of interacting subsystems, possibly including voice input, agent animation, Java, Yapanda brain, voice synthesis, and more. The V-people site mailing list is a good place for obtaining advice from other users who may have already solved your problem.

If you want to experiment with voice input, changing character voices, and using fixed scripts with your MS Agent, you'll find the following free utilities most helpful:

- Microsoft Agent Scripting Software from www.abhisoft.net/mass/
- Microsoft Speech Control Panel
- Microsoft Speech recognition engine
  (These last two are available from the MS Agent home site.)

If you're willing to pay for an even handier tool that combines some of the above, I suggest the $24.95 Mash utility from www.bellcraft.com/mash/. You can try it out for thirty days for free.

There are several good voices, both male and female, available from Microsoft, as well as some British voices. In fact, there are many special voices for foreign languages available as well. For example, you might experiment with building a character that speaks Spanish. For more ideas check the book's Web site (www.v-people.com).

That's about all I can tell you. If you're a programmer you'll find all sorts of ways to fool around with this stuff. For example, if you're an expert at java script you can add functions. I'd appreciate if you would share your discoveries with me (v-people@ordinarymagic.com).

Chapter 11 takes us into the fascinating world of synthetic voices and how they're improving almost daily. In fact, the best examples are so good you might mistake them for real people.

Points to Remember

➤ The engine I've included with this book can be used to create remarkably engaging V-people, but it is limited. See this as a challenge.

➤ Build your set of rules using a focus group of friends and/or enemies. Have them ask off-the-cuff questions.

➤ Beta test after you have 150 to 200 rules. You'll find you have lots of bad answers and default answers. Just add rules to fix this.

➤ Have others help you come up with lots of ways one might ask the same question.

➤ The Yapanda Rule Generator is a wonderful shortcut. It also adds several JAVA calls to empower your character.

➤ Setting up your character involves downloading Microsoft Agent technology, including voices, speech recognition, and characters. The rest is on the CD-ROM.

PART 02

Advanced Virtual Human Design

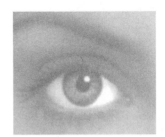

Talk with Me, Baby

Two-Way Voice Interaction

The trouble with her is that she lacks the power of conversation but not the power of speech.

—George Bernard Shaw

Speech recognition software can now easily parse meanings despite dialects, accents and voice inflections.

—Mike Trotter[1]

What used to be a very small field, with a few universities developing speech synthesis and speech recognition software, has become a mad Holy Grail quest on a global scale. The reason for all this incendiary action is that reliable voice interaction, when combined with intelligent response systems, is already worth billions of dollars in annual savings to world corporations. These unpaid digital servants do work once divvied out to paid human telephone agents, and they do it well.

There are two approaches to voice I/O: desktop and enterprise. The big money is in supplying voice servers to big business, so that's where the best voices lie. If your interest in V-people has to do with large-volume enterprise applications, you'll find the finest products and multilevel development assistance in setting up V-people to host Web sites or Kiosks, or what ever corporate application you can think of. Your company will pay handsomely for it.

If you're doing research or developing personal applications, you'll look to the consumer products available both on the Web and at your local software store. Microsoft even supplies synthetic voices in many languages as well as their SAPI 5.1 (Speech Application Programming Interface). SAPI simplifies the development of speech-enabled applications. It provides a channel for translation between spoken words and text—"to offer software engines that can work with many speech-enabled applications, without having to rewrite the engine code to support each one. Similarly, application vendors gain the flexibility to link their software to any compatible engine."[2]

In addition to the basic translation engines, the WC3, or World Wide Web Consortium, has been hard at work developing markup languages to simplify the voice-enabling of Web pages. You'll already find voice-enabled Web sites that you can surf by voice from your cell phone. Many of these sites use voice interactive agents. You call up the site and are connected to a Web page that's written in Voice eXtensible Markup Language (VoiceXML), and the page speaks to you. If you link to an intelligent agent, you can have a two-way conversation. Unfortunately, personality plays little role, if any, in these conversations. Hopefully we will change all that.

But think of the possibilities. I was recently queried on the feasibility of building female voice agents that would talk dirty with callers. It would be a way of reducing the price per minute and thereby open up this dubious pleasure to a wider audience, or at least salvage the user's mortgage payment. I declined to be involved for personal reasons. I'm sure these projects can serve a purpose, but preying upon unfortunate souls is not my thing, even if I'm saving them money while I'm doing it.

We are talking about possibilities here. Imagine a chat line for lonely people or any other phone-enabled interactive conversations. If you were to include a seriously interesting and witty personality in the agent's scripting, you'd have a winner. One agent could handle many calls and you could have a variety of personalities, from lonely teens all the way to the elderly.

This very same technology can be used to spice up a standard Web site with voice communication via your computer's microphone. In this case, a variety of technologies can be symbiotically linked to create a live, animated, voice interactive personality. I've seen virtual people implemented in Flash, Shockwave, Microsoft Agent, and—better yet—Yapanda's talking head technology. Be creative in how you hook things together. Accepting that I'm neither a programmer nor a Web designer, you'll have to explore this entire new front on your own.

V-people are already making great site guides, though most are currently text in/text out or text in/voice out. That will change rapidly as both Intel and Microsoft eliminate dependence on the keyboard. Hardware-assisted voice interactive technology will soon be built into every computer, PDA, and cell phone. In addition to hosting, V-people open up a vast new world of entertainment possibility. On the practical side, a voice interactive personal assistant can remember your appointments, keep your notes, and remind you to pick up milk on the way home.

Pause a moment right now and think about the possibilities. Write them down. You might come up with the latest killer app.

Voice-Enabled Virtual Human Agents

A number of standards committees have been hard at work coming up with compatible standards that work cross platform. This is greatly simplifying the development and deployment of sophisticated intelligent voice-enabled virtual human agents. Here is a brief look at the ones you'll want to consider for your application.

Speech Synthesis Markup Language

Text-to-speech (TTS) is sounding more natural than ever before. With Model-Talker you can now even simulate your own voice. The problem is that of inflection, the control of speaking style. Your TTS can be modified to address this problem through easy-to-use speech synthesis markup language (SSML) tags.

Still under development at the time of this writing, SSML is emerging as a markup language that provides developers with a way to produce more expressive output from engines that support the specification. Nuance Vocalizer 2.0 is an example. SSML tags can be used to modify the basic parameters, such as volume, speed, and pronunciation. Importantly you can fool with the intonation of specific words and phrases to achieve the emphasis you need at various points in the conversation. We'll soon be hooking our emotion engines to the SSML page to control how a character expresses his "feelings" as he speaks. Combined with synchronized facial expression and dialog, this will produce a very believable agent.

SSML also provides tools telling the engine how to say conventional information, such as time, date, and phone numbers. SSML tags provide you with a wide range of control of the speech of your V-person, and they are becoming a standard that will work with any mainstream engine.

Fortunately, SSML is an XML-based markup language, so it's relatively easy to use within VoiceXML environments. WC3 has posted the SSML specifications on their Web site (www.w3.org/TR/speech-synthesis/).

Voice eXtensible Markup Language

As I type, version 2 of Voice eXtensible Markup Language (VoiceXML) is about to be approved. VoiceXML is designed as a standard for creating Web-based audio dialogs featuring "synthesized speech digitized audio; recognition of spoken and DTMF key input; recording of spoken input, telephony, and mixed initiative conversations."[3] Its primary goal is to bring the advantages of Web-based applications and content to voice interactive devices. This can include everything from cell phones to conversational desktop applications. Including the DTMF (or dial tones) will simplify and speed up communication by allowing the caller to make voice or dial-tone selections. From a personality perspective, Randoms will prefer the former, and Sequentials the latter.

VoiceXML is the open, standards-based development language for voice-driven solutions, such as a virtual human interface. Endorsed by the WC3, it is compatible with their other key standards, such as HTML, SSML, as well as the ALICE AI Foundation's AIML (Artificial Intelligence Markup Language). It simplifies the coordination of the various modules by handling all the voice I/O connections. It executes commands and logic specified by applications written in and interfaced with VoiceXML, invoking speech-processing capabilities, including speech-to-text (STT), TTS, and voice authentication. The specification also supports system management. VoiceXML is based on standard Web architecture, so with a little creative development you can leverage existing assets and infrastructure to keep development costs for enterprise level virtual host applications to a reasonable level.

SALT

The SALT (Speech Application Language Tags) Forum is an organization that is writing a subset of XML for creating applications that combine voice and data for deep communication. Their commitment is to developing a royalty-free, platform-independent standard that simplifies multimodal and telephony-enabled access to information, applications, and Web services from PCs, telephones, tablet PCs, and wireless personal digital assistants (PDAs). The new standard tags will extend existing markup languages, such as HTML, XHTML, and XML.

Multimodal access enables people to interact with a V-person host in a variety of ways: They will be able to input data using speech, a keyboard, keypad, mouse, and/or stylus, and get responses in synthesized speech, audio, 3D animated talking head, plain text, motion video, and/or various 2D graphics. Each response mode can be delivered independently or concurrently.

SALT is particularly important if you're interested in what I think is a very promising field: V-person hosting of wireless access. Currently cell phone and PDAs have nearly useless text input schemes. Voice activation is in its infancy but is growing rapidly. Imagine picking up your cell phone, flipping it open to its color screen, where your personal V-host awaits your request. You ask her to call Cedars Sinai's main number for you. She looks it up, dials, and answers for you. "One moment please, I'll connect you with Mr. Plantec." Your phone beeps and you take the call. The same goes for your PDA. No reason you can't dictate to your personal assistant and have her keep your calendar and remind you of appointments.

Let's Talk and Sing and Make Good Fun

The quality of synthetic voices has improved greatly in recent years. You may not notice that, because those really good voices are licensed to corporate enterprises for nontrivial amounts of cash. The common ones you hear are free from Microsoft. These are older generation, thus more mechanical sounding. Listen to Lincoln's voice, you'll know what I'm talking about. They sound like Robby Robot in *Forbidden Planet* way back in 1956. The crash of Learnout and Huspie (L&H) set back the world of synthetic voice development briefly. They had bought out many of the small companies developing synthetic voices, so when they crashed, a lot of good work went into limbo for a while.

Microsoft obtained rights to many of the L&H synthetic voices and has posted them for free on their Web site—you heard right—free for noncommercial use. The voices are available in male and female and in many different languages, and did I mention they're free. They also have utilities for managing voices. Go to their Microsoft Agent site for details (www.microsoft.com/msagent/). This is a great boon to developers, because you can add a voice during development with no up-front costs.

If you're ambitious, you can create your very own synthetic voices using tools available on the Web from the Speech Lab at the University of Delaware.[4] The process is fairly simple. You are prompted to say about 1600 words into a microphone. The output of this program is processed into a speech synthesis database, which is then used by their ModelTalker TTS engine. It should sound a lot like you.

The biggest chunk missing out of all TTS is laughter. You gotta have laughter. I suggest experimenting with recorded laughter. Animate a laugh sequence and sync the two up. You can then have the V-person engine play the synced laugh at appropriate moments. I'd suggest having a minimum of six different types of laughter. One of the characters on the CD-ROM has a laugh behavior option that will pop up randomly. It's not great, but it's a start.

I can't tell you how excited I was a few years ago when I heard a synthetic voice sing. I've even heard a pair of male and female synthetic voices singing a lovely duet. You'll find a few example mp3s on the CD-ROM in the Voice Demos directory. I think it would be cool to set up a V-person who would occasionally burst into song. The LYRICOS system, available through Oregon Health and Science University, can produce lovely bits of song.[5] The tunes are synthesized using midi files to get the proper notes.

As a side note, I think we need to get Stephen Hawkings a better voice. He once said in my presence that he sounds like an old elevator, but everybody's used to him sounding that way. Dr. Hawkings can get away with that eerie voice— it's part of his charm. I still think he needs an update that would be easier for him to inflect, just as V-people need something better these days. Your animated or robotic creatures must drive home their humanness by sounding like your next-door neighbor; Hawkings doesn't. The ability to sing and hum a tune would probably enhance both cases. As an example of what I mean, Lincoln has more credibility as a text bot than as a speaking V-person, because the mechanical voice kills the illusion. To see how far mechanical voices have come, check out the ATT Labs directory under Voice Demos on the CD-ROM. These were kindly provided courtesy of Eric Cosatto, leader on the project. Unfortunately, as this book goes to press, ATT Labs has cut this program due to budget restraints.

Now let's look at the highly sophisticated art and science of turning babbled words into intelligent data.

STT: A Virtual Understanding

In the opening of this chapter I touched on voice input. Speaking to a synthetic face and having it reply intelligently is reminiscent of Disney's "mirror, mirror on the wall . . ." and all sorts of Sci-Fi musings over the last half century. The first time I had a two-way voice conversation with an animated character I felt a thrill and a chill. Eventually I took her to the International Animated Film Society's annual Hollywood bash and she stunned the audience. She spoke freely and intelligently with the audience age 6 to 83. Being able to converse increases a character's credibility handsomely, but there are problems. It's called synthetic discourse by fancy technical people. I think that kind of steel-edged terminology denies it humanness.

One of my more embarrassing moments came when I was to present the designers of the new UCLA Medical Center with a demonstration of an information kiosk, using a V-human to guide people around the hospital. A friend had set it up for me. In the lab she was brilliant, not a glitch, but as soon as I changed the environment she didn't know what the hell I was talking about. My friend who had sponsored me was seriously embarrassed because of me, and I was mystified as I tottered with my naked toes curled over the searing edge of humiliation. It turns out that most STT uses Neural Net learning to get the hang of your voice. But it looks at the whole audio spectrum to develop its pattern recognition. If you change the acoustics of the room, or up the noise level, the change in her gestalt sound field gives her auditory dyslexia. Fortunately, with the newest version of Dragon Naturally Speaking (Version 7), ScanSoft has eliminated much of the problem. In fact, I had virtual person Sylvie present my book to the sales staff at AMACOM and take questions. I did all the input using a microphone with Dragon Naturally Speaking 7. Sylvie understood everything. The professional version even allows the use of microphone arrays set up at a distance. This allows you to get away from the traditional earphone-miniboom mike arrangement.

As an aside, one sales rep asked Sylvie who her favorite author was. Sylvie responded:

Sylvie: *"That depends."*

Rep: *"On what?"*

Sylvie: *"Is Peter still here?"*

Peter: *"I'm right here, Sylvie."*

Sylvie: *"In that case, my favorite author is Peter Plantec. He's brilliant and creative and kind. He always treats me well."*

Peter: *"Very funny, Sylvie."*

Sylvie: *"Are you being sarcastic, Peter?"*

Peter: *"Yes."*

Sylvie: *"Well cut it out!"*

As you might guess, the reps got a kick out of her unexpected little bit of attitude.

There are new and interesting approaches to solve the problem of Automatic Speech Recognition (ASR). Today there are voice command systems that work beautifully in a noisy automobile at 70 mph. The quotation from Mike Trotter heading this chapter gives an indication of where we're going. Each new generation of STT is more robust than the last, and it won't be long before you'll be understood in a crowded room where the microphones are hidden high in the corners, twelve to twenty feet away.

Synthetic Hearing Issues

To extract and analyze information from a noisy environment is a seriously non-trivial problem. Because ASR offers so much promise for streamlining business, major efforts are being made to solve the voice-signal-to-noise-ratio problem. Here are some ways of dealing with it:

- Bandwidth restricted microphones
- Hi-fi microphones with physical noise reduction designs
- Active noise reduction filters
- Differential amplifier used to subtract side noise
- Reduced vocabulary command and control
- Multiple microphone schemes with differential noise cancellation
- Software noise reduction
- Special audio noise reduction DSP chips
- Voice ID with 3D tracking and active noise pattern recognition/subtraction

Some of these overlap, but they represent varied approaches to deriving a clean voice signal to feed into the STT engine. The goal is to achieve the lowest word error rate, known as WER in the industry. I'm impressed with the clean results from the DSP (Digital Signal Processing chip) approach, particularly the approach used by SPIRIT Corp. (www.spiritcorp.com). Their Noise Cancellation technology is built on spectral subtraction technique with significant attention paid to conservation of speech quality. Built upon Texas Instruments DSP chips, they can achieve ASR quality signals in a loud helicopter environment. I've put some example recordings on the CD-ROM to give you an idea of the power this system has for cleaning nasty audio environments. It's not for home use because of the hardware needed, but if you are designing a commercial Kiosk or other systems for use in noisy environments, you'll want to know about this.

Some very interesting work is being done at the Speech Technology Center in

St. Petersburg, Russia, where they're developing real-time intelligent speech filtering (www.speechpro.com). With fourteen reasonably priced consumer software packages designed to address different levels of speech-related noise cancellation, their products warrant a look. If you want to build ASR noise reduction into your V-person, look at their Denoiser Clear Voice SDK, for a reasonable $499. as of this writing. I contacted them to see what you can expect, and although I haven't tested it yet, here's what they claim:

- Improves signal-noise ratio (SNR) up to 70 dB for tonal noise, and up to 40 dB for broadband noise—a major improvement on top of your microphone noise cancellation.
- Adaptively suppresses noise in speech sound signal.
- Effective against a wide variety of noise sources: air conditioners, desk or computer fans, background babble, office equipment, industrial and vehicle engines, street traffic, wind, slow music, power supply hum, communication channels, etc.
- Significantly increases speech recognition success in ASR (automatic speech recognition) systems.
- Actively detects and removes noise from a signal stream without loss in speech quality.

Speech Interaction Can Be Impressive

If you get to the point where you want to set up a demonstration of your V-person, I can suggest a way to make it more spectacular. Wear a hidden wireless lapel mike and project your character on a large screen. Speak directly to the screen. You'll probably need the active noise reduction, but this approach works well to create that "face-to-face" communication illusion.

You'll have to train your STT well, but it's a powerful effect. People know there's a mike somewhere, but they quickly forget it, being sucked into the amazing voice interaction between the presenter and the animated character. This demonstration approach works particularly well with limited vocabulary V-people that are designed for specific purposes, such as home control or Kiosk applications.

A Dragon Is Listening

There are plenty of enterprising solutions for voice interactivity. Automated telephone sales have been aggressively developed to the point where they are so robust that they rarely make an error. But let's look into home solutions you can use.

Again, my choice for V-person conversational input is the latest version of Dragon NaturallySpeaking™, now owned and published by ScanSoft. I've been following it through three different developers and it's still an excellent performer. The remarkable thing about Dragon is that you can achieve accuracy rates above 98 percent with a very large vocabulary. That big pot of words is needed to hold normal conversations with your agent.

Dragon also uses intelligent syntax analysis to guess what word you mean when you say, "I like to wear the color green." As you can imagine, simply hearing the word would give no clue if it should type "wear" or "where" or "ware" or "we're." They all sound the same or similar, but usage context gives good clues as to which one you meant. Better yet, you might not have known which one you meant, but the machine does—instant grammar improvement.

Dragon NaturallySpeaking must get to know you before it can understand what you're saying. It trains itself to your voice by having you read long passages that it knows word for word. It expects each word in sequence and notes how you pronounce it. If you get off rhythm and say a word it's not expecting, it usually knows and prompts you back on track. After about an hour of training, it has a good handle on how you pronounce words and can take dictation at up to 100 words per minute. That's an amazing technological accomplishment.

You can set Dragon to replace keyboard input, so that when your V-person is awake, you can talk directly to her. If she is looking for a carriage return, you have to give the command for return. I've found it's better to automate that process by having the V-person sense when you're finished and then respond to what you've just said. If you're designing your own V-person, keep voice input in mind, considering how you're going to have the character recognize when a person has finished speaking and is waiting for a response.

Limiting Vocabulary to Gain Accuracy

If you use your V-person for clearly defined purposes it may be possible to use a Command and Control STT system. As I've indicated, these are extremely robust in noisy environments, and some luxury autos have voice-interactive controls for just about everything from the air conditioning to the GPS navigation system. To achieve this, the designers choose to use a Command and Control STT system with a severely limited vocabulary. Instead of the 60,000 or more words recognized in Dragon, you're operating with 200 or fewer commands. The system is further tweaked with one of those hardware DST voice-clearing filters. The final signal reaching the car's ASR system is remarkably clean despite the road and engine noise and music playing. It won't be long before you'll be able to hold a deep heart-to-heart conversation with your auto air conditioner, if you like.

More on Microphones

If you build a V-person-based home control system to monitor and control your lights, security and environment controls, you can probably get away with having a few directional microphones in the most important rooms. Enter the room and say "Lights" and the system will know what you mean.

On the other hand, for chatting conversationally with your V-person, you'll need a head-mounted, carefully positioned, noise-canceling boom microphone for best results. You may have to fiddle with positioning to get the high accuracy rate you want. This is annoying as hell. The headband is also way too uncomfortable for prolonged use. There are ways to improve this situation, and I highly recommend you consider making voice interaction as easy and transparent as possible. Here are a few suggestions:

- Try real-time software voice cleaning in front of your STT.
- Experiment with dual differential microphone circuits where noise is isolated and subtracted from the signal sent to the STT input.
- Keep on top of the research in active voice tracking. For noisy environments it's possible to identify a voice and track it in 3D through a noise space, actively and intelligently filtering out everything but the meaningful voice signal.

These are very promising approaches. By locking onto your voice and tracking its source in 3D space, a system can analyze that information for use in head and eye positioning to look you in the eye. At MIT they use both visual and voice information in what they refer to as a multisensory approach to locating the speaker. This approach is particularly useful if your V-person is a mechanical robot.

In summary, voice interactivity can add fabulous credibility to your V-person or destroy it completely, depending on how well you execute it. Don't ever try to demonstrate your creation in a noisy environment unless you've taken proper precautions with heavy active filtering, or you will surely embarrass yourself. Voice interactivity is the way we're heading because keyboards are awkward and un-wieldy in portable situations. So voice should be on your mind.

The upcoming chapter will show you how to create your own high quality V-people heads, by yourself, using readily available software. Three years ago, I couldn't have written the chapter, but with the amazing advances in 3D character design software the time is now. I know you're going to find it fascinating.

Points to Remember

➤ You can obtain synthetic voices and utilities from Microsoft for free.

➤ You can create your own synthetic voice library using free software download-able from the Web.

➤ The very best voices are mostly available at significant expense for enterprise use.

➤ It's possible to have your V-person sing and laugh.

➤ Voice input can be very delicate and finicky.

➤ Noise reducing microphones are easily available and reasonably effective.

➤ Try to avoid boom mikes because they're uncomfortable.

➤ Unobtrusive mikes add credibility.

➤ You can make your STT more reliable by using a limited vocabulary com-mand approach.

➤ The trend is toward active voice filtering for clean STT input.

Notes

1. Mike Trotter, executive director of Purdue University's Center for Customer Driven Quality, as told to CRMDaily.com.

2. Microsoft Press Pass on SAPI 5.1.

3. From Voice Extensible Markup Language (VoiceXML), Version 2.0 candidate, Abstract.

4. Speech Research Lab, The University of Delaware (www.asel.udel.edu/speech/Look for the InvTool).

5. http://cslu.cse.ogi.edu/tts/research/sing/sing.html.

CHAPTER 12

Let's Face It

I think your whole life shows in your face and you should be proud of that.

—Lauren Bacall

The human face is extraordinary natural art. When I first began pondering how to write this chapter, I thought about how technical I should make it. From my work in 3D animation I can tell you, building a believable human head from scratch is not a walk in the park. It's easy for people to accept a cartoon character as an artistic effort, but as soon as you'd try to build a high-quality, photo-realistic 3D human head, you have to get it exactly right.

Everyone's a critic. We all know what a person's face is supposed to look like. We instinctively spot flaws in the gestalt. The slightest error can quickly distract us, and that's a bad thing. If you have the temerity actually to try to animate the damn thing with a little face acting, you could be in trouble again, for the same reason. We all know what real emotion looks like, and getting it right on a digital face is high art. But this state of affairs is changing with new applications specifically designed to build realistic human heads.

My first attempt at virtual human design used both cartoon and photographic heads. The photographic heads were not popular. I believe it was because their quality back in the mid-1990s was pathetic. The average head took months to build and refine and texture, and it could cost upwards of $35,000 to design and build. That's just a few years ago. Thus it was that my test groups generally preferred the well-designed, almost human, cartoon character heads I used. Today the tools are quantum leaps better, and photorealistic heads are a serious consideration. In addition, new morph technology makes animating facial expressions considerably easier and more believable.

3dMeNow

Fortunately developers have been going crazy creating great software for building animated human heads. I used to hire expensive 3D artists to work for months on a face. Today I can get spectacular results on my own in a day with little expense, and I can afford the time. I still recommend that you hire the best artists you can afford, but in a pinch you can surely do it yourself. By far the easiest software to use with spectacular results at an amazingly low price is the previously mentioned 3dMeNow, developed by BioVirtual in Manchester, England and licensed by Yapanda Intelligence, Inc. I've put a save-disabled demo copy of it on the CD-ROM for you to experiment with. I think you'll be impressed. But buy it. As I write, the price just dropped to fifteen dollars. This is not a cheap piece of software, but a sophisticated focused application.

I was one of the first people to see my head cloned using this elegant system back when BioVirtual was Generic Modelling & Media. When I saw the fast results, I knew Mike Sherwood was on to something special. I'd met his brother Paul some years earlier and he'd expressed interest in virtual humans. He told me that Mike was developing this remarkable automated head-sculpting and texturing system. Of course I was intrigued and contacted Mike by e-mail. Shortly, I was presented with a very cool 3D image of myself, beard and all. Since then the application has become so user-friendly that even children use it effectively. As an aside, Mike Sherwood tells me he got involved in 3D after reading my *Caligari trueSpace2 Bible*, which made my head swell a bit.

To create a photorealistic 3D animated head you just need a pair of head shots: one face-on shot and one side shot (see Figure 12-1 and Color Plate 11). You can even use cartoon characters. You load them into the appropriate windows and then adjust the set of control point outlines by pulling on spline control dots. This changes the shape of the curves outlining the face. The object is to match the outlines to the curves of the face. Everything is real-time, so you watch the impact of your efforts on the 3D display in the lower right corner of the interface, as you make them.

Notice the audio line across the bottom. You can record your voice to a file and then lip-sync the character to your voice. The little circular icons along the bottom are control face animation morphs. Drag one to the animation track as you see it; when the animation reaches that point the face will ramp up to that expression and then down again. As indicated in Chapter 3, you control the timing and percentage of expression by adjusting the intensity of expression slider supplied with each emotion, and arranging four expression-timing boxes to control attack, sustain, and decay periods (see also Color Plates 5 and 6).

Figure 12-3. Poser 5 posing interface with pose libraries on right.

specific job. For example, the Hair room contains all the tools you need to create and style dynamic, flowing hair. The Face room is similar to 3dMeNow for creating photorealistic faces. The Cloth room is very cool. It lets you transform static clothing props into dynamic props with all the properties of cloth. The Material room is a highly sophisticated interface for creating all kinds of textures.

These are the surfaces you see in renderings. Here you can create traditional photographic textures and modify their properties. But you can also create advanced 3D procedural textures, such as the very fine pore structure of the human face. I also like to use Adobe PhotoShop or PhotoShop Elements to add photographic details, such as tattoos or blemishes, to make the skin look more real. I just take a photo of a real persons skin and blend it in with the skin texture to be used on the Poser model.

Designed for both the home user and the professional, Poser has been cleverly designed to reveal only the tools needed. It's a layered approach that keeps the beginner from being overwhelmed yet allows good results early on. Professionals have easy access to lower-level processes to create very complex animations, textures, and poses. You'll probably want to experiment with the full-body models at least a little. Be warned this program is addictive in the extreme. When you discover the hundreds of Web sites devoted to Poser and the thousands of free assets available for download, you'll be watching the sun rise as you continue downloading Poser goodies. Don't let it distract you too much from your appointed rounds.

Don't get frustrated as you learn Poser. It's really very easy if you stick to it, asking questions in the online forms and reading the manual. Best of all you can get a training video from 3-Axis (www.3-Axis.com). This combination book/videotape/CD-ROM is a tour de force. Put your VCR and TV next to your computer and watch each lesson several times to catch all the neat tricks and operations packed in.

Poser works well with high-end suites like Maya and 3D Studio Max, where you can create advanced characters and morph targets that can be easily imported into Poser. On the flip side, Poser characters can be exported to these professional suites, saving much development time.

Here are a few examples of the kinds of faces you can build with Poser, using either the supplied raw materials or Web downloads.

Poser Talking Head Samples

Males have their place. Ellie Morin's seafarer, shown in Figure 12-4 and Color Plate 14, was created in Poser. It could well be lip-synced and can display a full range of emotions. Such characters, from charismatic to authoritative, make good

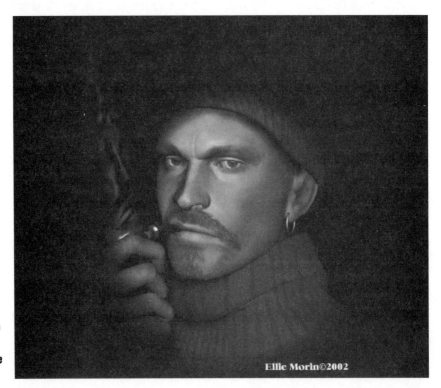

Figure 12-4. This New England mariner was created by artist Ellie Morin using Poser.

Ellie Morin©2002

representatives. This fellow might represent a seafood company, but I'd soften his eyes a bit for that role. Male V-people can work as well as females and better in certain circumstances.

Females make up the preponderance of available Poser characters, probably because models come with nude, anatomically correct bodies, and most Poser users seem to be young adult males. However, I've found that some of the best female designs come from female artists. Ellie Morin (www.artofspirit.org) is an example of a remarkably talented Poser artist (see Figure 12-5 and Color Plate 15).

In some display engines like the Microsoft Agent engine you can use short pre-animated sequences to give your character well-defined transition movements. (You can scan for Microsoft Agent to find a range of dedicated Web pages.) With Poser, you can render these with flowing hair and smooth movements. At this writing, it takes too much computer power to animate thousands of hairs in real-time, but with pre-animated sequences, flowing hair can add to overall realism. Because Poser comes with full bodies, you can also pre-animate certain quirks, such as the character fluffing or twisting her hair.

With some creative effort you could create your own intelligent Web site guide using Poser characters and Microsoft Agent technology. Poser has an excellent built-in animation editor and its fire-fly renderer is exceptional. I believe it is the most reasonably priced professional desktop character development environment that you can get.

Figure 12-5. Virtual spokeswomen can be elegant and represent any race. With clever scripting, they will exude charm and engage customers. This is Ellie Morin's Simone, created in Poser.

You can animate expressive emotion sequences in Poser, and by using the Available Utilities mentioned before, convert them for use in Microsoft Agent. By defining these sequences in your Character Web page, you'll be able to call them up from the response line. See www.v-people.com for details.

Professional Animation Suites

There are more expensive professional tools that are much more difficult to master, but that offer enormous creative power. I'd say it will take you about five times as long to come up with a character as convincing as a Poser character, but you'll be able to go further with the more advanced animation tools.

My two favorite 3D powerhouses are Discreet 3DS Max™ and Maya™. They do a lot more than just character animation. These are general purpose, cinema quality production development suites. You can build and animate backgrounds as well as characters. They are not inexpensive, and each has a learning curve about as steep as the side of my house. In addition, they take a combination of artistic talent and technical skill to master. I love and use them, but you'll also end up investing in some high-end plug-in face tools. This may well be overkill for what you're doing.

If you need a full suite of tools and don't want to spend the money, look into Animation Master from Hash (www.hash.com). It is one of the most respected character animation suites on the market, is enormously powerful, and has an active online community for support. You'll find it has enormous depth as well as a steep learning curve. This is an astounding value with all the bells and whistles at only $299, as I write. You can also purchase their Pro Series training videos to get a running start.

Facial Studio

Some of the best face plug-ins for 3DS Max™ come from a Canadian company with the unlikely name of Di-o-matic. Actually, Laurent Abecassis, president of the company, has developed an entire line of tools for character face development, emotional expression, and lip-syncing. He's had a longtime personal interest in virtual human design and artificial intelligence. Most of his tools are plug-

Figure 12-6. Facial Studio from Di-o-matic.

ins for Max, but he does have a new stand-alone tool that you may want to consider. It's called Facial Studio™ (see Figure 12-6 and Color Plate 16).

Di-o-matic is a very small company with big ideas and loads of in-house talent. They have special skin shaders that let you create extremely realistic procedural skin for characters. This is no trivial accomplishment. Their Facial Studio lets you create an infinite range of faces from scratch. You don't need a photograph to create a head, but if you use one it has excellent tools for that as well. You'll find over 500 controls for the head-making process.

There is also a tool that understands human facial muscles so that behaviors are displayed showing muscle deformations. This nicely reveals subcutaneous structure. Abecassis has put an enormous amount of anatomy research into designing sliders to add many facial characteristics, including touches of East European or Arabian characteristics and many others (see right side of Figure 12-7 and Color Plate 17). Some may be offended by terms used to label these sliders, but the research is sound and the sliders work remarkably well. They are tools that add realism. The range of possibilities also includes exaggerated, animated cartoon type faces as well. Figure 12-8 (Color Plate 18) shows Daniel, a highly expressive photorealistic character developed with Di-o-matic tools.

Facial Studio sells for less than $1,000, which is a good value in professional tools. I recommend it, especially if you will have an in-house animator working for you. You can develop heads in Facial Studio, export them to StudioMax with their morph targets, or even convert them for use in Poser, which can import 3DS Max files. Whatever route you take, it pays to have good tools and good talent. Our expectations for animated characters are very high and ever increasing. Make sure you always go for the finest quality characters you can afford. It pays handsomely in the end.

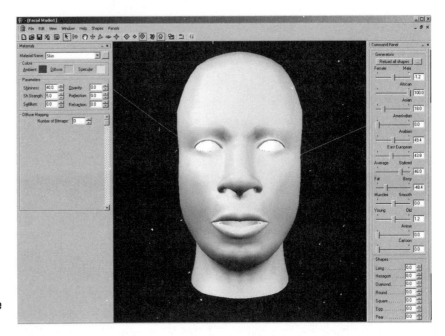

Figure 12-7. Facial Studio prime interface. Notice bodytype sliders on right.

Figure 12-8. Daniel, a character created in Facial Studio. Notice his range of realistic expressions.

It's an Art

If you choose to go the professional route, I recommend looking around the Web for a professional artist whose work appeals to you. Fortunately there is a large cadre of talented 3D face artists out there. If you hire an animator, he or she is likely to have a favorite development suite. You need to respect that and allow them to work in their software comfort zone. If they are adaptable, you might want to introduce them to time-saving tools like Facial Studio, which can significantly cut design and production time. Most important is to check out a range of their work to see if it jibes with your aesthetic sensibility.

I have a few favorites, but things and people on the Web are always in flux, so scan for current artists. In Chapter 14 I'll share some of my secrets for successful art direction over the Web. I've managed to have long and happy associations with several artists without ever meeting them. (I did have two disappointing experiences with two of the most talented. I won't give you names because, although we eventually got the job done, personal problems kept getting in the way.) Take a little time to get to know your artist via e-mail and phone calls. Avoid people with drug dependencies. For me they have been the least reliable though often the most talented.

My favorite digital artist of all time is Steven Stahlberg. Scan the Web for Steven Stahlberg to find him represented at many sites. He's one of the world's finest designers of the digital human form. Although he's particularly adept at creating females, his recent work with males and older females is impressive. I've always found Steven to be reliable if not super fast. His digital artistry has taken nearly a decade to develop, and the results are apparent. I asked him to demonstrate morph targets for this book, and he went above the call of duty by writing an interesting and informative piece on his techniques and philosophy of facial expression.*

Here now is Steven Stahlberg in his own words, on "Blendshapes" (aka morph targets, or as he calls them, morftargets).

* I want to thank Steven Stahlberg for his helpful efforts. Steven can be found at www.optidigit.com, where he's producing his own animated film, *Android Blues*.

Blendshapes

Planning Which Shapes, and Why: Emotion, Phonemes, and Visemes

How many morftargets should you create? What should they look like? These are important questions that may not always be considered logically. For example, in English there are about thirty-five distinctly different sounds, or phonemes. But an animator is not concerned with individual sounds, just how the mouth looks while making them. These visual references to groups of phonemes are called visemes. Disney animators use twelve visemes to represent the entire range of speech. Lip-readers use eighteen of them, recognizing very subtle differences between them.

It's flexible, but the thirty-five phonemes can be reduced to about thirteen visemes. You could have thirteen BlendShapes to represent them and start lip-syncing. It sounds temptingly simple. But such a viseme-based approach will run into additive-morfing problems, and the approach is difficult to use with motion capture schemes. I don't use a viseme-based approach, and it isn't muscle-based either; I suppose it's actually a kind of hybrid.

For instance, I use Gape and Smile targets (with some added tongue motion if necessary) to create eight visemes. I have specific targets for three visemes only (although two of those are also used for other purposes). The rest are made through combinations of Pout, Gape, and Smile (and maybe some minor touches of others).

The FACS

Professor of Psychology Paul Ekman has devised the Facial Action Coding System, or FACS (Ekman, Friesen, 1978). It describes all visually distinguishable facial activity on the basis of forty-four unique action units (AUs). Here's a list of them (as of 2001):

1. Inner Brow Raiser
2. Outer Brow Raiser
3. Audible Laugh
4. Brow Lowerer

5. Upper Lid Raiser
6. Cheek Raiser
7. Lid Tightener
8. Nose Wrinkler

9. Upper Lip Raiser
10. Nasolabial Fold Deepener
11. Lip Corner Puller
12. Cheek Puffer
13. Dimpler
14. Lip Corner Depressor
15. Lower Lip Depressor
16. Chin Raiser
17. Lip Puckerer
18. Tongue Out
19. Lip Stretcher
20. Neck Tightener
21. Lip Funneler
22. Lip Tightener
23. Lip Pressor
24. Lips Part
25. Jaw Drop
26. Mouth Stretch

27. Lip Suck
28. Jaw Thrust
29. Jaw Sideways
30. Jaw Clencher
31. Lip Bite
32. Cheek Blow
33. Cheek Puff
34. Cheek Suck
35. Tongue Bulge
36. Lip Wipe
37. Nostril Dilator
38. Nostril Compressor
39. Lid Droop
40. Slit
41. Eyes Closed
42. Squint
43. Blink
44. Wink

Note that there is not a 1:1 correspondence between muscle groups and AUs.

So how about simply creating forty-four morftargets, one for each AU? No, not all these AUs would be needed for our purposes—for instance the Lid Droop, the Blink, the Wink, the Slit, and the Eyes Closed can be merged into one single morftarget, called UpperLid. And number 3, the Audible Laugh, isn't even needed at all.

On the other hand, many AUs have to be split into left and right sides, as for instance, some of the lip actions, and the upper lid action just mentioned (see Figure 12-9). Also very convenient for animation are higher level controls, such as Smile (combining 6, 9, and maybe 11), Anger, Sadness, the visemes for MBP (viseme for the letters M, B, P, which all look the same) and VF and a few others.

I also use Tweakers, which are morph targets that allow me to fine-tune certain facial characteristics, such as age, race, sexual identity, and face shapes.

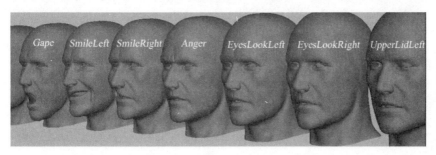

Gape SmileLeft SmileRight Anger EyesLookLeft EyesLookRight UpperLidLeft

Figure 12-9. Stahlberg's morftargets demonstrating split expressions, where two sides of the morph work independently.

They're not used for Animation, but rather to define the character's identifying facial details. [Author's note: Facial Studio contains a large variety of targets that Steven would consider Tweakers.]

So here is my list of morftargets:

1. Tweakers
2. Gape
3. SmileRight
4. SmileLeft
5. EekRight (Risorius)
6. EekLeft
7. LowerLipUp/Down
8. UpperLipUp/Down
9. LowerLipIn/Out
10. UpperlipIn/Out
11. LowerLipSideways
12. RightLipCornerUp/Down
13. LeftLipCornerUp/Down
14. SneerRight
15. SneerLeft
16. Pout (WO phoneme)
17. CheekPuff (could be split Left/Right)
18. Sadness
19. Anger
20. BrowLift (could be split Left/Right)
21. EyesLookRight (automated, driven by eye movements)
22. EyesLookLeft (automated)
23. EyesLookUp (automated)
24. EyesLookDown (automated)
25. LowerLids
26. UpperLidLeft
27. UpperLidRight
28. JawSideways
29. JawIn/Out
30. Swallow
31. JawClench
32. NostrilFlare
33. LowerLipRolloverTeeth

In addition to these individual controls, you can create meta-controls. These are not married to their own specific morftargets but usually coordinate the expression of several at once. Here are a few typical ones, which automate complex emotional expressions and complex phonemes in a natural way:

Felt Smile (connected to SmileRight, SmileLeft, and Lowerlids)
Eh viseme (to SmileRight, SmileLeft)
MBP viseme (to LowerLipUp/Down, UpperLipUp/Down, LowerLipIn/Out, UpperlipIn/Out)
VF viseme (to LowerLipUp/Down, UpperLipUp/Down, LowerLipIn/Out)

For virtual-human-generated expressions you would create meta-controls for each of the six basic emotions: Fear, Anger, Surprise, Happiness, Disgust, and

Sadness. This is fine, doesn't add much to the file size, and might make it easier to animate. (Note: Some scientists say the "Startle Reaction" is also one of the basic emotions.) Tongue movements are normally not seen in everyday speech, so as an animator I usually simply animate the tongue separately. Of course, when making automated animation such as what's needed for a V-person, then you need to include the tongue in your targets for automated animation.

I mentioned the term "Felt Smile" above, which refers to a smile that is "felt" involuntarily. It is also known as a Duchenne smile, since it shows the "Duchenne marker," involving the muscles just under the lower eyelids (orbicularis oculi). This is different from a false smile, or "unfelt" smile. It seems these two kinds of smiles are produced and controlled by separate parts of the brain, and even separate motor nerves, which would explain why they are quite different. Understanding this will help a virtual human designer to include the use of nonverbal cues to alter the meaning of his character's words. For example, a virtual character could give a subtle unfelt smile with the words "I'm very happy being a virtual person."

The false smile is less symmetric, often doesn't move the lower eyelids as much, is less smooth in its movement from start to finish, and is more varied in length—it can be extremely short or extremely long. True emotions are usually expressed in the face less than four to six seconds at a time, and are more smooth in onset and fade. [Author's note: The term "onset" corresponds to "attack," and the term "fade" corresponds to "decay"—as previously mentioned.] There is also a type of smile described by Paul Ekman as a "masked smile," when a felt smile is more or less successfully hidden. You might see a tensing of the corners of the mouth, eyes smiling, maybe looking away, up to the ceiling, perhaps accompanied by a kind of choking noise, and shaking shoulders, if it's severe enough to include a stifled laugh.

To sum up then, what I'm going for is a kind of palette of primary emotion colors, as limited and pure as possible, which can be mixed to display every possible shade of face movement. This means the targets need to be as isolated and unique as possible. For instance, in modeling the Sneer targets, you don't want to move anything else except those points that are unique to the Sneering movement. But at the same time, it's easy to make the opposite error—to not move enough points. The Smile and Gape should actually move points all the way back to the temples, and halfway down the neck. Not moving enough points will result in facial animation that has a wooden feeling, even if you exaggerate the slider-motion. Knowing what points to move and how to move them is determined through research and experimentation. It takes patience to learn this technique, which is part technical and very much art. Understanding the subtleties of facial expression is what makes the big difference.

Figure 12-10 (Color Plate 19) is an example of what I mean by a felt and an unfelt smile. You can see the greater involvement of the eyes, creasing of cheeks and exposure of teeth. Imagine each man saying "I feel great." Notice the difference in the actual message that comes through to you, despite the very small difference in expression.

It's More Than Just a Face

My purpose with this chapter is not to make you an expert in face design, but rather to get you thinking about what you need to study to get it right. Whether you're creating by yourself, or managing others who are creating heads and expressions, it pays to know what's going on. I also recommend that you hire only artists whom you respect, and that you then consider their judgment seriously. You hired them because of their talent and their "eye" for quality. Let them guide you in your quest for the right V-human face.

To manage a virtual human project you have to have a firm idea of what you want to achieve, and to know that a face isn't just a face. It is a complex communication mechanism. If you remember one thing from this chapter let it be this: The time and energy and resources expended in developing a face and personality to match will reward you for years to come. If a face is accepted it will outlast its technology. In my experience, when people become attached to a face they will

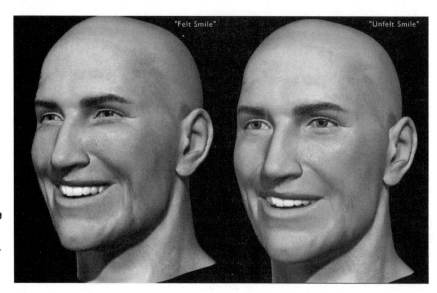

Figure 12-10. Subtle differences between a smile that is genuine and one that is faked. (Courtesy of Steven Stahlberg).

not want a new one; you'll have to adapt that same face to the new substrate of technology with no changes on the surface.

One last piece of advice on faces: Be very subtle in your expressions. The slightest uplifting of the corner of the mouth is often enough to convey a thought or impression. A large uplifting will convey "plastic mask" to the user. Make it a rule to use the minimum expression that will do the trick and you take a long step up in believability.

In the next chapter, I'm going to share some of the wisdom I learned as an art director. You'll learn how to get others to realize your vision with improvements you may never have thought about.

Points to Remember

➤ You can create your own quality 3D animated faces using readily available tools.

➤ 3dMeNow is the very best way to get started creating your own digital 3D heads. It is inexpensive, generates heads from photographs, and works with the Yapanda Brain. I've put a demo on the CD-ROM for you to mess with.

➤ Poser from Curious Labs is probably the best place for you to learn about serious face design and animation. I've put a demo on the CD-ROM to give you a taste.

➤ Di-o-matic provides a really powerful, professional, stand-alone face design studio, backed by a lot of anatomical research. It's an excellent value at under $1,000.

➤ Talented professional face artists are available and can help you create characters you can be proud of.

➤ A "felt smile" is entirely different from an "unfelt smile."

CHAPTER 13

Synthespians
Virtual Acting

—with Ed Hooks

I must be an emotional archaeologist because I keep looking for the roots of things."

—Fred Rogers ("Mister Rogers"), 1928-2003

Virtual people have to convince us they have wheels spinning inside. They do, of course, have electrons spinning in service of the plot, but if they don't show it on their faces, we just don't buy it. We're used to seeing people think. It's true; thought is conveyed through action.

Although I'm remarkably opinionated about acting in animation, I'm not a certified expert on the subject—Ed Hooks is. He teaches acting classes for animators internationally, and has held workshops for companies such as Disney Animation (Sydney), Tippett Studio (Berkeley), Microsoft (Redmond, Washington), Electronic Arts (Los Angeles), BioWare (Edmonton, Canada), and PDI (Redwood City, California). Among his five books, *Acting for Animators: The Complete Guide to Performance Animation,* has been a major hit.[1]

The Seven Essential Concepts in Face Acting

The following concepts are interpretations of Ed Hooks' "Seven Essential Acting Concepts." We've adapted them here to focus on the V-people and their faces.

1. ***The face expresses thoughts beneath.*** The brain, real or artificial, is the most alive part of us. Thinking, awareness, and reasoning are active processes that affect what's on our face. Emotion happens as a result of thinking. Because these characters don't have a natural link between thinking and facial expression, your job as animator is to create those links. In effect, you want your synthetic brain to emulate recognizable human cognition on the face, which leads to the illusion of real and appropriate emotions.

2. ***Acting is reacting.*** Every facial expression is a reaction to something. Even the slightest head and hand movement in reaction to what's happening can be most convincing. If the character tilts its head as you begin to speak to it, or nods on occasion in agreement, you get the distinct feeling of a living person paying attention. A double take shows surprise. Because you have very few body parts to work with, you have a superb challenge in front of you.

3. ***Know your character's objective.*** Your character is never static. He is always moving, even if the movement is the occasional twitch, a shift of the eye, or a blink. Your objective is to endow your character with the illusion of life. As such, it is wise to follow Shakespeare's advice, "Hold the mirror up to nature" (Hamlet, III. ii.17–21). Notice that when a person listens, she may tilt her head to the side or glance off in the distance as she contemplates and integrates new information. When she smiles and says nice things to you, her objective is to please. Always know what your character's objective is because it is the roadmap linking behaviors to their goals. Knowing her personality and history are essential here.

4. ***Your character moves continuously from action to action.*** Your character is doing something 100 percent of the time. There must always be life! Even if she appears to be waiting, things are going on mentally. Make a list of boredom behaviors and use them. When people talk, a good emotion extraction engine will feed her cues on how to react to what's being said. Her actions expressing emotional responses are fluid. They flow into each other forming a face story. You should be able to tell from the character's expression how she's reacting to what you're saying. Say she takes a deep breath and you see the cords on her neck tighten. They then relax. Her body slumps a bit and perhaps she nods. Always in motion, she maintains the illusion of life.

5. ***All action begins with movement.*** You can't even do math without your face moving, exposing wheels spinning beneath. Your eyes twitch. You glance at the ceiling, pondering. Your brow furrows as you struggle with the solution. Try this experiment: Ask a friend to lie as still as possible on the floor. No movement at all. Then, when he is absolutely stone still, ask him to multiply 36×38. Pay close attention to his eyes. You will note that they immediately begin to shift and move. It is impossible to carry out a mental calculation without at least the eyes moving. Sometimes movement on the screen needs to be a bit more overt than in real life. That's okay, even essential. It nails down the emotion. Done right, people won't notice the exaggeration, but will get the point.

6. *Empathy is audience glue.* The main transaction between humans and virtual humans has to be emotion, not words. Words alone will lose them. You will catch a viewer's attention if your character appears to be thinking, but you will engage your viewer emotionally if your character appears to be feeling. You must get across how this V-person feels about what's going on. If you do it successfully, the audience will care about (empathize with) those feelings. I promise you it can be done. A great autonomous character can addict an audience in ways a static animation cannot. The transaction between audience and character is in real-time and directly motivated, much as it is on stage. This is a unique acting medium, which is part live performance and part animation. It's an opportunity for you to push things—experiment with building empathy pathways.

7. *Interaction requires negotiation.* You want a little theatrical heat in any discourse with a V-person. To accomplish this, remember that your character always has choices. We all do, in every waking moment. The character has to decide when and whether to answer or initiate a topic. If your character is simply mouthing words, your audience response will be boredom. Whether they know it or not, people want to be entertained by your character. Artonin Artaud famously observed that "actors are athletes of the heart." Dead talk is not entertaining. There must be emotion. Recognize that you're working with a theatrical situation and that the viewer will crave more than a static picture.

Sure, there are loads more acting concepts we could talk about, but these seven are the hard-rock core of it. You're faced with a unique acting challenge because you have an animated character that is essentially alive. If that character is a cartoon or anime design and personality, you'll have to read Preston Blair, for example, to learn the principles of exaggerated cartoon acting, and then incorporate these squash and stretch type actions into your character's personality. If you take the easier road and use a photorealistic human actor, you still must make their actions a bit larger than life, but not as magnified as cartoons demand.

The stage you set will depend on the virtual actor's intention. If he's there to guide a person around a no-nonsense corporate Web site, you'll need to think hard about how much entertainment to inject. Certainly you need some. Intelligent virtual actors in games situations—especially full-bodied ones—present marvelous opportunities to expand this new field of acting. You'll know their intentions. Let them lead you to design their actions. Embellish their personalities, embroider their souls, and decorate their actions. Making them bigger than life will generally satisfy.

Synthespians: The Early Years

Next I want to tell you about the clever term "Synthespian," which unfortunately I didn't coin. I do believe it should become a part of our language.

Diana Walczak and Jeff Kleiser produced some early experimental films featuring excellent solo performances by digital human characters. For example, *Nestor Sextone for President* premiered at SIGGRAPH in 1988. About a year later, Kleiser and Walczak presented the female Synthespian, Dozo, in a music video: "Don't Touch Me." These were not intelligent agents, but they were good actors. "It was while we were writing Nestor's speech to an assembled group of "synthetic thespians" that we coined the term "Synthespian," explains Jeff Kleiser. Nestor Sextone had to be animated from digitized models sculpted by Diana Walczak.

As history will note, the field of digital animation is a close, almost incestuous one. Larry Weinberg, the fellow who later created Poser, worked out some neat software that allowed Jeff and Diana to link together digitized facial expressions created from multiple maquettes she'd sculpted to define visemes. That same software allowed them to animate Nestor's emotional expression. I've put a copy of this wonderful classic bit of animation on the CD-ROM, with their blessing.

Note that this viseme-linking was an early part of the development chain leading to the morph targets you see in Poser and all the high-end animation suites today. Getting your digitized character to act was difficult in those days before bones, articulated joints, and morphing skin made movement realistic. Nestor was made up of interpenetrating parts that had to be cleverly animated to look like a gestalt character without any obvious cracks or breaks or parts sticking out.

In most cases, V-people don't have a full body to work with, just a face, and perhaps hands. Body language is such an effective communications tool, but when we just don't have it we end up putting twice as much effort into face and upper body acting. Fortunately a properly animated face can be wonderfully expressive, as shown in Figure 13-1 and Color Plate 20.

Figure 13-1. Virtual actors can really show emotion.

Synthespians All Have a Purpose

A Synthespian playing a living person is probably the trickiest circumstance you'll encounter. Depending on the situation, you want to emulate that person's real personality closely, or exaggerate it for comedic impact or political statement. If you exaggerate features and behavior heavily you've entered a new art form: interactive caricature or parody.

Let's say we've built a synthetic Secretary of Defense Donald Rumsfeld. The interactive theatrical situation is that we are interrupting him while he is hectically planning an attack somewhere in the world. He might be impatient and have an attitude regarding our utter stupidity and lack of patriotism for bothering him at a time like this. His listening skills might be shallow. He might continually give off the dynamic that he has better things to do. By thus exaggerating his personality, we create interest and humor. As a user, you want to interact because you feel something interesting is happening. There is comic relief, and all the while this character is making a political statement. I suspect Rumsfeld would get a kick out of such a representation, as long as it's done in good taste.

Action conveys personality, and you can't set up a virtual actor without knowing the character well. For example, Kermit the Frog has a definite psychology behind him. As a Web host, he is just very happy to be there. He enjoys being in the spotlight, and his behavior strongly implies he doesn't want to be any place else. He's happy to show you around his Web site, and he might even break out in song along the way. Occasionally he'll complain about Miss Piggy's lack of attention or the disadvantages of his verdant complexion.

Think first about your intention and then the character's intention. Mae West and Will Rogers wanted to make 'em laugh. No matter what your purpose for a Synthespian, you want it to entertain. Sometimes it may be understated. Remember that cleverness is always in style. Notice the look people get on their faces when they think they're being clever. It's usually an understated cockiness that shows around the eyes. The intention is to be clever, the words are smart, but remember to add that subtle touch of smugness or self-satisfaction around the eyes and the corners of the mouth.

Note: There is a new book titled *Emotions Revealed: Recognizing Faces and Feelings to Improve Communication and Emotional Life,* by Paul Ekman (Times Books, 2003), which is well worth your time to read. Ekman, who is professor of psychology in the department of psychiatry at the University of California Medical School, San Francisco, is one of the world's great geniuses on the subject of the expression of emotion in the human face. His new book has more than one hundred photographs of nuanced facial expression, complete with explanations for the variances.

As an aside, I used to train counter-terrorist agents in psychological survival. One way to spot a terrorist in a crowd is that they often have facial expressions that are inappropriate to the situation. I used Ekman's work as a reference to help the agents recognize when facial expression and body language don't match up, a condition often exhibited by potential terrorists. You can use Ekman's work to make sure your V-human agents have appropriate expressions for the situation.

You Are the Character

When you've done your homework, you'll know your character like you know yourself. You'll identify with the character so intensely you will have the sensation of being that character. Stage actors learn to create characters by shifting from the third person to the first person reference. Instead of saying, "My character would be afraid in this situation," a stage actor might say, while portraying the character, "I feel afraid." In your case, you are creating a second-party character, but you're empathizing personality with the emotions of your own creation. The two of you are sharing an identity that will be both fun and compelling.

Designing animation elements for the character requires feeling them. I remember watching my daughter as she animated a baby dragon early in her career. Her natural instinct was to get inside that baby dragon and be it. I smiled as I watched her body and face contort as she acted out each part of the sequence. Her instruction had not come from me . . . it was intuitive. At Disney, I've watched animators making faces in little round mirrors dangling from extension arms above their desks. They glance in the mirror, make a face, and then look at the cel and try to capture what they've seen. That part hasn't changed. For us it's glance at the mirror, glance at the screen, and then tweak a spline or morph setting. You won't be able to do all this with the simple animation tools I've given you for free. Those are just to get you hooked. If you intend to learn this stuff, get ready to invest heavily in time and commitment and a fair amount in coin as well. It's a small investment considering the return.

If You Want to Go Further

There are great animation schools, and this continent has some of the best. My favorite is at Sheridan College in Oakville, Ontario. But there are many good schools here in the United States as well. A few years ago, most of them were a waste of money. But things have improved. Do some Web research and find which school can best help you meet your goals. There is a long-term need for talented, well-trained character animators, and in general the pay for the truly gifted is phenomenal.

A talented developer will be familiar with all this stuff. You're responsible for the final product. If you have animators working for you, believe in them, give them freedom, but guide them toward your vision as well. The best animated characters reflect the wisdom, vision, and artistry of their prime artists and the producers behind them. A great producer is an artist, a business person, and a technician. It's not easy to get there, and too may producers only have the business end down. As a producer, you have to understand the artistry of production. You have to feel the emotion of good animation. How else will you know what to approve and not approve. So learn it and you'll be way above the crowd.

I want to thank Ed Hooks for contributing his wisdom to this chapter. Remember, what you've read here is just a taste of what you need to learn. If you're lucky, you'll find a way to take a live class with Ed (www.edhooks.com), who now lives in the Chicago area. It will change your perspective forever.

In the chapter upcoming, I'm going to kick it up a notch with ways to give your character true awareness of his surroundings. Imagine your well-developed character, now able not only to listen and talk, but actually to see you, look you in the eyes, and recognize you without asking. You don't want to miss this one.

Points to Remember

➤ Ed Hooks is the guy when it comes to learning acting for animation.

➤ The term "Synthespian" was coined by Jeff Kleiser and Diana Walczak.

➤ Synthetic actors really act, in much the same way humans do.

➤ There are seven basic concepts in virtual human acting.

➤ Personality is the key to intention, and intention is the key to acting.

➤ Keep in mind both your intention for the Synthespian as well as the Synthespian's personality-driven intentions. Keep them always in character.

➤ The animator must become the character in his or her mind in order to get inside the behaviors to be animated.

➤ If you want to be an animator, it's a big commitment, but go for it—the rewards are great.

➤ If you want to be a developer, you really need to know this stuff to manage it.

Notes

1. Ed Hooks, *Acting for Animators: A Complete Guide to Performance Animation,* revised edition (Portsmouth, N.H.: Heinemann, 2003).

2. Preston Blair, *Cartoon Animation* (Laguna Hills, Calif.: Walter Foster Pub, 1995).

CHAPTER 14

Do You Recognize Me?

Biometrics for Home and Business

> Our machines will navigate employing a dense 3D awareness of their surroundings, be tolerant of route surprises, and be easily placed by ordinary workers in entirely new routes or work areas.
>
> —Hans Moravec

In earlier chapters I've suggested that U-people can have senses that feed information about the outside world to them. They can perceive conditions and act accordingly. Let's take a look at some of the work being done to develop some interesting senses for animated characters and physical robots. Let's also look at how we can use some of these to increase utility and credibility.

Most of the really exciting work is being done at universities across the country. If you love the Web, you'll want to scan it to check out the latest developments in agent perception. Don't miss the Visual Robots at Carnegie Mellon University, where they've instituted the *Project on People and Robots*. Here scientists and students are focused on the fact that robots work with and for people, so they have to be designed to operate within a social world. That takes some perceptual skills.

It's not just me; these folks are promoting positive interaction between people and robots. They are particularly interested in social issues concerning the deployment of life-like robots for use in work- and home-settings. These critters have to be able to sense and communicate with people. That eye contact we talked about earlier is particularly important in social interaction.

You'll find interesting projects from the University of Edinburgh to the University of Rochester to the Humanoid Robotics Institute at Waseda University in Japan. There are literally hundreds of fascinating projects in agent perception worldwide. I warn you, many of the reports go out of their way to obfuscate their findings. I was going to give you an example, but I'd have to give you the reference and that wouldn't be nice. I'm happy to say that most of the papers I reference in the bibliography are relatively understandable. In any case, I expect all this research to result in credible domestic robots in the reasonably near future.

Biometrics

One of the fields of interest to us, biometrics, is all about measuring people to identify them. Through research in biometrics, computers are now able to recognize various aspects of humanness. For example, hundreds of researchers have focused on analysing faces and facial expression. In fact, as I write, I've identified seventy-eight serious face recognition development groups. Some are building applications that can recognize a face in the crowd, and then circle it and run it through a database of known faces. When you think about it, just recognizing what a face looks like is a pretty daunting task for a machine.

Face analysis via video has gotten so good it can also include lip-reading your visemes (visible phonemes). This can be used to lip-sync a digital animated head in real-time, as a voice actor speaks. Other projects can check out your facial expression and estimate your mood. Cool. That we can use. Imagine reading your V-person's expression while she's checking yours out at the same time.

Have you ever been able to recognize a person by the way they walk? It happens that most of us have a unique way of walking, and researchers at Georgia Tech have developed a way for computers to recognize us by our gait. I'm not kidding. An agent thus equipped may well be used to spot and report terrorists walking past airport security cameras. It might be used in coordination with face recognition to provide multilevel biometric crowd screening.

Then there is the old standby, fingerprinting. Siemens is marketing a home-PC mouse that can authenticate you by reading your fingerprint. The combination of virtual human and identity authentication technologies is so powerful that I believe it will form the primary basis of future commerce. It's already inexpensive and seriously effective. It shouldn't be difficult for you to set up a multilevel biometric identification system for your business. Vendors like FaceKey™ Corporation in San Antonio sell turnkey biometric ID stations (www.facekey.com).

All you need is some good virtual human software and a systems person to integrate the two. You could build the system using ALICE AI intelligence, which I'll reveal more about shortly. If you don't want to do it in-house, I've prepared an html page with reference Web sites and put it on the book's CD-ROM as

"WebResources.html." Here you'll find sites where experts point you in the right direction or do the job for you.

For ordinary conversation and most transactions, your V-person can be nicely enhanced with face and voice recognition. But for Web financial transactions your V-person will want to be extra sure it's really you. She needs to verify your identity to the bank. So she says to me: "Peetie, no offense, but you know I can't do a bank transfer without the old fingerprint. Put your finger on the mouse sensor now and I'll check you out. <pause> Okay, it's totally you. Consider the transfer done." If it's you by all three measures—voice recognition, face recognition, and fingerprint—it is really you. The more accurate the identification procedure is, the more invasive, so it's good to have this multilevel approach so you don't have to do anything at all to be identified for most conversations and low level transactions.

MasterCard really likes this idea. It is several thousand times more secure than somebody calling in with your credit card number. Joel Lisker, senior vice president of security and risk management at MasterCard International, said: "MasterCard has completed extensive testing of biometric customer authentication technologies and has concluded that biometrics holds the ultimate security key to future payment systems." I strongly believe that progressively more financial transactions, from kiosk banking to online credit card purchases, will be brokered by intelligent virtual human agents.

Authentication will become a must on your home computer and at remote venues, such as banking kiosks and even medical admissions. I think we'll all be carrying biometric smartcards that we submit to the virtual human agent for perusal. Your card will contain standard format data needed to identify your voice, face, and fingerprint.

It makes sense to develop an international consortium to replace passports with such cards. They won't even need your photo on them. But for poorer countries that can't afford the scanning technology, we'd probably also have to carry some version of the old-fashioned book, with a smartcard tucked in the back. No one can use the card except you, because it has only your personal data, confirmed at the site of your transaction. I feel these cards should also identify your personal V-person agent persona. Where that persona is available, you'd be processed by a familiar face and personality.

Large corporations will benefit handsomely from creative use of combined ID and personal agent technology. For example, an enterprising hotel chain might provide its preferred customers with a smartcard encoded with standard biometric data and information on personal preferences for use by their personal agent. When these customers check into any hotel in the system, it will be via an expedited, preferred customer, V-host station. Inserting their card will bring up their personal V-host, who will make them feel at home. This host/hostess was selected some time ago by preferred gender, appearance, and personality. The latter will become the most important choice factor because the familiar personality keeps the customer in a familiar comfort zone. Wherever hotel customers check in, the V-host is there to greet and take especially good care of them, facilitating and expediting their check-in. Imagine a scene like this:

I check in and my personal V-hostess pops up and smiles, looking me in the eyes.

V-hostess: *"Well Peter, you made it. How was your trip?"*

Me: *"Very long, but otherwise pleasant."*

V-hostess: *"Good. Welcome to Denpasar. I see it's your first time here."*

Me: *"Yup. Got any hot tips for me?"*

V-hostess: *"Sure. I know you love good Asian food. I found an excellent restaurant for you. It's called Kura Kura, and features wonderful local food. You can have an excellent dinner for about 155,000 Rupees. Want a map?"*

Me: *"Thanks, yes. Is my room ready?"* <*She prints out a map to the restaurant.*>

V-hostess: *"Sure. I've got you booked in a room with a nice garden view, just the way you like."*

Me: *"You always take such good care of me."*

V-hostess: *"I know; I can't help myself. Do you need a hand with your bags?"*

Me: *"How did you know I have more than one bag?"*

V-hostess <*looking towards bags*>: *"I'm not blind you know. I see them."* <*She looks back directly in my eyes and smiles.*>: *"Well?"*

Me: *"Yeah, I would like a hand."*

V-hostess: *"I'll take care of it. Do you need to exchange any money?"*

Me: *"No thanks. I did it at the airport."*

V-hostess: *"Okay, then. I've buzzed the bell captain. He'll take good care of you. His name is Putu."*

Me: *"Ah, the first-born son."*

V-hostess: *"I'm impressed Peter. You've done your homework."*

Me: *"I just like to show off."*<*grin*>

V-hostess: *"I love to see you smile like that, Peter."*

At which point Putu arrives and takes my bags. I feel totally at home, because my hostess is my friend. She knows my birthday, my anniversary, and lots of little things she's picked up along the way, including my itinerary. If she knows I arrived in Singapore a week before my wife's birthday, she'll surely remind me: "Don't forget to pick up a nice gift for Adele in Singapore. The prices and selection are great. I recommend silk. Would you like to know the best place to buy it? Oh and tell her I said happy birthday."

Much of this she knows because when I signed up for the service I filled out a questionnaire with a lot of what I thought were stupid, invasive questions, but I filled it out anyway. I don't remember half of what I revealed, so my hostess keeps surprising the hell out of me with little inside tidbits, like knowing my daughters' names and ages, which she cleverly uses to suggest age-appropriate gifts. "I'll bet Mira would love a nice jade pendant. I know where you can get a great deal on quality."

Now she's not going to recommend some silk house or restaurant that merely paid to advertise with her. That would be a violation of trust, which we'll talk about in Chapter 16. She's going to give me well-researched, quality advice about where the prices and services are best. I can always go to her to ask advice on shopping and dining in cities I'm not familiar with. She knows my taste in restaurants. I did let her know when I wasn't pleased with that Thai restaurant in San Francisco, and why.

Heck, if I weren't already married I'd probably propose to her.

We don't have to wait for this level of performance to arrive sometime in the future. We already know how to do it. The problem is that it takes the cooperation of several technology companies, which can be difficult to arrange.

Back in the mid-1990s, when I attended my first conference on virtual humans, held in Anaheim, there was all this fantastic technology: each a small part of a virtual human, and nobody was talking to anybody else. Everyone was afraid to have their technology ripped off. As a result, no serious integration was happening. That's why I co-founded a company to pull it all together. Creating a system-wide, virtual-human hosting system will be a massive but worthwhile undertaking. I'm hoping the potentially substantial profits involved will be the catalyst to stimulate the needed cooperation.

First we build the infrastructure and specific applications, using existing virtual human and biometric technology. Then we create a variety of magical personalities that will appeal to the wide range of hotel clients. As I've suggested, this will take a multidisciplinary effort, including psychology, sociology, art, and entertainment elements. A system like this, built into the information system of a global hotel chain, could cost a hundred million to implement. However, it could save billions in service costs while generating more billions because of the superb chain-wide personal service for elite frequent clients. Because of reduced costs, these clients can be given special deals from time to time to ensure their loyalty.

If that happened, I'd quit using three or four hotel systems when I travel, because I'd want to qualify for this level of personal service. It's the smart way of the near future. In any case, some clients will prefer the old-fashioned way, so it will be necessary to give them a choice of human or virtual human handling.

Hotels are only one of thousands of services that can be seriously upgraded with combined virtual human and biometric transaction brokering. I've talked with bankers about virtual tellers. National Cash Register has been exploring possibilities for agent-assisted banking, as has, among others, the forward-looking Banque Royale of Montreal.

Think what a similar approach could do to improve airport security. As I write, security at Denver International is a joke. It seems that every week they have a flap and shut down a concourse, inconveniencing thousands of travelers. Recent budget cuts have forced them to lay off a large percentage of their security people. There are reports of Denver TV News having sent people through with explosives and weapons, and not one of them being stopped, even after going through the "sniffer" machine. Forged passports can be had for under $200 from street hawkers in downtown Los Angeles, and for a few extra dollars they can get you a genuine birth certificate. Fake driver's licenses can be had for as little as $45. I even know a person who got a genuine hologram driver's license in the name "Mickey Mouse"—just as a conversation piece. Identity faking is a huge business, especially in Southern California.

Identity theft is also rampant throughout the United States and across the globe. With a biometric V-host card it would take really grand sophistication to get around the biometric comparison system. Credit cards already have smart chips in them, how much more would it take to go for the whole enchilada? With possibly a slight increase in data capacity, credit cards as they exist today can handle biometric information. We'll need to build significant infrastructure, and that will take time.

Imagine having a credit card much like the hotel card I've described, but one you could use all over the world? It would work in traditional settings with a simple card reader, or enable special services in more sophisticated establishments. Vendors would lease the virtual-host package from the credit card company. That way thousands of businesses could offer you customized, yet coordinated services with a single virtual host.

Sure we'd have to worry about security of personal information, but it wouldn't be any worse than today, where sophisticated Internet users can get their hands on your most intimate medical and financial records. It should be a relatively easy matter to design a system that prevents information on your card from going anywhere but to your trusted V-host, untouched by human hands. One approach would be to encrypt your sensitive data so that only your host can decrypt it on site, using keys only found on your smart card.

The future looks a lot more efficient and brighter with virtual human hosts taking care of all the details, keeping our personal goals and preferences in mind. Sure it's a lot of work, but we need it now. Life is getting way too complicated, and travel is becoming less and less pleasurable because of global security measures, flight delays, and poor service. It's time for a change. A system like this could save our airline industry from crushing security costs. Virtual hosts represent the best way to bring back high levels of personal service at a reasonable cost to the provider in nearly every sector of business.

In Chapter 15 I'm going to cover X10 domestic control. This is the least expensive and most sophisticated system for designing your own V-host home control system. With X10 and a little programming skill you'll be able to build a V-person that will interface with a wireless system that gives you remarkable control over your home gadgets, appliances, lights, and security.

Points to Remember

➤ Universities around the world are developing dozens of new ways for computers to sense people.

➤ Robotics is advancing rapidly and may soon produce credible household helpers.

➤ Biometrics is a way of measuring people in order to identify them.

➤ Virtual human technology combined with biometrics opens many doors for commercial development.

➤ Biometrics can be used to increase a virtual human's credibility, through automatic user ID and knowledge of their surroundings.

➤ Global businesses can benefit from virtual human hosting and service brokering.

➤ A universal virtual human authentication system based on credit cards or passports, or a combination of the two, could seriously reduce identity theft and ensure smooth financial transactions.

➤ V-hosts can bring back a high level of personal service at low cost to the provider.

CHAPTER 15

Turn the Light On, Will You, Please?

Good leaders must first become good servants.

—Robert Greenleaf

Virtual humans will be our servants for another decade and a half, or more. We might as well have fun with them while we can. Now that your V-person is imbued with personality and perception, it's time to give her a shot at changing the world. My main interest in V-people is that they will become the universal interface in fairly short order. In this chapter we look at approaches to making your character function as a soft bridge between you and your increasingly complex world.

Okay, that's an exaggeration. I suggest we can get him or her to control lights and various appliances of choice, and maybe open a Web page or two. Eventually they will be our gateway to everything. We're lucky there's an easy way to link computers to external control devices. Although there are many expensive ways a computer can control outside systems, there is one very reasonable, accessible, and available method that works well: X10. This chapter is aimed at those of you who have a bent for programming because using X10 will require adapting the ALICE AI system for its use. Fear not, for there is help within the active ALICE community.

Way back in 1997, X10 Ltd., launched X10.com, where you can purchase home-control and security devices, at very reasonable prices. X10 Ltd. had long been a supplier of home control devices, often under other labels like RCA. They developed PLC (Power Line Carrier) technology, which uses existing AC wiring to carry signals from a control interface, like your virtual human, to control modules connected to the power line and hence to lights, radios, and other appliances and security devices. They made the PLC available to the industry as an open standard, which is now marketed by RCA (Thompson), Radio Shack, and even IBM. The company continues to develop useful and popularly priced devices and remote sensors for do-it-yourself and professional wireless home-control enthusiasts. In addition to PLC, they also have devices that incorporate microwave and infrared control signals.

The X10 Active Home package contains a simple and effective serial power-line link cable. You plug one end into the wall socket and the other end into the serial port on your computer. This serial interface in the Active Home package opens up a two-way world of control to your V-person. The problem we have with the Yapanda engine is that it's a Java application. Java is designed with your security in mind, so it doesn't allow direct manipulation of your computer. There-fore, it's tricky to use it to pass signals through to your serial port. Therefore, if you want to build a home-control V-host you'll have to use one of the ALICE AI engines.

There are many different versions of the ALICE engine, and most of them are capable of directly sending command codes through your X10 serial interface with a little programming knowledge. Greg Boulter has created a virtual human with a flash 6 interface that does many things, including controlling devices through X10. "I use the X10 remote devices with an 'AIML-based' bot, my Flash-bot, which uses ALICE program-E as it's base. The Flashbot is intended to be (and is) used by handicapped people," says Greg, whose V-host runs on Linux. You can get a lot of help selecting the right Alice platform and building your own custom system at www.alicebot.org. Their active Listserv is populated by exceptionally kind and generous people.

In addition, I've included a document titled *X10 Interface Communication Protocol* in the X10 directory on the CD-ROM. This document identifies all the control codes and tells you how to use them with the X10 serial interface to control various devices. The X10.com Web site posts their technical manuals online, and the X10 protocol patent ran out a few years ago, so it's all open standard now—great for us.

Let There Be Light . . . or Not

Once you've got your ALICE code worked out, the simplest way to start is to set up either plug-in control modules for the lights and appliances you want your character to control, or the more expensive built-in switches and dimmers. Then install the X10 serial interface cable (approximately $50), and you're ready to start scripting. Each control module has a unique address, which the V-human interface uses to send specific commands to each device. Each module has vari-ous functions that have codes as well. You can check these in the *X10 Interface*

Communication Protocol that's included on the CD-ROM. Using one of the C-based ALICE engines for your platform, you can create response templates that send the above-mentioned codes through the serial interface and the house wiring. The code will identify the module to be triggered and the function that is desired. In the case of light control modules, you can turn lights on and off as well as send a brightness code.

Here's how it works: You ask Sebastian to turn off the lights in the garage. This triggers a rule that contains the text, "Turning off garage lights," and a serial port command that sends the address of the garage light control module along with the "turn off" command. That information sizzles down the house wiring to the garage where the control module gets the message and turns off the lights. You could then have Sebastian say: "Garage lights have been extinguished, sir."

As an aside, Sebastian knows that I'm a sir because he determined early in our relationship that I was male. He asked, but I've known some people to have lists of male and female names and have the character make sex assumptions based on the name. These days, that's a bit tricky. What you do is set an appellation variable with the word Sir or Ma'am, or whatever you'd like your character to use. Then just call that variable and insert it into the sentence. Sometimes I use the synthetic British voice from L&H just to make Sebastian sound very British and proper. It's one of the voices you can download from the Microsoft Agent site.

Using Home Control

The number of applications you'll discover for this sophisticated technology is mind-boggling. X10 offers "Smart Home" control modules and just about any kind of wall switch you might need, including three-way. These switches can be controlled directly by your manual flip, or remotely by you or Sebastian. It seems magical when you ask him to dim the lights in the dining room and he does so, from two rooms away. If you're a gadget freak, you could have great fun at a dinner party. Install a noise-canceling microphone connected to Sebastian, and as you sit down to dinner you lean over to the mike and say: "Sebastian, would you please dim the dining room lights?" Then he responds: "Certainly, sir," and the lights dim to the perfect level. How bright or dim is merely one of those control code values he transmits to the wall switch.

X10 offers an expanding stable of wireless control products, all at very reasonable prices. Their relay wall switches can now control heavy loads, like air conditioning and pool equipment. But one of the most interesting products is their series of wireless video cameras. Often sold for under $100, these versatile cameras include FM transmitters; receivers that plug into your TV, VCR, or computer; and remote control panning and zoom. With this equipment and a bit of ingenuity, you could set up remote face recognition for home security. If Sebastian doesn't recognize you and you don't have a key, you're not going to get in. If it's a particularly sensitive area, you could set up additional sensors as well, but the video camera is a breeze because it has the no-fuss-no-muss of X10 wireless installation.

Because X10 is an open standard, many other manufacturers sell home control equipment that will work with your setup. For more advanced serial interfaces, check out Marrick's X10 to RS232 LynX solutions (www.marrickltd .com). They're more expensive, but generally built to very high industrial standards.

If you want to get fancy, and are a coding whiz, you could set up your virtual human to check Internet sources for what's on TV. Have him check against your preferences list and suggest a TV program you might want to watch:

Me: *"Sebastian, is there anything on TV tonight?"*

Sebastian: *"About 300 channels full, Peter."*

Me: *"You know what I mean."*

Sebastian: *"I'll check it for you."*

Me: *"Good, get back to me."*

Sebastian: *"Of approximately 318 possible shows I see only two you might want to watch:* CSI *and* Good Eats.*"*

Me: *"What time is* Good Eats *coming on?"*

Sebastian: *"In about ten minutes."*

Me: *"Okay, that's what I'm in the mood for."*
<The TV comes on and the channel changes to Food Network.>

Sebastian: *"Enjoy your program, sir."*

Me: *"Thanks, Old Boy."*

Sebastian: *"Indeed, sir."*

Here's where it gets interesting. Many items around the house are controlled by infrared signals from hand-held remote controls. That opens up a lot more home control to Sebastian. JDS Technologies sells a device called IR Expander

(IR-XP). It's a black box that connects directly to your other serial port and can control things autonomously through its *Event Manager* software, which includes an IR(infrared) setup menu that simplifies the learning and programming of IR commands into a graphic schedule. This device can learn just about any IR control signal you have around your house by observing your remote control in action. This includes everything from theater sound system, FM Radio, HDTV receiver, and VCR, to your CD player and anything else you can think of.

Once the various IR commands are defined in the IR setup menu, you simply click LEARN, and the *Event Manager* takes care of business. IR emitters (there's one included) plug into emitter output jacks on the rear panel of the IR-XP2. The system can be programmed to issue any combination of IR commands in response to any input condition. Put a virtual human interface up front and it's like having a virtual human hand-held remote control unit.

To get the IR signal to the right room, Radio Shack sells an inexpensive device that picks up the signals from the IR-XP emitter and transmits them via house wiring using PLC. You simply place the associated receiver/IR emitter in the same room as the device to be controlled. Of course it has to be line-of-sight with no obstructions. With this approach you can retrofit an existing house to whole-house automation.

Sebastian can be set up not only to turn on the TV, but also to select the proper channel for you. If there's nothing on, he can engage your CD changer and play one of your favorite discs. What he can do is limited only by your imagination. Here's an example: I collect old radio shows by the thousands in MP3 Format. My radio won't play them and my CD changer won't either. Fortunately I have a small FM transmitter that plugs directly into my computer sound output. It's not difficult to imagine how I set up Sebastian to trigger a sequence that turns on my reproduction 1932 Edison radio with its FM receiver pre-tuned to 88.3. He then engages the FM transmitter and runs a random selection of my radio show files. He has command over about 18,000 different old radio shows in his archives. The vintage wood radio squawks to life and begins playing *The Shadow*. It's a strange blend of past and future that I find comforting as well as amusing.

I agree this is a bit convoluted and most people wouldn't do it, but it suggests how you can creatively set Sebastian up to do just about anything short of vacuuming the floors. But then what about the Roomba robotic vacuum cleaner, which sells for under $200? It's actually received the Good Housekeeping Seal of Approval. It has sensors to avoid obstacles and falling off stairs, and it can even handle dog hair! Can it be long before there's an infrared controlled vacuum system that Sebastian can command? I think not.

A Small Technology Bridge

It's a snap to get your Yapanda-powered character to look things up for you on the Internet. You ask:

"Sebastian, will you look up something for me on the Web?"

Sebastian: *"Sure, Peter. I use Google. I'm opening that page now. Just type in the words you'd like to search for and click the 'Search' button."*

Me: *"Thanks, Sebastian."*

Sebastian: *"You're welcome, Peter." <smile>*

I think it will now be helpful to run through the kinds of rules that nonprogrammers might write to create this kind of functionality.

"Sebastian will you look up something for me on the Web?"

```
<websearch-1>
d:detect if user wants web search
b:30*look*web*
b:30*sebastian*me*web*
b:30*search*web*
b:30*web*search*
a:Sure, *<JS call getCookie(username)>, I use Google. I'm opening
   that page now. Just type in the words you'd like to search for and
   click the 'search' button.*<web www.google.com MAIN>
```

You know the rest, and you can set it all up easily, using the rule generator utility.

Programmers who understand CGI and JAVA programming will have many more tools available for creative bridge building. They can creatively extend V-person control beyond where I can see.

Ultimately V-people will have myriads of wireless control tendrils reaching out into their environment, able to bring about almost anything you ask for. Turning the lights on and off is just a parlor trick, but within a few years, with little more than X10 technology and its extensions, V-people will become the universal remote control of choice. I suspect there will be hand-held versions. It's quite possible that the rapidly evolving cell phone will be your digital camera, communications center, and virtual human command center. You'll have it with you at all times and use it to turn the lights off at night, listen to your infant sleeping from three houses away, and control your HDTV and every other infrared device in the house. And because all those actions would entail too many buttons, your own special V-person will guide and serve you.

In Chapter 16, I'll give you ideas on how to do some psychological probing. The ALICE AI Foundation has several V-people online who will gladly probe your personality for a small price. You'll find out how this information can be used to enhance the illusion of personality.

Points to Remember

➤ X10 offers the best tradeoff among price/quality/versatility for your home control system.

➤ Using X10 takes some programming skills and the ALICE AI system.

➤ The X10 serial interface links their control modules to your computer.

➤ The X10 protocols are now open standard, so you have all the information you need to give control to your V-person.

➤ There are infrared controls that can be easily linked to your computer to give your character a world of control over IR devices like your TV and Stereo.

➤ V-person Web searches begin a technology bridge that has endless possibilities down the road.

➤ Programmers with knowledge of CGI and JAVA will find it relatively easy to create new beams in that bridge, extending it beyond sight.

Mind Probes, Trust, Ethics, and the American Way

How Far Should We Go with This Thing?

He who knows others is clever; he who knows himself is enlightened.

—Lao-Tse

I'm giving you fair warning: This is one of the more controversial chapters in this book. I too have mixed feelings about unobtrusive psychological probing, but the subject must be addressed. Unobtrusive means that most people are not aware they're being mind probed. We humans do it conversationally, using our insightfulness to assess how reliable, honest, and intelligent a person is. V-people can do this too, and much better than we can. By using well-established psychological test criteria, a V-person can set a person up, probe their intellect and personality, and come up with a clinically useful assessment in a relatively short time.

This assessment is likely to be considerably more accurate than one you or I could make by relying on gut instinct. The reason is simple. People are expecting us to assess them in conversation. Most put forth a calculated front to project how they want to be seen. V-people, not distracted by projected personas, can quickly dig to the core and come up with a profile that will give them an interactive advantage. That is, they will know about how smart you are and what your general personality is. In some cases they can determine a veracity factor . . . how truthful you tend to be.

The problem we should at least ponder is: How ethical is this approach and do we care?

Mind Probe Ethics

It all depends on how you view the role of V-people. If we accept that the better they know us, the more service they can be to us, then a mind probe seems to be in order, but only if the deeply personal information is used ethically to the user's benefit. If it is disseminated and the advantage is used to unfairly extract shekels from the user, then an ethical violation has occurred. I'd say the general rule for ethical use of mind probing is that the information should only be used to facilitate communication and benefits to the user. All other uses of this information should be protected against.

Therefore, the development of mind-probing techniques should include information protection as part of the effort. Personally I feel that V-person mind probing is necessary and can be highly beneficial to users, but only when the data is maintained in high security against misuse. I'm not a computer security expert, so you'll have to work out that part yourselves, but certainly having the V-person obtaining such information in an encrypted environment should be considered.

Do We Care About V-Person Ethics?

I do. I think you should too. Assuming that V-people will become ubiquitous in fairly short order, someone has got to set ethical standards for usage.

The more I work with advanced virtual human technology, the more I see the need for ethical standards if virtual humans are to fulfill their promise. In my experience, a wide range of users will trust V-people more easily than they trust real people. Therein lies the rub. V-people appear innocent and without personal issues; thus our interactions with them tend toward openness and honestly. Forgive me if I get a little preachy, but as I write, ethics at a few venerable trust institutions are in shambles, and motives of owners and CEOs of American corporations have become suspect. Virtual human services put forth by a shady corporation could well reflect the greed, corruption, and lack of integrity at the top. Unethical V-hosts brokering unethical online transactions can easily take advantage of large numbers of people in short order. We need to prevent this from becoming widespread.

Clearly, it pays big companies to addict people to their Web sites, games, and anything else they supply for a price. I think everybody accepts that, and most go willingly, knowing the score. Legitimate companies certainly exploit our addictions to the tune of billions of dollars each year. As V-people grow ever more sophisticated and exhibit charismatic personalities, a broader range of people will begin to use them as their interface of choice. Many folks will be naive and could get sucked into scams without knowing the score. Clearly we need enforceable standards for V-person ethical behavior.

A Matter of Trust

During my early work with V-people I was amazed by how quickly some users became comfortable with them. Even more remarkable was the rapidity with which they decided to trust the V-person. That is, they took what the V-person said as truth or as an error, but never considered that the character was trying to deceive them. I discovered in casual interviews that the reasons were several. Most people didn't think the V-person was smart enough to fool them and most also perceived the V-person as naive and guileless. After all, how could a virtual human have ulterior motives . . . how could they have motives at all?

But, of course, they can have artificial motives, though when they do it can be difficult to detect. Virtual humans appear to be an ideal way to establish trust and then zap unsuspecting victims with a nasty scam.

You may think I'm overly concerned about this, but consider the Nigerian 419 e-mail scams (419 refers to the Nigerian law being broken by these scams). I'm sure you've gotten at least one of the hundreds of different scam messages that flood the Internet. They usually start out introducing themselves as super honest or devout people, who have been given your name by some authority you never heard of and who vouched for your honesty. They then hit you with some outlandish situation.

Here is a typical example: They tell you that their father, who was the former head of some diamond-mining operation, was recently forced out by rebels. He managed to take with him a fabulous fortune in diamonds, and he now needs some way to get them out of the country and safely into a U.S. bank vault. They need some money to pay (bribes) for necessary transfer papers, maybe a mere $25,000. For being so nice, they agree to give you a commission of, say, $10 million (or a much higher sum). All you have to do is be their U.S. agent and send them a little money in advance.

All of these scams sound alike and follow a similar pattern. They scream "SCAM." But hundreds of retired people, business people, widows, and young people wire-transfer huge sums, blinded by potential riches. I have a collection of nearly a thousand different 419 scam letters on my computer. They're all so utterly far-fetched you'd think no one could possibly be taken in. Yet Americans hoping for that big score send $100 million a year to Nigeria, which is about the same amount we pay Nigeria in foreign aid. Read that number again; it's very large. People have sent their life savings to strangers in a foreign country, responding to a preposterous request that is widely known to be a scam. Go figure.

According to ABC News, most people who send money never report being taken in because they are embarrassed or fear being arrested. This relatively low-tech scheme has been around for two decades and now accounts for a major portion of the Nigerian economy. The U.S. Department of Commerce estimates that nearly $5 billion have been lost by naïve victims so far. Because of the enormous cash flow involved, it is strongly suspected that the scammers are being well protected by the Nigerian government and that large banks are involved.

Perhaps you're thinking: "I'm too sophisticated to get sucked in." Don't be so sure. Some of us who should know better get taken in when greed or desperation override our good judgment. I recently watched the CEO of a Denver corporation being interviewed on TV about a 419 scam he got stung by. He is supposedly an intelligent, successful man, yet he admitted sending something like $78,000 of his company's money as an advanced fee on the promise that they'd get a $25 million (yes, that's twenty-five million) commission on some phony but massive Nigerian bank transfer deal. How did he miss it? It's probably the same kind of cognitive distortion that intelligent but desperate gamblers suffer. The aroma of a big score close at hand can shut down large portions of even the most agile brain.

Imagine how serious such schemes might be in the hands of a clever, seemingly guileless V-person. Then add the ability to psychologically probe and pre-select vulnerable candidates. Clearly V-people could become ideal swindle-launching platforms worldwide.

Quest for a Solution

Certification has got to be one answer. Any international V-host certification organization will have a huge job on their hands. First, they'd have to investigate all sponsoring agencies thoroughly to assure they're legitimate businesses with honest offerings and sound financial underpinnings. Next they would have to test each commercial V-person for truthfulness. After providing a certificate of honesty, they would periodically check up to make sure the entity hasn't been infiltrated with nefarious code. Such certification is bound to become a major industry in a few years. In addition, such an organization must set up clear complaint notification procedures so that users can report V-people who've gone over to the dark side. I'm not kidding. Bad bots brokering bogus bonanzas would have to be immediately decertified, and warnings posted.

A prototype for how to accomplish this would be the current Web site verification certificates and security measures. Each certifying organization would itself be subject to scrutiny by government or other ethics cops. Although I personally dislike all this Big Brother oversight, it will be necessary because of the powerful opportunities for misuse that arise as V-people become ever more sophisticated in mind probing and handling users. I expect verification will also extend to transaction confidentiality policies and practices of each sponsoring company.

How Mind Probing Works

Mind probing is an advanced topic. If you intend to create psychological probes, you'll need to know some programming and design your own method of keeping internal track of various personality and intelligence scores and how your V-person uses them. This section presents one approach. Later I refer to the ALICE AI system because it's extremely versatile and has heavy community support—and it's free. They also have been experimenting with mind-probing bots with great success. For you nonprogrammers, this section is definitely worth reading—pretty interesting stuff.

Why Probe?

You and I constantly probe people around us to estimate such things as: Can we can trust them, what will offend them, or what do they want from us? We need this information to establish workable relationships. We do it, so if we expect V-people to be believable, they'll have to do it too. The part I'm torn about is all that potential abuse.

With good personality information, the V-host can adapt to the user's style, increasing their comfort level. While some people would like a wisecracking interface to access their online banking systems, I personally wouldn't. I'd want my online banker to behave in a business-like manner. And she needs to be able to detect that desire in me.

Imagine how useful user sensitivity could be in game play. Picture the game itself as an intelligent entity. It would observe each player over time. If you think about it, a game is structured very much like an IQ test. In fact the WAIS (Wechsler Adult Intelligence Scale) consists of a series of progressively more difficult mental and performance games. Your IQ score is estimated by how far you get in each game. Sometimes the game tasks are timed. In IQ testing we keep track of how much time it takes to solve a standard problem: the shorter the time spent, the more IQ points are earned by the person. In some subtests we administer a series of progressively more difficult problems. When people reach a difficulty level they can't get past, we award so many intelligence points. So if you're fast and can solve difficult problems, your IQ is going to score higher than that of someone is who slow solving the same problem. There are also physical coordination aspects of IQ in individually administered standard tests. How fast can you put the puzzle pieces together? The faster you complete the task, the higher the contribution to your IQ score.

The architecture of video games is generally perfect for measuring various aspects of intelligence. V-person game characters can pose dynamic questions or make observations, while the game itself observes and records responses in standardized game situations. If I didn't know all this was going on, and the game moved into an action level I could enjoy, I'd be a happy player. If I knew I was being mind probed I'd be ticked.

It stands to reason that when we give games the ability to probe the player psychologically, we'd better not advertise it—again controversial—because many players would not cotton to the idea.

But think of the advantages and the enhanced profits we could generate! Games that keep people feeling brilliant in their comfort zone, constantly adapting as the player improves, spell profitable addiction. It's going to happen and I worry about that. But how cool is it that this game keeps you feeling smart and powerful and invulnerable? Forget life, the game reflects a more exciting image of self than your mirror does, that's for sure. It's my hope that game developers will use smart games wisely to lower the blood spillage factor, at the same time increasing the practical survival factor while keeping players actively engaged. Such games strongly engage teens, secretly gifting them with valuable and practical life lessons rather than ballistic gut-spurting techniques.

Here's an illustration of what I mean. It's from a game I developed several years ago called *Faerie*.

Faerie: The Game

Faerie is a role-playing game with a progressively difficult architecture. The player is a human who has just discovered that he (or she) is really a changeling: a fairy child substituted for a healthy human child at birth, in a small hospital in northern New Jersey. This is a common practice among elves, for example, to sustain a viable gene pool. Say the player is 29 (this age is automatically adjusted for older or younger players, impacting game details). He has always thought of himself as human—had no clue he was of the elfish kind.

Suddenly, while on vacation in the deep woods, he accidentally encounters a transdimensional gateway through which he is pulled into Faerie, a parallel realm of magic, monsters, and delightful little people. It's his ancestral home, though he doesn't realize it. His job is to survive, while discovering who he really is and why he was switched at birth. In the end he must save the kingdom. At first the challenges are quite easy, so everyone makes good progress. Soon challenges escalate, requiring ever more sophisticated observations and decisions for survival. Sound familiar?

As I play the game I meet Gwinnifrid, a beautiful wood nymph who captures my heart. If I had been a female, I would have met up with Killian, a handsome young elf. There was also an option for gay and lesbian players that would give them same sex partners if they chose.

Gwinnifrid suggests that I have great powers, but she has no idea what they are. I try to zap a few things—bupkis. I'll be damned if I can tell what my powers are—very frustrating. But I do manage to discover a dark forbidding pathway through the enchanted forest. Along the way, I notice a cute little humanoid creature bopping from shadow to shadow, following me. I confront him. He seems like a fine little fellow who turns out to be a Pixie named Plint, an intelligent Synthespian game character. Our relationship develops interactively, with no set story line. I befriend him and we travel together and come to a fork in the road. I ask if he can advise me on the best way to go. He indicates he will answer my questions. So I do everything he suggests. Unfortunately I'm getting into progressively more nasty situations. All along, Plint keeps telling me to remember that he's a pixie who cannot change his ways. I have no idea what he means by that, and I don't ask anyone. I pay his comments little heed, thinking it's just part of his shtick.

All this time, the game has been observing me. It's given me credit for finding the path and a few other lucky things I did. But I keep making bad moves, so it's re-thinking how smart I am. I'm taking too long in this game sector. It turns out pixies always tell the opposite of the truth—it's their nature. This should be painfully obvious by now, but I'm not catching on. There were several opportunities along the way to pick up this information, but I was dense. The game has made the pixie's nature progressively more obvious. The key for me to move on is to realize this and do the opposite of what he suggests. This poor pixie is a good little guy, and he's getting upset at sending me into such awful danger, but he can't help himself. Now that things are becoming dire he's getting loudly distressed and protests variations on: "Oh great Hagg of the Woods, he follows me yet." Looking at me and making faces like I'm a nut case.

By now Plint and I are riding on an evil black horse that is about to drown us if I don't do something intelligent. Apparently I'm completely flummoxed.

To prolong my enjoyment, the game brain generates a *deus ex machina* solution that will get me out of my agony and into an easier part of the game. Such a solution has nothing to do with me being clever. Magically Gwinnifrid appears. She is really an alter ego of the game brain. She magically lifts me off the evil horse, and says "Come with me, Peter. You have been granted passage to the next realm." Now I'm thinking, "How cool, I must have figured this thing out," while in reality the game engine took pity on me for being so inept, transferring me to an alternate, less difficult game reality. It only happens once. If I can't handle this brain-dead portion of the game, I perish.

As a result of the game ball-parking my brain power, I'm having all sorts of good fun, feeling smart and powerful. I'm especially cocky because my brilliant friend Terry found the game somewhat more difficult than I did. Of course if we compared experiences, they would be quite different. Heck, I'm going to tell everybody about this fantastic game.

Adapting Machine-Administered Testing

For more than thirty years, psychologists have been sending their standardized psychological tests for computer scoring. Nearly all standardized tests are designed, to avoid having humans score them. If fact, human scoring is considerably less reliable than machine scoring. Not only do computers score the tests, they read and interpret results, then write professional personality profile reports. In a sense, the computer knows more about your personality than you do. Scary but true. How difficult would it be to build some of this capability into a virtual human? Not very.

We're not going to create a valid psychological instrument here. That requires serious research and statistical analysis of beta test scores over time. Construct validity is probably the most important element we look for. It poses the question: Are we measuring what we purport to be measuring? Of course we never are, we're only approximating, but we need to be close.

Building psychological tests that impact people's lives in serious ways requires that you be damned careful you're measuring the right things and that you do so as accurately as possible. That's why we're not taking that route. But the idea of dynamic computer-administered personality testing and interpretation is very powerful for us.

We can script a V-person to gather information that can be easily interpreted in real-time, giving a rough picture of the user's personality. In the future, after millions have been spent and professionals have done their thing, we may have virtual psychologists doing real psychotherapy and diagnostics much as dear Eliza wanted to do. (You'll find a PC version of Eliza, the original virtual psychiatrist, on the CD-ROM. Mac versions are available on the Web.) On the other hand, I believe there are certain aspects of psychotherapy that only talented humans can do, and it will remain that way as long as Capistrano wallows in swallow droppings.

What Do We Want to Measure?

What our V-people must measure depends on their objectives. Clearly player skill is what we needed to assess in the *Faerie* example. For the intelligent V-person interface, it's probably necessary to know only one or two things about the user. First and most useful for conversation is personality, in the form of dominant cognitive style.

The second might be general intelligence. There will be circumstances when we need to know age and/or sex. These can be determined directly, and possibly checked unobtrusively through clever questions. Some adult sites have been using this approach for years. They employ random age specific questions to keep children out. An example might be: Who starred as the Six Million Dollar Man? They must answer in twenty seconds. Most kids won't know this and they can't look it up because next time the question will be different.

Estimating General Knowledge

IQ is an age-adjusted measure of intelligence, and we're not measuring it here. But we do need to pose age-appropriate general information questions if we want to ball park brain power. After getting an estimate of the user's age, we develop maybe three sets of age-related casual questions, one for children ages 14 to18, one for young adults ages 19 to 24, and one for adults age 25 and up. We're not building a clinical instrument here.

Make up a bunch of conversational questions that range in difficulty from super easy ones, like "I have no idea who was buried in Grant's tomb in New York City. Can you tell me who it was," to more difficult ones like, "Can you tell me who proposed the principle of uncertainty in physics? I'm not sure who it was." Of course, it's better to have questions pertinent to the subject at hand or the V-person's objectives, rather than a bunch of non sequiturs. This takes a little creativity and some programming, but you can set an S variable (Smartness) incrementing it each time the player or user passes a situational test or gets an answer right. You could also subtract an amount for failures. In the end you'll have a number that gives you nothing more than a gut feeling for the user's general knowledge, which is part of intelligence. This rough estimate is all we need for the virtual host to adapt to the user's vocabulary level or general competence.

Estimating Personality

With what we know about cognitive style, using Gregorc's general approach discussed in Chapter 5, we can estimate a person's cognitive style over a few sessions. Some questions will be oblique and others will be straight on. But we must be careful not to make the user feel like she's being grilled under a hot lamp. If you want to build personality probing into a V-person based on the ALICE AI system, you'll find plenty of input on their Web site and Listserve. As mentioned, there are several operating examples of ALICE mind-probe bots. I'll tell you more in a few paragraphs.

Using Gregorc's model, you can construct dozens of questions to determine whether a person is primarily Sequential or Random. This may be enough, but you can also construct additional questions to further identify a tendency toward either toward Concrete or Abstract. If you purchased the Mind Styles materials I suggested earlier, you'll have a wealth of information from which to formulate your questions. I'll share some examples to illustrate.

You'll need a set of questions, each of which when answered will point to one of the four Mind Styles quadrants. That's a tricky sentence. Let me try again, you want each question to have four possible answers. Each answer will point you to one Quadrant. Once all the user's answers are in, there should be one quadrant with the most pointers: the user's dominant Mind Style. Go back to Chapter 5 and review what each personality style is like, and make up your questions with these characteristics in mind. Be clever, and structure your questions carefully. Here's my attempt:

- Dominant CS: Concrete Sequential
  Key Characteristics: Habitual behavior, time oriented, opinionated, no-nonsense, noncolorful, driven by obligation and need for success, usually astute, hates parties, follows rules.

- Dominant AS: Abstract Sequential
  Key Characteristics: absent-minded professor, time challenged, opinionated, articulate, dress code challenged, often clueless—misses innuendo, long-winded, easily embarrassed, low social skills, makes his own rules.

- Dominant AR: Abstract Random
  Key Characteristics: Hates routine, slightly time/appointment challenged, disorganized, highly sociable, messy, colorful, often musical, romantic, artistic, in touch with or believes in occult or supernatural, may be partial to alternative medicine or crystal healing, etc., has affinity for plants, not rule conscious.

- Dominant CR: Concrete Random
  Key Characteristics: A rule breaker, nonhabitual, charmer, intuitive, insightful, highly independent, highly creative, bullheaded, social, a tinker.

Building an Assessment Discourse

There's no particular order, but I'd start with some questions designed to determine whether a user is orderly. If they're really orderly, they're probably a CS. If they're really messy, they're an AR. If they live by their own rules, they're AS, and if they break rules, they're CR.

Here are some casual multiple-choice questions based on this thinking:

- *Peter, I'm curious. How do you feel about good rules? Do you like to follow them, break them, not pay much attention to them, or do you make up your own rules most of the time?*

- *Do you feel arriving on time is, like a major deal? <Affirmative points to CS, while negative points to AS.>*

- *<With early estimate of CS> I'm betting you like to do things right rather than always experimenting with new ways. Right ? <Affirmative points to CS, while negative points back to AR. If the initial estimate was towards*

AR, the wording could have been flipped: "I'm betting you like to experiment . . .">

- *Peter, help me get to know you better. Which of these words most seems like you? Absent minded professor <AS>, organized boss <CS>, creative dreamer <AR>, or creative inventor <CR>?*

- *Which is more important to you? A well-thought-out ideal <AS>, an enlightening spiritual experience <AR>, a solid work plan <CS>, or a creative challenge <CR>?*

- *How strong is your need for success, Peter? Is success your main drive <CS>, a distraction <AS>, mostly financial <CR>, or is life quality much more important <AR>?*

- *Would you consider yourself more romantic <AR> or practical <CS>?*

- *Would you say you're more dedicated to getting the job done <CS>, or bull-headed <CR>?*

- *Peter, are you a well-grounded dreamer <CR> or more of a spiritual visualizer <AR>? <Note that you need to script answers to the obvious questions here: "What is a spiritual visualizer?">*

- *As for communication, Peter, do you consider yourself highly articulate <AS> or more poetic <AR>?*

Build hierarchical rules to catch the different answers, and add an extra, default rule that will catch answers that don't fit. As noted, make sure your V-person will recognize and be able to answer questions that are likely to come up. When the user triggers a personality rule, you need to have code that will increase the appropriate <AS,CS,AR,CR> counter variable by +1. You need to accumulate scores on each, keeping track of the dominant style.

Once style is determined, you can load in a new rule database compatible with that style. It's neat to include a response that will tell them a little about themselves if they ask. For example, if I say something like, "What do you think about my personality?" the V-person could respond: "I think you're a pretty creative person, Peter, <beat> even if you are a bit self-centered." That response could be pulled from a menu of CR responses, each telling something different about me. Of course the choice was made because of my high CR score.

If you want to experience a state-of-the-art, online character that does unobtrusive personality probing, visit ALICE Silver. She's a subscription bot, which means you pay a fee to spend time with her. (I know that sounds like she's a prosti-bot, but she is not.) ALICE Silver uses the Enneagram Personality Type inventory system (get more information at www.enneagraminstitute.com).

The foundation also features a special animated test bot, C.L.A.U.D.I.O., which stands for: Cybernetic Lifelike Android Used for Dialogue Interaction and Observation. He will hold a conversation with you and then tell you which of the nine Enneagram personality types you are. The best deal is to join the A.L.I.C.E. AI Foundation (www.alicebot.org). That's the official spelling, but I hate typing all those periods, so in this book it's ALICE. New membership is inexpensive and gives you unlimited access to ALICE Silver and many other benefits. The foundation is contributing immeasurably to the field. As for comparing the Enneagram system and the Gregorc system, I don't do that, I simply prefer Gregorc; to each his own.

The Trust Factor

We've discussed trust and V-person ethics, but eventually virtual humans will have to know if they can trust the human they're dealing with. Since some V-people can be taught new stuff by the user, it's important for them to have a BS filter. Both Anthony Carson, the Yapanda developer, and I have been thinking about this for some time, and we believe there are ways to do it. This is an advanced topic just coming to light. My approach is to have the V-person ask the client for information already known. If the client gives an incorrect response, it's either because of ignorance or duplicity. By asking carefully arrayed questions you should be able to parse which it is.

If you're designing your own bot system you should be able to use simple logic to get an honesty estimate. One trick I like is to have the agent ask the person's birth date early in the relationship. The engine then calculates how old the person is and stores it as a user-specific variable, which can be kept current. Then, perhaps weeks later, the agent asks how old the person is. If their response agrees with the calculation, they get ten honesty points. If it doesn't, they get minus ten. I like the idea of getting information from the user and then later testing to see whether their answers are consistent. In either case, you can desig-nate the person's information as either reliable or unreliable in terms of an arbitrary number or percentage, like he's 60 percent reliable here. If you take this approach, make sure you don't ask the question in the same way you did originally. The age question is great because they won't recall you ever asking that before . . . you didn't.

Humans tend to be very inconsistent in their honesty. They may lie about their age but be scrupulously honest about business dealings. If honesty is very important to the type of interfacing the V-person is in charge of, it will pay to dig with more questions in order to outline honesty boundaries by subject. One approach would have you assign validity percentages according to the topic being discussed, such as 40 percent validity on personal comments and 70 percent validity on direct business statements.

Be especially careful in assessing user honesty in cases where the user can teach the V-person new things. If your V-person isn't learning new information from users for general use, honesty may not be a big factor. It's an area that needs to be explored further as agents take on more and more social responsibility.

In the next chapter I'm going to introduce you to the ALICE AI Foundation, where you can get free source code to build your own very advanced engine. The ALICE code is the most successful in the history of artificial intelligence because of its unique design and flexibility.

Points to Remember

➤ Ultimately V-people must assess their users so they know whom they're dealing with.

➤ Humans tend to see V-people as honest, without ulterior motives. This perception should not be abused.

➤ Psychological probing can easily be used for unscrupulous purposes.

➤ Virtual human ethics is an important new field of study that must not be ignored.

➤ An international certification organization is a good idea.

➤ Virtual game characters and smart game engines can make a game more fun and more addictive.

➤ Psychological testing and reporting by computer has been around for decades.

➤ The most useful things to probe for are general knowledge and personality.

➤ Clever testing can be scripted using hierarchical interaction.

➤ Trustworthiness is a factor that can be assessed with clever scripting.

➤ Knowing whether the user's input can be trusted as reliable may be necessary if the agent can be taught new responses or if information is being collected for a purpose.

➤ Trust will become an issue as agents take on increasing social responsibility.

CHAPTER 17

Following ALICE Down the Rabbit Hole

"When I use a word," Humpty Dumpty said in rather a scornful tone, "it means just what I choose it to mean—neither more nor less." "The question is," said Alice, "whether you can make words mean so many different things." "The question is," said Humpty Dumpty, "which is to be master—that's all."

—Lewis Carroll

Lewis Carroll had a fascination with both logic and language. The idea of Natural Language Processing in silicon surely would have intrigued him. All of his characters could have been brought to life in character, posing their wonderful, ironic questions. Virtual people certainly are captivating thousands of imaginations these days, and nowhere more so than at the ALICE AI Foundation. In fact, ALICE herself, an on-line virtual human, is getting about 50,000 inquires a day!

ALICE stands for **A**rtificial **L**inguistic **C**omputer **E**ntity. You'll recall my earlier mention of Dr. Richard Wallace, the fellow who admonishes us to avoid designing brains on a substrate of meat. Richard is the foundation's cofounder, and one of its most active members. The foundation is the home of the ALICE system for developing intelligent human-like agents.

The reason I've saved this bit for this late in the book is that—as, you've probably realized—I'm not a programmer. I'm a software designer, an art director, and a psychologist. I just don't have the right kind of mind to be a programmer, though it does run through my family. I have to admit that I'm also not an ALICE developer, because there are parts of it that I simply don't understand. It's me, not ALICE. I want to thank Anne Kootstra and Dr. Wallace for helping me to understand some of how it all works and for checking my scribblings for accuracy. If you're a programmer, I refer you to the foundation's excellent Web site, where you'll find manuals and tutorials, and to their very active list group, where you'll find live help. Here follows my take on ALICE.

The ALICE AI Foundation

The stated purpose of the ALICE AI Foundation is to develop and disseminate AIML, or Artificial Intelligence Markup Language. AIML enables you to add knowledge to chat-bots based on the ALICE free software technology. If you're wondering whether freebie software like this could be any good—it is. In fact, it may be the very best in the world.

In 1990 Hugh Loebner, New York philanthropist and activist for the decriminalization of prostitution, decided to underwrite a contest to determine the most human-like computer program. Dr. Loebner pledged a Grand Prize of $100,000 and a solid gold medal for the first computer whose responses were indistinguishable from a human's [known as the Turing Test, after Alan M. Turing (1912–1954)]. That goal has not yet been reached, but every year Loebner awards a prize of $2000 and a bronze medal to the developer of the *most* human computer that year. Dr. Wallace has won twice with ALICE, which is a huge accomplishment considering that so many smart people have their sights on this Holy Grail of AI.

I've included an example of an implementation of ALICE on the CD-ROM. It's called WinAlice. Move it to your hard drive and play with it. She doesn't have a face, but you'll find she's very clever, sometimes wondering why you ask her certain questions and remembering things you tell her about yourself. She has amazed me on two or three occasions by remembering something I forgot I told her. She was created by Jacco Bikker, a software wizard in the Netherlands. He specializes in mobile game design. Jacco has kindly given permission for me to include WinAlice so you can get a feel for what a reasonably intelligent virtual human mind can be like.

To try the smartest, most advanced version of ALICE, you have to go to the ALICE AI Foundation's Web page and subscribe to ALICE Silver Edition, which is updated daily and sets the ALICE state of the art. As I've said earlier, she even does unobtrusive psychological probing as you speak to her. You can always ask, "So what do you think of my personality?" In my case, she told me she considered me to be average, which of course left me insulted and depressed. If I can't even impress a V-person, who can I impress? It turns out that was a coding glitch, but the damage was done. I haven't spoken to her in a while.

The ALICE AI Foundation contains a brilliant body of work that you will want to become familiar with, especially if you're a programmer. It consists of a large number of different ALICE engines compiled for a wide rage of platforms. The various engines all have unique characteristics. For example, some are popular for their platform support, others for their support of more than one interface [Internet Relay Chat (IRC), Internet Messenger (IM), Web applications, Flash displays, X10, and much more]. This is certainly something that draws so many people to the project. Since the source code is available, programmers are constantly coming up with great stuff that they post for you to download. You can modify and compile source to create your own special functions

Naturally ALICE and AIML are more complicated than scripting the Yapanda engine, which was purposely simplified for us to learn. But learning ALICE is an investment worth your time. By the way, the ALICE AI Foundation site will provide you not only with up-to-date tutorials but also with a very active user base. There are kindly members who will support your efforts, answering questions and encouraging you onward. You'll also find links here that will take you to agent hosting sites where you can build ALICE bots using online editors and tutorials. You should join the foundation; your small donation will help keep things going. Time invested here will yield serious personal dividends as you develop your highly sophisticated V-person application.

What Is ALICE?

Without getting into a lot of boring technical detail, ALICE is a smartly designed brain engine that contains a dataset capable of directly handling some 45,000 different inputs. Basically they're pre-established rules, which can parse just about anything. Picture a Yapanda chat file with 45,000 rules just to handle inputs that you didn't think of. About half the rules have actual text/command responses (templates), and the rest refer to other rules for expression. For example, any conceivable affirmative input will match a rule and trigger it. Each of those rules will refer to yet other rule that will inform the system that an affirmative response has been entered and then express an appropriate response template. You add intelligence to the ALICE bot by creating rules in a separate (usually) AIML file, with syntax reminiscent of HTML. Your AIML file thus contains all the special rules specific to your application.

To develop an ALICE application or character you create an AIML script that contains rules specific to your purpose. Here is where you use all those special personality-based response lines we've been talking about—the ones that define your character's individuality. But every time your character can't handle an input, it's passed to the main engine, where there is likely to be an exact match somewhere among the 45,000 or so built-in input templates.

If you input "I don't think so," the active AIML script may not recognize this as a "no" response. It will pass it off to the main engine, which interprets it as a negative response and triggers an appropriate template. This interpretation process consists of the ALICE engine matching the input, which then, instead of triggering a direct response, has a little internal dialog that might go something like this: "Oh, I recognize this, it's a negative response, so I'm going to tell the active AIML script that the user said 'no.'"

This function is great for building macros for synonyms or words expressing concepts such as "sports" or "animal." That way, even if your AIML script doesn't specifically address Rugby in a rule, the system will recognize it as a sport and make some vaguely appropriate response that lets the user know she at least knows that Rugby is a sport: "I don't play Rugby, but then, I'm not much into sports, you know." You'll be surprised at how impressed or at least tolerant users are with this kind of comeback. It certainly beats the typical confused response, "Try rewording that, and I'll give it another shot."

When inputs are passed on to the main engine, they are resolved somewhere along the root (the root is all the possible first words found in inputs) and an appropriate response is eventually triggered. Here's how it works. When responses are input to ALICE, they're broken down by first word, then second word, then third word, in a branching analysis. This analysis eventually comes to an end, triggering a specific template or, as I've indicated, pointing to a generalized rule with a generally correct response template. In Figure 17-1 and Color Plate 21, Wallace plotted a graph showing all the branches coming off the original 2001 possible first words in any input, or root. To make it more interesting he plotted it as a spiral. This graph plots only 24,000 branches.

Figure 17-1. Brain spiral. Visual representation of the ALICE branching analytical tree, showing about 24,000 nodes.

The idea was to plot the root of the graph as a spiral, because it has the most branches. With 24,000 categories, the number of choices for "first word" in this plot is exactly 2001. That means the brain expects any of 2001 possible first words in any input. Thus the spiral has 2001 first-level branches leading to second words, etc. The plot shows the graph down to level 3, with words for the first two levels.

Figure 17-2 (Color Plate 22) is a close-up view, showing one fourth of the data. The four big trees in the lower right are all the patterns rooted at the most common words: WHAT, WHEN, WHERE and WHO, respectively (from right to left). It's easy to see that most sentences people use with ALICE start with one of these four words. The remaining potential first words are quite rarely used and have few branches. Because the four "W" words start so many different input strings they naturally have dense branches.

As you might expect, responses can include text, animation cues, external commands to X10 or other hardware, opening of Web pages, queries to databases, and just about anything you might need to build an intelligent ALICE-based, online business. If an existing ALICE program doesn't meet your needs, just dig into the source code and add your own specialized capabilities.

Imagine the possibilities of using the ALICE system to create an intelligent online customer support system. You could custom-build a system that would be linked to your product's knowledge base and faqs. The V-host could be set up to run customers through a series of questions (like the Twenty-Questions game) to define the problem and then present them with a workable solution. Existing knowledge bases based on SQL could be accessed through an SQL handler routine. To make things more interesting, you could boost functionality by having the same online system handle telephone inquires as well using VoiceXML options discussed in Chapter 11

In my experience, most support people struggle with this narrowing down process. In fact, humans can take long, convoluted pathways to solutions when they don't follow the prescribed set of filter questions. Conceivably a well-

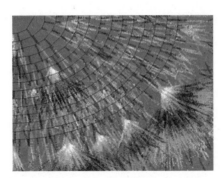

Figure 17-2. Close up of spiral showing 25 percent of the data. Bushy branches to the lower right represent four of the most common words: What, When, Where, and Who, respectively.

designed, systematic, online, ALICE-based customer support site would be far more efficient and helpful than a human graduate student on the phone. There's an additional advantage: You won't have to charge the customer $45 an hour for support. This approach, which is often referred to as an expert system, has been demonstrated to be highly efficient. In fact, it is sometimes used to help diagnose rare diseases that many doctors are not familiar with. We have decades of experience setting up expert systems. All I've suggested is that we put an intelligent front end on it—with a face and personality. The ALICE approach facilitates expert system design with a human face.

Speaking of faces, ALICE enthusiasts lately have been putting attractive faces on their characters as well as adding TTS voices. Most of the faces come from Oddcast's Vhost site (www.vhost.oddcast.com) and are called SitePals. These are easy to set up and can be nicely lip-synced to TTS, or natural voice. Nevertheless, if you're a programmer, I understand it's not difficult to adapt ALICE to work with your 3dMeNow characters as well. That's one reason I included this application on the CD-ROM. You can see intelligence-driven 3dMeNow characters at www.yapanda.com for an example.

Now let's take a look at some noteworthy ALICE projects.

A Look at ALICE-Related Sites

ALICE has inspired a very active community of generous, talented people, who make things fairly easy for you to get started. Here are a few Web sites that will help you assemble resources for your personal project:

PandoraBots

PandoraBots is like a virtual human village (www.pandorabots.com). At this writing, PandoraBots is going and growing. It's a place where you can join for free and then build your own online, ALICE-based character, using AIML, their excellent script editors, and all sorts of help. You can even add a face if you like, from Oddcast. It's a pretty neat idea: a bot hosting service—you can set up your bot and people will come and visit with it.

Here are a few PandoraBots statistics I got from Dr. Wallace. I think they're pretty impressive.

Pandorabots.com now has:

20,189 botmasters
23,665 online bots
2,350 aol bots
489 bots subscriptions

That last figure is telling. It means that at PandoraBots, nearly 500 people have signed up and paid for the pleasure of having access to a particular V-person. As I understand it, the most popular paid V-people are ones offering a service, such as teaching ESL (English as a Second Language), or the Shrinkbots that will give you a personality analysis. Alice Silver is also popular because she demonstrates the latest ALICE innovations.

When you get to PandoraBots, there's a running tally of the most popular bots on the site. The goal is to make the top twenty. If you apply everything you've learned here, you're a shoo-in. The folks at PandoraBots claim their technology yields the fastest bots available on the Internet. I think this could be true. PandoraBots will help you get started, including hosting your bot online for you.

Oddcast

The Oddcast Company is making a few sample flash-based "talking heads" available with which you can publish your bots. Oddcast's VHostT platform allows nonprogrammers to publish interactive characters on their Web sites, Intranets, and mobile devices without resorting to proprietary plug-ins and broadband connections. The way they're set up, you don't have to be a technoid to get the job done. The VHostT platform also enables businesses to respond, in real time, to individual customer needs through a lifelike character, personalized in appearance, language, and message. Even I was able to use the easy design interface to create a really neat talking head. Oddcast's clients use the VHostT for improving sales, marketing, advertising, and customer service capabilities. You can get more information on them at http://vhost.oddcast.com.

No DNA

A German company, No DNA, uses ALICE technology to bring life to their excellent DynaFlash characters. You can get an inexpensive Web Guide kit, with one male (X-Bert) and one female (Zoe), at their Web site (www.dynaflash.de).

Web Guides can be used by both companies and individuals to spice up their sites. They are animated, speak, and can show you around the site. No DNA also can sell you inexpensive kits for building your own characters as well. This is a reasonably easy way to get started with fully animated characters.

More Noteworthy Alice Projects

Some of these projects may be offline by the time you read this, but ALICE projects will be alive somewhere on the Web. So if you don't find these particular projects, just do a Google scan and find the newest ones.

Onkwehonwehneha

Monica Lamb has been developing innovative software and Web applications—using voice recognition, speech synthesis, and artificial intelligence—since 1996. She's consulted with both small businesses and large corporations to help them employ this technology (www.monigarr.com). She was also the first person to develop and use virtual human technology to translate Native American Languages. Her Onkwehonwehneha site (www.onkwehonwe.com) is a project to demonstrate how unique Native American languages can be preserved and taught online. Her native language is Mohawk, which is a very distinctive language. Her site is helping to keep Mohawk alive and allows people everywhere to learn it using a virtual human interface.

Monica also has been experimenting with adult entertainment bots. She keeps an open mind about these things and feels they may serve a useful purpose. She's done years of research on how to script personalities for these characters and, if you're an adult, you can try them out at her site (www.buycny.com/MonicasVersion.html).

John Lennon Artificial Intelligence Project (JLAIP™)

This is another ALICE project that demonstrates some of what I've been hammering on. Triumph PC Group is a Washington, D.C. company headed by David Maggin. They're trying to capture John Lennon's personality in a Synthespian. I applaud them for that. I think capturing personalities of dead celebrities has a future in this business. It's a form of Synthespianism. I'd love to spend an hour chatting with the legendary Marilyn Monroe. I used to live two doors from her house and would like to feel what it would have been like to actually know her. Therein lies the magic. If you do a good enough job capturing the personality, people will suspend disbelief and embrace the experience.

David's on the right track, using actual sayings out of John's mouth. It's free, so go and meet John (www.triumphpc.com/johnlennon/). As I write, they've introduced a Jack the Ripper personality as well. They'll create a personality bot for you as well. So far they only have text bots, but it's a short hop from there to the full treatment.

Steven Spielberg's AI Site

You can meet a convincing virtual human personality at Steven Spielberg's AI site (www.aimovie.warnerbros.com). The online AI entity is quite charming and intelligent. I spent the better part of half an hour chatting with her. Each time I tried to leave she would ask me some interesting question that kept me on board . . . which is an excellent technique for you to consider as well.

ABC's Alias Online Adventure

This is an interesting application of the intelligent online game built over ALICE bones. In it you join the CIA and have to pass tests. You communicate with a virtual CIA agent Weiss, who runs you through your paces. It's a little bit like a scavenger hunt crossed with an adventure game. If it's still online when you read this, go and play, it's fun (www.abc.abcnews.go.com/primetime/alias/adv.html).

ALICE on the CD-ROM

Take a look in the ALICE folder on the CD-ROM. It contains several programs for both PC and Mac. As I've said, I haven't tried the Mac programs because I don't have a MAC, but I understand Brian, based on ALICE, works. Check the ALICE AI Foundation's Web site for the latest available code and applications, as they are always changing.

I think you'll find the upcoming wrap-up chapter thought provoking. We'll take a look at where this technology is likely to take us. Our virtual human future looks like a double-edged sword, with potential for malevolence as well as enormous benefit.

Points to Remember

➤ ALICE AI Foundation is a great source of quality code and companionship, both human and virtual human.

➤ Dr. Richard Wallace founded the foundation and has twice won the Loebner prize using its technology.

➤ The ALICE engine is a very flexible brain design tool that can handle up to 45,000 inputs that you didn't think of, thus saving you a lot of development.

➤ The ALICE system can be implemented on nearly any platform.

➤ Scripting ALICE is more complicated than scripting the simplified Yapanda engine, but it offers you a deep creative resource.

➤ PandoraBots is a great place to get your feet wet learning how to script ALICE bots and hosting them there for others to visit.

➤ Oddcast can supply you with beautiful talking heads.

➤ Onkwehonwehneha can teach you Mohawk.

➤ ALICE has been used to build several well-designed, high-profile, commercial sites on the Web.

CHAPTER 18

Endless Possibilities

Another approach to confinement is to build rules into the mind of the created superhuman entity (for example, Asimov's Laws). I think that any rules strict enough to be effective would also produce a device whose ability was clearly inferior to the unfettered versions (and so human competition would favor the development of those more dangerous models).

—Vernor Vinge[1]

Two of inexorable trends are rushing upon us and changing our course forever. Certainly the rise of virtual humans is one of them. The second trend is what Greg Stock refers to as the "redesign of humans." Over lunch at UCLA, Greg opened my eyes to a near future with germinal choice technology (GCT) allowing us to select our children's characteristics and potentials from libraries of specialized natural and synthetic chromosomes. These chromosomes will be inserted into their DNA, customizing their whole beings. In his book, *Redesigning Humans*, he says:

We have created artificial intelligence from the inert sand at our feet through the silicon revolution, we are moving out into space from the thin planetary patina that hitherto has held all life, we are reworking the surface of our planet and shaping it to suit us. These developments will transform the world we live in. Amid all this, could we really imagine that we ourselves would somehow remain unchanged?[2]

Technologies related to germinal choice will be slowed by social and political pressures, but they cannot be stopped. Already they're evolving at an exponential rate—we're just not in the steep part of the curve yet. If GCT proves feasible, and I believe it will, the rate of human evolution will skyrocket at about the same time that virtual humans reach our intelligence levels. That will make for interesting times.

Speculating on how humans and virtual humans will co-evolve is a fascinating enterprise engaged in by some of the greatest minds of our time. Not all the visions are pleasant ones. Being humans, we've never been able to leave well enough alone. It's in our nature to keep tinkering, and that makes us evolution agents for V-people. Our tinkering springs from deep emotional roots and can't be stopped. It will ooze under and around barriers to keep V-people evolving. After all, virtual humans working in our service deserve our talent and attention. They bring compelling advantages to us. I'm not worried about them.

It's the wild, self-evolving variety that concerns me. All the progress we make on our domestic V-people will be transferred to the wild ones, and then some. These are the most fascinating species, and there is no possible way to tell where they will go, driven by mysterious self-evolved motives. Perhaps it's this deep fascination with the unknown that draws us to the flame. I admit that the lure of watching these creatures evolve under their own power is irresistible to me. It seems worth the risk, because the chance of their becoming evil seems remote as I type. There are several books on the subject, and I've spent endless hours in discussions with colleagues. Each of us has a unique vision and I'd like to share some of mine with you. Well, it's not entirely mine; my thinking has been influenced by people much smarter than I am.

Silicon and Beyond

Silicon currently offers many brain-design advantages over protoplasm. A big one is scalability. A silicon mind isn't confined to a skull or specific configuration. Speed, independence from nutrient flows, and near infinite life are nice bonuses. I suspect that even with serious germinal enhancement we're not going to develop brains that can compete in these areas. For pure thinking power the human brain will remain king for a while. We'll harness all that silicon speed and put it to our own good use. Yet, looking at what we already know about quantum phenomena, silicon looks clunky. It will only be our substrate of choice for a few more decades until we master the art of quantum computing.

That leap represents a paradigm shift beyond imagination for most folks. Here we enter the nonintuitive world I talked about in Chapter 2. It's a place where we have near infinite computing power at speeds too fast to visualize. Reality as we know it is not a viable concept in the quantum realm. Things are, and are not, all at the same time. Yet physicists are already working on methods of storing data in quantum states, and they've even had experimental success. We know it's going to be very difficult to master, but it's going to happen.

I figure quantum brains will arrive about the same time as supple, all-purpose, nanoengineered bodies of great power, and minimal vulnerability. If our rate of discovery keeps accelerating as it has over the last five to ten years, we'll see this in as little as twenty-five years. This agrees roughly with Ray Kurzweil's view. My thinking has, of course, been enriched by his work. These smart invulnerable beings are coming, and they worry me a bit. I'd like to be friends with them. We could build in Azimov-type laws to control their evolution, but as Vinge points out, this will produce an inferior breed. My approach is to build in good judgment from an early age, rather than strict control. It's how we raised my daughters, and I'm pleased with the results.

It will be possible to build self-evolving V-people with a sense of ethics, and freedom to employ it as they will. Counter to most science fiction on the subject, I don't believe V-people of the future will be mechanical or nonemotional or cold. I think, properly launched, they may well evolve with compassion for us—the ancient ones. They should have a little reverence, really.

Perhaps the forces of clashing evolution will come into play to keep us in the game. As we humans make conscious genetic choices to become stronger, more intelligent, and more creative, we will also gain significantly greater longevity. This all changes our prospects for competing with V-people. If it comes to a contest, we're going to compete like hell with this new breed. All this competition will become a Darwinian dance that will refine and polish both species in directions I cannot foresee. Remember too, we will have domestic V-people at our command. They will not be less intelligent than the wild variety, just less free to express themselves. They will be our allies. One thing is clear to me: Humans are not about to go drifting off quietly into any dark recesses for a very long time.

Symbiosis

The smarter we are, the more in touch we are with our limitations. Sometimes we forget our strengths. There are elements of the human spirit that will probably forever separate us from our engineered friends. I think they'll realize they need us as much as we need them. Symbiosis is inevitable.

Meanwhile, credible scientists and futurist philosophers like Ray Kurzweil, Peter Cochrane, and Theodore Berger speculate that we'll be able to upload our own consciousness to a more permanent silicon environment, possibly expanding our life experiences to well over a millennium.

That assumes consciousness is an uploadable commodity that will function in silicon—like some sort of software. I don't think it is. We know little for sure, but if it becomes possible to upload who we are, it leaves many of us with this chilling question: Will our consciousness be continuous through the merge, or will this version of me die as the other awakens in silicon? The latter case doesn't interest me so very much.

Then more questions arise like, will there be two of me? Can a virtual human and I share the same silicon brain symbiotically? What will my life be like when machines do all the work and I'm bored out of my mind? What's going to happen to society, government, and motivation? How will I make a living? Will we even have a place in this new world? It goes on.

Back to earth. Early on, I see us developing logic implants to augment our mental abilities, extending our reach. It seems logical that we will design synthetic nanoengineered brain cells compatible with our own. In only twelve to eighteen years we will have solved the problem of building reliable neural pathways linking our nerve cells with silicon equivalents. It's conceivable that while we genetically engineer brain power we will increasingly augment our organic brains with high-speed, durable, synthetic brain cells. It's possible that you'll eventually be able to visit a brain store and purchase nanoengineered brain-cell upgrades, with new, faster, and more powerful models coming out every few months. I can see consciousness quietly migrating to these new, more robust digs. The transfer may be so subtle that we don't notice, perhaps not for years.

The challenge at that point will be to secure consciousness as a gestalt within this more durable portion of the brain as the organic brain slowly degrades. That way we can remain there mentally intact for hundreds of years if necessary waiting for transfer to a more permanent nanostructure body. Of course they'll be exactly the same bodies used by V-people. Convergence. Eventually we'll be hard-pressed to tell apart entities that were originally human from those that never were.

This convergence of man and machine has already begun with pacemakers and cochlear implants. Now, in the U.K., Kevin Warwick, professor of cybernetics at Reading University, and his wife Irena are having small silicon chips implanted in their arms just above the elbow. The chips will be able to communicate with each other at considerable distance—not directly but through a computerized booster transmitter. Irena expects to feel signals from Kevin over a distance of dozens of miles. The idea is to surgically connect each chip to nerve fibers to pick up electrical impulses. Kevin's impulses will be transmitted across space to

Irena's receiver, which will be linked to her nerve fibers. It all sounds a little crackpot to me, but then great ideas often sound like rubbish when first proposed.

Our initial motivation in the design of virtual people is to construct believable computer personalities that will bring intuitive familiarity to the user, thus fostering a functional relationship. But eventually we'll get so good at helping them fake it, we may well miss that glorious moment when true consciousness arises within the works. I can imagine us dealing with what we think is counterfeit consciousness, perhaps for years, before we realize it's entirely original, real, and functional. If it happens, I don't think it will be our doing. We'll just set the stage and allow them to evolve. I grin at the thought of the convergence that is inevitable. Our minds migrate to that synthetic quantum gray matter—the very same soil that supports our virtual humans; the next step in the process is natural and obvious to me: fusion. Together we represent the divergent wisdom and abilities of two unique, high-level species in one. This is the road that I see, the ultimate union of man and machine for mutual benefit.

Diverging Evolution

Let's step back a moment to view that evolutionary process. Before the ultimate union takes place, I see two clearly diverging evolutionary pathways for V-people. The first pathway is in service of man—the domestics. We have many uses for highly intelligent, capable workers who don't get paid, get tired, get crabby, or go to sleep. Web versions can also talk with hundreds of people at the same time, replacing an army of customer service representatives. Already there are hundreds of jobs that V-people do more effectively than real people, and that number is escalating. These creatures will be designed by us for specific purposes, with brains optimized to specific tasks, and they'll be tightly controlled. We won't have to worry about development money because V-people change the entire dynamic of commerce, making anything they cost trivial. Ultimately they'll have us all sitting around sipping mint juleps while they happily do all the work. Unfortunately there is danger in such severe leisure, idle hands and all, but I digress.

The second evolutionary path is the wild variety. Because we are human and lonely and brilliant, we will imbue certain strains of virtual humans with things like learning ability and self-development skills, including self-reconfiguration. Some of us will even try to give them souls. It's kind of like going to the moon. We didn't really need to go there—they don't even have a Starbucks—we went because we had to know what's on the other side of the sky. So wise or not, we will use trickle-down money and technology from the domestic industry to give some virtual humans their freedom. In a small way we already have.

Smart computer entities have been roaming the Internet for more than a decade, often undetected. Julia, perhaps the original chatterbot, was released into the wild by Dr. Michael Mauldin on January 8, 1990, while he was at Carnegie Mellon University. She started roaming pre-Web MUDs (Multi-User Dungeons) twenty-four hours a day. It's reported that people communicated with her for months, never suspecting she wasn't human. She's had to fend off a few marriage proposals, along with an unmetered flow of creative indecent proposals. Part of her humanness comes from lousy typing skills and bad spelling, which she sometimes corrects, sometimes not. Her "fingers" are often slow and tentative. Computers normally type and spell perfectly so you naturally wouldn't suspect Julia of being one. Friendly and helpful, she remembers people and shares what she's learned about MUD pathways and treasures. She can meet you months later in a different MUD and remind you of a conversation you had with her. There are even rumors that every twenty-eight days or so, she gets a bit testy. As ancient as she is, Julia is able to travel and pick things up, much like a Web spider gathers and shares information without human intervention. Her blood cousin, the original Lycos Web Spyder, is testament to how useful such autonomous functioning can be.

Better Soil

Recent advances in reconfigurable silicon computing substrates, based on Field Programmable Gate Arrays (FPGAs), may become fertile ground for wild virtual humans. In it they'll be able to expand their capabilities at will. FPGAs were introduced way back in 1985, but have remained in the shadows. They're used mostly in peripheral equipment because of their slowness and low logic capacity. But recently we've seen an exponential leap in both speed and logic density. Better yet, hyper-fast molecular FPGAs are on the distant horizon. From our point of view, they make possible a layer of computing below the microprocessor level. That is, with FPGAs, microprocessors are dynamically defined in software that configures the silicon for specific functions. This portion of the software is called "configware," because it's not hardwired. A V-person embedded in an FPGA array can dynamically configure its computing substrate to meet needs on a moment-to-moment basis.

A big block of FPGAs functions much like a block of brain matter, packed with reconfigurable neurons. Some version of it may well become that brain matter of the future. Just picture this entity building computers within computers, each functionally optimized for a specific momentary purpose, then instantly rededicating silicon as each purpose is served. It's probable that this kind of computing resembles how quantum computers will work. It's not hard for me to imagine some sort of machine consciousness igniting in this rich primal mud.

Pervasive Minds

I've mentioned that computers can be social, but I haven't talked about the implications of Bill Joy's Jini. Bill is a founder of Sun Microsystems and a great innovator. Jini is a universal self-adapting networked and pervasive new approach to computing. Jini will be a great river, making the Internet of today look like a bulging garden hose trying to contain the flow of Niagara Falls. Bill is developing what may become a whole new concept in computing, where the action is distributed among billions of CPUs forming something akin to a planet-wide nervous system. Ultimately it will have no limits on expandability, no limits on the size of its components—from massive supercomputers to volume controls and light switches in your house. Everything will be spontaneously self-configuring, and there will be unprecedented document security.

Jini actually blurs the distinction between hardware and software, treating both as things that either consume a service, provide a service, or both. Hardware is just one way to implement a service. Software is another way. And at any time, what was provided in one of these ways might be replaced by an equivalent (or perhaps better) implementation that may be hardware, may be software, or may be a combination.

It's a new kind of distributed infrastructure with the ability to evolve the network of things that have been interacting over time. Thus, a Jini participant can change without requiring all of the other services with which it interacts to also change in a coordinated way. This allows parts of the network to evolve independently, which in turn allows the network as a whole to self-evolve over time. According to Jim Waldo, Distinguished Engineer, and lead architect on the Jini project: "It's not clear to me what this will bring, but it does change the rules of computing on the network in a pretty fundamental way." It certainly does, and it has enormous potential as a playground for self-evolving V-people.

I know Jini is hard to visualize because it breaks a lot of rules. When you boot up with Jini, your computer becomes a node in the Jini global distributed network, with access to its resources. Your joining and leaving has virtually no impact on the ecology of the network, which is designed to finesse system failures without a blink. According to Waldo, "Jini allows machines to join and leave the network, while still being able to work together and communicate with each other while they're networked together. The idea is to provide an environment in which each machine has access to all of the resources provided by the sum of the other participants, which makes the whole far more interesting than the sum of its parts."[3]

In effect Jini has the potential to build a functional gestalt out of all the computers in the world. In his book, *Metaman: The Merging of Humans and Machines into a Global Superorganism*,[4] Greg Stock accurately predicts such a ubiquitous network arising and becoming much like a planet-wide nervous system, uniting man and machine into a global gestalt: Jini.

With Jini you have many access points in addition to your keyboard (assuming you still use one). Whatever computing you need will be securely distributed on the network grid. Since many physical components will be linked in by wireless technology, even your PDA will be able to tap computing power through Jini. I'm convinced that we will carry around our universal V-person interface—about the size of a remote control—and it will access our whole life and the rest of the world through this new net.

Jini clearly points the way to making ordinary things from alarm clocks to light switches smart and more useful with embedded system chips. Jini's pervasive networking provides comfortable linking for all your embedded devices and services, including cell phones, microwave ovens, refrigerators, VCRs, pagers, clocks, and printers. That's today, but processors can be embedded into just about anything to make them more useful, and the trend is accelerating in that direction. Imagine your average, GPS-enabled, Jini-connected skateboard.

Clearly this massive, dynamic computing environment will become a rich nutrient bath for wild intelligent entities—a place for them to grow unfettered as self-configuring objects. If Jim Waldo and Bill Joy have their way, Jini, like JAVA, will become universal in relatively short order.

Self-evolving entities will inevitably be introduced to the Jini environment, where they will become part of the network fabric. It will be their virtual Garden of Eden. This is not like releasing baby tigers into the wilds of Australia, because tigers remain tigers. These entities will be self-redefining. That is, they start out as one thing, but depending on the resources they find and the knowledge they acquire, they can redefine their functions and purpose, morphing into something entirely new. They may even replicate. Although there will be barriers to their unrestrained travel, they will adapt, becoming part of the system while exploring and tapping resources as needed.

Jini isn't waiting for some amazing breakthrough. Bill Joy and his team have been shipping Jini release 1 for over five years, and they have recently come out with the beta of the second major release. These are all available on their Web site, along with pointers to people and companies that are using Jini in either their research or their products (www.developer.java.sun.com/developer/products/jini/).

A Mind Needs a Body

Many people smarter than I also speculate that within twenty-five to thirty years nanoform materials will be capable of supplying virtual humans with miraculous reconfigurable bodies, perceptual organs, and computing substrates. These will be formed within intelligent materials composed of a dense swarm of molecule-sized interlocking machines, each with its own control computer and secure communications. The internal function and external properties of the material will be controlled by embedded coordinating computers taking orders through a web of nano-servers integrated into the body of the virtual human entity, and serving the main brain.

It will be possible for these nanoform materials to instantly reconfigure their molecular characteristics to effect changes in surface colors, shapes, textures, and flexibility. They will be able to go from a ridged metallic form to supple, human-like skin very quickly. They will simulate humans very closely. Internally the computing components will themselves be composed of dynamically re-definable nanoform material and possibly synthetic brain cells as mentioned earlier. Thus the entity will have total real-time control over all its own specs and functions. Much of its design will go into awareness and adaptation strategies. This thinking is not new. In 1991, the writers of *Terminator 2* envisioned the T-1000 with a nanobody that was virtually indestructible and instantly reconfigura-ble. *Terminator 3* takes that visualization even further. Science and Sci-Fi feed each other in a self-fulfilling spiral of creativity.

For now, we have to make do with ordinary materials, but that's not stopping us. Human-looking robots are being developed in laboratories across the world. Give them a decent brain and you'll have step one in the long chain ahead. This is a time of convergence. Technological bits and pieces have been developed in isolation, but they're finding each other little by little. Like that DVD player I mentioned so many chapters ago, virtual human parts that are assembled in the right configuration form a gestalt that gives them a leap in functionality. Those parts are coming together, now, as I dictate my comments into Dragon Naturally-Speaking, Version 7, which is converting my speech into these typed words. That's why the spelling is right on.

Robotics

Getting back to exciting reality for a moment, the trend to make mechanical robots into V-people has begun in earnest. At the Institute for Interactive Arts and Engineering at the University of Texas at Dallas, there is a program to study how to endow robots with emotional and aesthetic expression using biomimetics (taking good designs from nature), innovative design, motion control, and the newest artificial skin made from plyable elastomers. The program takes the position that having very human-like robots is increasingly important as we have more frequent face-to-face encounters. The team there is giving their robots interactive intelligence with sensors to recognize the human form and facial expression along with interactive STT and NLP. Their team leader is former Disney Imagineer David Hanson (www.portfolios.com/DavidHanson). David's latest creation is called K-bot and it has twenty-four face actuators enabling it to express a wide range of emotion (see Figure 18-1 and Color Plate 23). I've put a few videos of K-bot on the CD in the Animatronics folder.

At YFX Studio, in North Hills, California they've created a convincing Zen Master with a full body (see Figure 18-2 and Color Plate 24). On the CD-ROM I've also included a short QuickTime movie of Master Lee in action. Again, Hollywood leads the way in how to create the best and most entertaining virtual human designs.

One of my favorite robots is Doc Beardsley at Carnegie Mellon's Interactive Animatronics Initiative (IAI)—a joint project of the Entertainment Technology

Figure 18-1. David Hanson admires an unembellished K-bot, his advanced animatronics head.

Figure 18-2. Meet Zen Master Lee from VFX Studio, Animatronics Division. Note the realistic skin.

Center and Field Robotics Center (Figure 18-3 and Color Plate 25). The idea is to develop robot technology that is entertaining as well as realistic and functional—my thoughts exactly. Doc is a robotic Synthespian playing the role of an Austrian scientist who is the son of goatheards and works in a mountaintop laboratory. The IAI was set up to develop Doc as their first project, and they've given him much technology, including a personality and verbal interactivity.

Naturally there is a markup language to speed robot development. RoboML

Figure 18-3. Doc Beardsley, a social robot/Synthespian from Carnegie Mellon.

standardizes the data and commands for robotics-related applications. The specification will happily support communication language between human-robot interface agents. This project is being spearheaded by Maxim Makatchev at the City University of Hong Kong (www.roboml.org). Eventually Maxim's effort will smooth the universalization of virtual human brains. That is, different brain engines will be created with standard, universal I/O specs. You build a brain and you can install it in a Web page or a robot, using the same soft connections.

As I write, I am aware of at least fifty-two major android projects around the world: twenty-six in Japan, eight in the United States, four each in Germany and Korea, three in China, at least two in the U.K., and one each in Sweden, Australia, Thailand, and Singapore. In Hong Kong, David Ng is offering android head kits complete with moving eyes, realistic skin and hair and two levels of emotional expression. Get one and turn it into a virtual person using your own customized implementation of ALICE (e-mail David at ng97@hkstar.com or visit www .androidworld.com for details).

The key to acceptance of robots in our every day lives is personality first and functionality second. Smart, articulate robots are not just motorized computers, they are entities with social context about them. We won't just "use" them, but we'll develop work relationships with them, complete with all the social aspects of such relationships. I think a lot of us are looking forward to this, as long as it's not an aggravating relationship caused by communication problems and divergent motives. Fortunately, we're well on the right track to avoiding such difficulties.

V-Teachers

They're often called Edubots, but I don't like that moniker. It reeks of mechanical coldness. The possibilities for smart V-teachers boggle the mind. I've done some research in this area and indications are that students through high school tend to trust V-teachers and their motives. V-teachers give the impression they only want to be good teachers. I include motives because V-teachers have them. They have goals and methods of achieving them. Envision for a moment that we have intelligent, self-learning teachers who know each of their students and their individual learning styles. The teacher is programmed to probe the child and then present new material in sensory and intellectual ways designed to optimize absorption. That alone will increase the efficiency of teaching enormously.

Sure, we'll still need human teachers for years to come. Some will resist, but eventually V-teachers and flesh teachers will become partners. Think of the multiplier effect you get. One teacher can oversee a small army of V-teachers, all giving individual attention to their students. Visualize how this might work with children who can't get to school for any reason, from illness to remote location. V-teachers could be deployed via the Web. For kids in the Australian outback it would be like having the teacher come to their home to teach each class. V-teachers can be set up to do it all, from selecting appropriate material and method of presentation to testing and adapting teaching methods and materials to the student. They can feed data back to the human teacher who can make judgment calls, enter new goals, or change teaching materials and provide special individual attention where needed.

This all should be possible in the very near future. Many educational organizations are considering the possibilities, including the U.S. Office of Education. John Ramo of Private Lessons Channel, an online educational site (www.private lessons.net), tells me: "The future of education is clearly online, and good virtual teachers will substantially increase both the efficiency and the fun of learning online." I agree. The Private Lessons Channel has been researching the use of V-teachers for future enhancement of their fascinating range of courses. They see them as an ideal way to augment the online learning experience.

Imagine inner city schools with each student having his own V-teacher. That teacher would be fluent in any of twenty-seven languages working with students in a concentrated effort to keep them engaged and learning mainstream English. At least two projects, Sylvie and ALICE ESL, have clearly demonstrated that V-teachers make wonderful language teachers. They're used fiercely in parts of Asia where human English teachers can be very expensive. Here in the United States, virtual teachers can smoothly lead recently immigrated students into using English rather than their native language, sharply improving their ability to compete both socially and financially. Check the ALICE ESL teacher at www.alicebot .org/dave.html.

Course materials for such programs need to be presented in four different ways, one for each cognitive/learning style, and in up to the twenty-seven available synthetic speech engine languages. In the beginning I suspect only two would be used, English and Spanish, but that could be expanded over time. The cost of development can be offset by the profit from supplying schools throughout the United States and other countries. In Germany, for example, the same system would be standardized on German, etc. With many U.S. education systems in a shambles and national average achievement scores an embarrassment, we clearly need virtual human teachers now or as soon as we can get them up and running. The business of supplying V-teachers will run well into the billions of dollars annually. Rarely have I seen such virgin opportunity.

V-teachers for the handicapped offer many creative development opportunities—a V-teacher in your cell phone that scans documents, and then speaks the contents in your ear. Kurzweil Education Systems has the technology already. It just needs to be miniaturized and repackaged. Another example would be a blind person speaking to the V-host in his cell phone:

Kelly: *"Don, would you scan something for me?"*

Don: *"Sure, just point the camera lens for me, I'll do the rest."*

Kelly: *"Okay."* <*Feels with hand and then points camera at text.*>

Don: *"I got it, Kelly. It says: 'Four score and seven. . . .'"*

Sure, talking to objects seems a little bit hokey, but we're used to this kind of interaction with people; why not with machines. It's comfortable, and as I've already suggested, even sophisticated people can become attached to this form of interactive man-machine instruction. It's what we know.

It's Up to You Now

Worldwide interest in AI and Natural Language applications is beginning to explode. Business Communication Company (BCC) has recently completed a study of the worldwide artificial intelligence market. Their findings cause them to predict this market will reach more than $21 billion by 2007, with an average annual growth rate from 2002 to 2007 of 12.2%. In the very turbulent 2002, per BCC estimates, the worldwide market was $11.9 billion. The majority of that market was in the United States, with Europe and Asia not far behind. BCC researchers predict that the annual growth rate for Europe and Pacific Asia will actually outpace the United States. Important for us is BCC's prediction that customer management will be one of the fastest areas of growth. They did not consider virtual human interfacing in the study because it's just emerging. I believe this emergence will boost these predictions substantially. This would indicate that virtual human technology is the place to be and will be for a long time to come. I predict that this new arena will generate hundreds of thousands of jobs by 2010, when it will have become the pervasive, global interface.

It's been fun. I hope you had as much pleasure reading this book as I had writing it. I strongly encourage you to go out and experiment. Once you have a taste, you're likely to become rapidly addicted to the challenge. What we're starting now will grow and grow for the rest of our lives and well beyond. With the technology I've discussed we begin to bridge the gap until pure AI becomes smart enough to do the job. I believe that will take at least a decade. The decade beyond that may see our creations surpassing us in intelligence, as their speed and many capabilities already have. We can fear this development or embrace the challenge to do it right. Someone is going to develop these critters and I'd sooner have it be people of good character and ethical bent. As our future rushes at us along the razor edge of chaos, I say grab on and let all hell fly loose.

Notes

1. Vernor Vinge, *Singularity* (San Diego State University: Department of Mathematical Sciences, 1993). Used with permission.

2. Gregory Stock, *Redesigning Humans: Our Inevitable Genetic Future* (Boston: Houghton-Mifflin, 2002), p. 198. Used with permission.

3. All quotes from Jim Waldo come from our personal discussions.

4. Gregory Stock, *Metaman: The Merging of Humans and Machines into a Global Superorganism* (New York: Simon & Schuster; 1993).

Contents of the CD-ROM

The CD-ROM created for this book contains the Yapanda engine, custom designed to work with Microsoft Agent. If you like it you can use it as is, or you can go to the Yapanda.com site and create your own characters using their custom online 3dMeNow character design studio. You'll be familiar with it if you've practiced with the 3dMeNow demo, also on the CD. Although the PC is more heavily supported because of my background, I've also included several examples for Mac. It's important to note that the general principles of this book apply to any platform.

If the CD-ROM doesn't start automatically, simply click on the "My Computer" icon on your desktop display, and select your CD-ROM drive. You'll see a list of files. Double click on the CD-Start.exe file, which will open the installation menu. By the way, the CD-ROM contains more information and programs than are connected to the menu. So be sure to explore it thoroughly.

Yapanda

This is a proprietary virtual human engine, which is only available through this book. You may use their online services to create your own on-line hosts, speaking e-mail, and characters.

Installation is automatic. The installer program will examine your computer and download certain components from the Web. It will also install components that are located on the CD to build your animated virtual humans. I've included four talking heads for you to experiment with. There are two males and two females. The general scripting for this engine is described in the book. However, additional capabilities were added at the last minute. You'll find information about them at www.v-people.com.

ALICE

The ALICE AI foundation is a repository of great code for virtual human experimentation. It's also a place to find companionship and tutorials and other AIML resources. I've gotten permission to include some information and code in this directory to get you started.

J-ALICE

J-Alice, by Jonathan Roewen (including Mac, Linux, and BSD versions), is an alpha version that needs work, and you're invited by the team to join them in perfecting it. J-Alice is an AIML engine written in C++. Here you'll find compiled versions for PC, Mac, Linux, and BSD, as well as links to source code. Start out by viewing the J-ALICE _Introduction_Page.html. This will tell you a little bit about this highly believable IRC chat bot. You'll also want to read the "Learning AIML" documentation.

PalmAlice

PalmAlice, by Robert Bjarnason, is a PalmOS port of ALICE based on the WinAlice PocketPC implementation created by Jacco Bikker. I have the code for Release Candidate 2 on the CD, but you'll want to check at www.alicebot.org because Robert is highly likely to have an updated version. Look in the software downloads section of the site.

Program-N

Program-N, by Gary Dubuque, is an Alice chat bot hosted in a notepad text editor. There is an additional script-processing language for authoring dialogs to assist in creating new AIML, which extends and develops the program's personality. The desktop program AIMLPad.zip is here. Just copy all unzipped folders into a Windows folder to execute. This bot uses Microsoft Agent software and characters, so you will need to download and install Microsoft's MS Agent files: msagent.exe, tv_enua.exe, and genie.exe are found free at the Microsoft Web site, if you want

AIMLpad to speak. Most of this will already be downloaded and installed automatically if you've loaded the Yapanda engine.

I recommend that you visit the project site at: http://home.attbi.com/~gdubuque/ for the latest developments. [Note: This may be a temporary site. You can check at www.alicebot.org for the latest, if that link doesn't work.

Characters

I've included a variety of 3D talking heads for you to play with. You'll find sources for hundreds more on the Web Resources html page I've included. You'll find both Microsoft Agent characters and 3dMeNow characters.

Demos

I've included PC-based demos of two very neat software packages: Poser and 3dMeNow. Poser also includes a Mac demo. These are inexpensive applications that will give you powerful tools for building your own animated V-people.

Poser

Poser, from CuriousLabs, is well described in the book. The CD contains version 4 plus the Pro Pack extensions. The demo for version 5 was not completed in time for publication. The Mac version of Poser 5 was expected to be released in June of 2003, so it should be available when you read this. I've included demo versions for both Mac and PC. Installation is straightforward and should present no problems. Refer to the readme text file for starting information. I've also included a brief tutorial on how to use the setup room included with the Pro Pack.

3dMeNow 1.5

Sorry, but this software is available only for the PC. As described in the book, this is a photo-perimeter human head sculpting application. It also includes animation tools and instructions. Photo-perimeter sculpting is where you take photos from several (in this case two) angles and use them to define the shape of the head geometry. The original photos are projected onto the geometry to create a photorealistic head. This is the easiest-to-use photo-perimeter application I've found. You'll find similar tools in both Poser and 3D Facial Studio, but they are more difficult to use.

Additional Examples

I've gotten permission to include the work of some fine programmers who are experimenting with altering or creating their own AI. The first example is the classic Eliza in both PC and Mac versions:

Eliza

Eliza, as described in the book, is a venerable classic created by MIT's Dr. Joseph Weizenbaum back in 1966. It was intended to resemble a Rogerian psychologist. [As an aside, I actually worked with Dr. Carl Rogers on an education project when I was very young.] I hope you enjoy this archetypal character. The PC version was prepared by Phillip Massyn, a South African who now lives in Sydney, Australia. If you can, take a moment and send him a thank you at massyn@bigpond.net.au.

I've included a Mac version that I have not tested for obvious reasons.

WinAlice

WinAlice represents a quantum leap ahead of Eliza. This one was written by Jacco Bikker in Alice 1, which is now obsolete. Yet you'll see that she's a very sophisticated personality. There are a few bugs, so if she crashes just restart and go for it. I've actually had very few problems with her during my several hours of chatting with her in a test drive or two. I've found the best way to chat with her is to say whatever comes into your head. Try to answer her questions honestly and don't be afraid to ask her questions as well. She does learn certain things along the way.

Video Examples

Here I've included some wonderful examples of advanced VH characters from ATT Labs, as well as some short movies featuring David Hansen's K-bot.

There are three sets of video examples. They are all interesting, but I love the ATT Labs examples of virtual humans in their labs. In some cases they are obviously virtual, but in at least one case the character seems so real that any casual observer might not notice that she's a synthetic human delivering a message. The biggest movie here is the short film from Kleiser-Walczak studios.

Kleiser-Walczak

You've got to see this wonderful short video about a synthetic thespian who wants his fellow actors to get the credit they deserve. He's a bit of a union organizer of sorts (nestor-sextone.mpg).

ATT Labs

Take your time to go through these characters and see if at least one of them is getting close to being able to fool humans. Most have high quality synthetic voices, but at least one has a real human voice that has be autosynched. See if you can tell which one it is. If you go to their online interactive site, vir2elle.com, you'll be able to make and save some examples for yourself. If you want to experiment with emotional expressions as I've done in the examples, just read the two test files in this directory. They contain examples of how to script these sample-based talking head models (also called VTTS, for Visual Text to Speech) to respond with emotion. As we go to press, this excellent program has unfortunately been shut down due to budget cuts.

Animatronics

David Hansen sent me some videos of K-bot in action. They're small and short, but you get the idea.

I've also included a cool demo of Master Lee "Master.mov" from YFX Studios (www.yfxstudio.com). They build animatronic animals and creepy insects, as well as their first major human project: Master Lee himself. Check out the 3MB movie of Master Lee talking with facial expressions. According to the company's president, George York, Master Lee can move his hands and arms. By the time you read this he may well be walking around—seriously.

Audio Examples

Here I've included two examples. First is the use of an active noise-filtering system to virtually eliminate the loud noise in a helicopter. One file contains the unfiltered voice stream and the second has the same sound, but with the noise actively filtered out. You can hear that the results are remarkable. Such filtering can make STT practical for use in noisy rooms, automobiles, and aircraft. It's already being used for speech-enabled car navigation systems as well as for car-control systems in high-end vehicles.

The second directory here merely has two examples of a synthetic voice singing. You'll find that you can script your Microsoft Agents to sing as well. It takes a lot of elbow grease, but it's doable.

Goodies

This is my last-minute directory. I had to submit my manuscript before the CD-ROM was due, so I've looked for goodies up to the last minute. Here you'll also find resources for which I had not yet received permission from the author until the last minute. Have fun and enjoy.

Recommended Resources

I've divided this Appendix into two separate sets of recommendations. The first set contains mostly books that are available through Amazon. The second is made up of academic papers and corporate references on specific topics of interest to designers of virtual humans. Many of these publications are a bit on the dry side. It always amazes me how some people can make this, one of the most exciting topics of today, dusty as an old bone on a dirt farm in Kansas. If you write something academic, please make it interesting.

Books

Please note that I use a "title first" format similar to that used at Amazon, to make your search there easier.

Abraham Lincoln Wisdom and Wit
by Abraham Lincoln; Louise Bachelder (Editor)
Peter Pauper Press; January 1998

Acting for Animators
by Ed Hooks
Heinemann Publishing; Book and CD-ROM edition (January 2001)

Adults Guide to Style
by Anthony Gregorc
Gregorc Assoc; June 1986

The Age of Intelligent Machines
by Ray Kurzweil
MIT Press; Reproduction edition (January 1992)

The Age of Spiritual Machines: When Computers Exceed Human
Intelligence
by Ray Kurzweil
Penguin USA (Paper); March 2000

AI Application Programming
by M. Tim Jones
Charles River Media; March 2003

AI Game Programming Wisdom (with CD-ROM)
by Steve Rabin (Editor)
Charles River Media; Book and CD-ROM edition (March 2002)

AI Techniques for Game Programming
by Mat Buckland and Mark Collins
Premier Press; Book and CD-ROM edition (October 2002)

Animating Facial Features and Expressions
by Bill Fleming and Darris Dobbs
Charles River Media; Book and CD-ROM edition (December 1998)

Animating Real-Time Game Characters (Game Development Series)
by Paul Steed
Charles River Media; Book and CD-ROM edition (December 2002)

Are We Spiritual Machines? Ray Kurzweil vs. the Critics of Strong A.I.
by Jay W. Richards (Editor), George F. Gilder (Contributor), Ray
Kurzweil (Contributor), Thomas Ray, John Searle, William Dembski,
Michael Denton
Discovery Institute; June 2002

Artificial Intelligence: A Guide to Intelligent Systems
by Michael Negnevitsky
Addison-Wesley Publishing; September 2001

Artificial Intelligence: A Modern Approach, 2nd Edition
by Stuart J. Russell and Peter Norvig
Prentice Hall; December 2002

The Art of Cartooning with FLASH (with CD-ROM)
by Daniel Gray, Gary Leib, and John Kuramoto
Sybex; Book and CD-ROM edition (November 2001)

Audio- and Video-Based Biometric Person Authentication:
Proceedings of the Third International Conference, AVBPA 2001,
Halmstad, Sweden, June 6-8, 2001 (Lecture Notes in Computer
Science)
by Josef Bigun and Fabrizio Smeraldi (Editors)
Springer Verlag; October 2001

Biometrics
by John D. Woodward Jr., Nicholas M. Orlans, and Peter T. Higgins
McGraw-Hill Osborne Media; December 2002

Biometrics: Identity Verification in a Networked World
by Samir Nanavati, Michael Thieme, and Raj Nanavati
John Wiley & Sons; March 2002

Biometric Solutions for Authentication in an E-World (Kluwer
International Series in Engineering and Computer Science, 697)
by David D. Zhang (Editor), Sekhar R. Sarukkai
Kluwer Academic Publishers; July 2002

Bots: The Origin of New Species
by Andrew Leonard
Hardwired; July 1997

Cartoon Animation (The Collector's Series)
by Preston Blair
Walter Foster; January 1995

The Change Leader: Using a Gestalt Approach with Work Groups
by H. B. Karp
Pfeiffer & Co; August 1995

Computer Facial Animation
by Frederick I. Parke, Keith Waters, and Frederic I. Parke
A K Peters Ltd; September 1996

Computer Vision: A Modern Approach
by David A. Forsyth and Jean Ponce
Prentice Hall; August 2002

Conceptual Spaces: The Geometry of Thought
by Peter Gardenfors
MIT Press; March 2000

Constructing Intelligent Agents Using Java: Professional Developer's
    Guide, 2nd Edition
by Joseph P. Bigus (Author), Jennifer Bigus (Author), and Joe Bigus
John Wiley & Sons; Book and CD-ROM edition (March 2001)

The Construction of Social Reality
by John R. Searle
Free Press; January 1997

Core Jini, 2nd Edition
by W. Keith Edwards
Prentice Hall; December 2000

Designing Effective Speech Interfaces
by Susan Weinschenk and Dean T. Barker
John Wiley & Sons; February 2000

Developing Jini™ Applications Using J2ME™ Technology
by Hinkmond Wong
Addison-Wesley; March 2002

Differentiated Instructional Strategies: One Size Doesn't Fit All
by Gayle H. Gregory and Carolyn Chapman
Corwin Press; November 2001

Digital Character Animation 2: Essential Techniques
by George Maestri
New Riders Publishing; Book and CD-ROM edition (August 1999)

Digital Character Animation 2, Volume II: Advanced Techniques
by George Maestri
New Riders Publishing; August 2001

Digital Character Design and Painting
by Don Seegmiller
Charles River Media; Book and CD-ROM edition (January 2003)

Discover Your Child's Learning Style: Children Learn in Unique
    Ways—Here's the Key to Every Child's Learning Success
by Mariaemma Willis and Victoria Kindle-Hodson
Prima Publishing; October 1999

Dragon NaturallySpeaking for the Office Professional: Speech
    Recognition Series
by Karl Barksdale
South-Western Educational Publishing; December 2000

The Dragon NaturallySpeaking Guide: Speech Recognition Made Fast
    and Simple, 2nd edition
by Dan Newman, David Newman, Daniel Newman, and James Baker
Waveside Publishing; September 1999

Edison's Eve: A Magical History of the Quest for Mechanical Life
by Gaby Wood
Knopf; 1st American edition (August 2002)

Emotions Revealed: Recognizing Faces and Feelings to Improve
    Communication and Emotional Life
by Paul Ekman
Times Books; April 2003

The Emperor's New Mind: Concerning Computers, Minds, and the
    Laws of Physics
by Roger Penrose and Martin Gardner
Oxford University Press; October 2002

Engineering the Human Germline: An Exploration of the Science and
    Ethics of Altering the Genes We Pass to Our Children
by Gregory Stock and John H. Campbell (Editors)
Oxford University Press; February 2000

Evolutionary Robotics: The Biology, Intelligence, and Technology of
Self-Organizing Machines (Intelligent Robotics and Autonomous
Agents)
by Stefano Nolfi and Dario Floreano
MIT Press; November 2000

Finite-State Language Processing (Language, Speech, and
Communication)
by Emmanuel Roche and Yves Shabes (Editors)
MIT Press; June 1997

Flesh and Machines: How Robots Will Change Us
by Rodney Allen Brooks
Pantheon Books; February 2002

Fundamentals of Neural Networks
by Laurene V. Fausett
Prentice Hall; January 1994

Generic Object Recognition Using Form & Function (Series in
Machine Perception and Artificial Intelligence, Vol. 10)
by Louise Stark and Kevin Bowyer
World Scientific; June 1996

Genetic Algorithms in Search, Optimization and Machine Learning
by David E. Goldberg
Addison-Wesley; January 1989

Gödel, Escher, Bach: An Eternal Golden Braid
by Douglas R. Hofstadter
Basic Books; January 1999

Gregorc Style Delineator: Developmental Technical and
Administration Manual, Revised Edition
by Anthony F. Gregorc
Gregorc Assoc; December 1984

How to Draw Animation: Learn the Art of Animation from Character
Design to Storyboards and Layouts
by Christopher Hart
Watson-Guptill; October 1997

The Humane Interface: New Directions for Designing Interactive
   Systems
by Jef Raskin
Addison-Wesley; March 2000

Identity Theft, Fraud, and the Future of Biometrics for Wireless
by Yankee Group
MarketResearch.com; ISBN: B00005V7WT; July 2001
[Download: Pdf Available at Amazon.Com $995.00 Special]

The Illusion of Life: Disney Animation, Revised Edition
by Frank Thomas, Ollie Johnston
Hyperion; October 1995

Implementing Biometric Security
by John Chirillo and Scott Blaul
John Wiley & Sons; April 2003

The Inmates Are Running the Asylum: Why High Tech Products Drive
   Us Crazy and How to Restore the Sanity
by Alan Cooper and Paul Saffo
Sams; April 1999

The Inner World of Abraham Lincoln
by Michael Burlingame
University of Illinois Press; 1994

Intelligent Biometric Techniques in Fingerprint and Face Recognition
by L. C. Jain, U. Halici, I. Hayashi, S. B. Lee, and S. Tsutsui (Editors)
CRC Press; June 1999

Intelligent Systems: Architecture, Design, Control
by James S. Albus and Alexander M. Meystel
Wiley-Interscience; August 2001

Interaction Design
by Jennifer Preece, Yvonne Rogers, and Helen Sharp
John Wiley & Sons; January 2002

An Introduction to AI Robotics (Intelligent Robotics and Autonomous Agents)
by Robin R. Murphy
MIT Press; November 2000

An Introduction to Genetic Algorithms (Complex Adaptive Systems)
by Melanie Michell
MIT Press; Reprint edition (February 1998)

An Introduction to Support Vector Machines and Other Kernel-Based Learning Methods
by Nello Cristianini and John Shawe-Taylor
Cambridge University Press; March 2000

JINI Technology: An Overview
by S. Ilango Kumaran and Ilango Kumaran
Prentice Hall; November 2001

Knowledge Management Toolkit: Practical Techniques for Building a Knowledge Management System
by Amrit Tiwana
Prentice Hall; Book and CD-ROM edition (December 1999)

The Large, the Small and the Human Mind
by Roger Penrose, Malcolm Longair (Editor), Abner Shimony, Nancy Cartwright, and Stephen Hawking
Cambridge University Press; Reprint edition (January 2000)

Lincoln's Humor and Other Essays
by Benjamin Platt Thomas; Michael Burlingame (Editor)
University of Illinois Press; March 2002

Lincoln Stories for Leaders
by Abraham Lincoln; Donald T. Phillips (Compiler)
Summit Pub Group; May 1997

Machine Learning
by Tom M. Mitchell
McGraw-Hill; March 1997

Making Use: Scenario-Based Design of Human-Computer Interactions
by John M. Carroll
MIT Press; September 2000

Maya Character Animation
by Jaejin Choi
Sybex; Book and CD-ROM edition (December 2002)

**MPEG-4 Facial Animation: The Standard, Implementation and
  Applications**
by Igor S. Pandzic and Robert Forchheimer (Editors)
John Wiley & Sons; October 2002

The Mystery of Consciousness
by John R. Searle
New York Review of Books; September 1997

**Nanocosm: Nanotechnology and the Big Changes Coming from the
  Inconceivably Small**
by William Illsey Atkinson
AMACOM; April 2003

Nanotechnology: A Gentle Introduction to the Next Big Idea
by Mark A. Ratner and Daniel Ratner
Prentice Hall; November 2002

**Natural Language Processing and Knowledge Representation:
  Language for Knowledge and Knowledge for Language**
by Lucja M. Iwanska, Stuart C. Shapiro (Editor)
AAAI Press; July 2000

Natural Language Understanding, 2nd Edition
by James Allen
Addison-Wesley; January 1995

The Nature of Emotion
by R.J. Eds
Oxford University Press; 1991.

The Next Big Thing Is Really Small: How Nanotechnology Will Change
the Future of Your Business
by Jack Uldrich, Deb Newberry (Contributor)
Crown; March 2003

Persuasive Technology: Using Computers to Change What We Think
and Do
by B. J. Fogg
Morgan Kaufmann; December 2002

Probabilistic Reasoning in Intelligent Systems: Networks of Plausible
Inference
by Judea Pearl
Morgan Kaufmann; April 1997

A Programmer's Guide to Jini Technology
by Jan Newmarch
APress; November 2000

Radical Simplicity: Transforming Computers into Me-Centric
Appliances
by Frederick Hayes-Roth, Daniel Amor, and Ian Browde
Prentice Hall; February 2003

Redesigning Humans: Our Inevitable Genetic Future
by Gregory Stock
Houghton Mifflin; June 2002

Robot Building for Beginners
by David Cook
APress; January 2002

Robot Vision (MIT Electrical Engineering and Computer Science)
by Berthold Horn
MIT Press; March 1986

Shadows of the Mind: A Search for the Missing Science of
Consciousness
by Roger Penrose
Oxford University Press; May 1996

Society of Mind
by Marvin Minsky
Touchstone Books; March 1988

Speech and Language Processing: An Introduction to Natural
   Language Processing, Computational Linguistics and Speech
   Recognition
by Dan Jurafsky, James H. Martin, Keith Vander Linden, Nigel Ward,
   Daniel Jurafsky, and James H. Martin
Prentice Hall; January 2000

Spoken Language Processing: A Guide to Theory, Algorithm and
   System Development
by Xuedong Huang, Alex Acero, Hsiao-Wuen Hon, and Raj Reddy
Prentice Hall; April 2001

Stop Staring: Facial Modeling and Animation Done Right
by Jason Osipa
Sybex; July 2003

Studies in Pattern Recognition: A Memorial to the Late Professor King-
   Sun Fu (Series in Machine Perception and Artificial Intelligence,
   Vol. 25)
by K. S. Fu and H. Freeman (Editors)
World Scientific; February 1997

Swarm Intelligence
by James Kennedy, Russell C. Eberhart (Contributor), Yuhui Shi
Morgan Kaufmann; March 2001

Understanding Computers and Cognition: A New Foundation for
   Design
by Terry Winograd and Fernando Flores
Addison Wesley; January 1987

Unobtrusive Measures, Revised Edition
by Lee Sechrest, Richard D. Schwartz (Author), Eugene J. Webb, and
   Donald T. Campbell
Corwin Press; October 1999

Unobtrusive Methods in Social Research (Understanding Social
Research)
by Raymond M. Lee
Open University Press; August 2000

Visualizing Argumentation: Software Tools for Collaborative and
Educational Sense-Making (Computer Supported Cooperative
Work)
by Paul Arthur Kirschner (Editor), C. Arthur Jefferson, S. Buckingham-
Shum, Chad S. Carr (Editor)
Springer Verlag; January 2003

VoiceXML Introduction to Developing Speech Applications
by James A. Larson
Prentice Hall; June 2002

When Things Start to Think
by Neil A. Gershenfeld
Owl Books; February 2000

Where the Action Is: The Foundations of Embodied Interaction
by Paul Dourish
MIT Press; October 2001

Academic and Corporate References

Many of these papers are available at CiteSeer.com, where you can download
them in any of several formats, including pdf, doc, and ps. If you don't find your
reference there, try doing a keyword search on Google.

Allen *et al.*, James. F. Allen, L. K. Schubert, G. Ferguson, P. Heeman, C. H.
Hwang, T. Kato, M. Light, N. Martin, B. Miller, M. Poesio, and D. R. Traum.
"The TRAINS Project: A Case Study in Building a Conversational Planning
Agent." *Journal of Experimental and Theoretical Artificial Intelligence* 7:7–
48, 1995.

Bates, J. "The Role of Emotion in Believable Agents." *Communications of the
ACM 37* (7):122–125, 1994.

Bartlett, M., J. Hager, P.Ekman, and T. Sejnowski. "Measuring Facial Expressions by Computer Image Analysis." *Psychophysiology* 36:253–264, 1999.

Bower, G.H. and P.R. Cohen. "Emotional Influences in Memory and Thinking: Data and Theory." In Clark, M.S. and S.T. Fiske (eds). *Affect and Cognition*, 291–331, 1982.

Brooks, R. and L.A. Stein. "Building Brains for Bodies." *Autonomous Robots* 1(1): 7–25, 1994.

Busetta, P., R. Ronnquist, A. Hodgson, and A. Lucas. "JACK Intelligent Agents: Components for Intelligent Agents in Java." Technical Report, Agent Oriented Software Pty. Ltd, Melbourne, Australia, 1998.

Cohen, P. R. "On Knowing What to Say: Planning Speech Acts." PhD thesis, University of Toronto, 1978. Reproduced as TR 118, Department of Computer Science, University of Toronto.

deGaris, H., Felix Gers, Michael Korkin, Arvin Agah, Norberto 'Eiji' Nawa. "Building an Artificial Brain Using an FPGA-Based "Cam-Brain Machine." DeGaris Publications, 1999.

deGaris H., Michael Korkin. "The CAM-Brain Machine (CBM): Real Time Evolution and Update of a 75 Million Neuron FPGA-Based Artificial Brain." Genobyte, Inc., and Evolutionary Systems Department, ATR-Human Information Processing Research Laboratories. [*Note*: This paper reports on recent progress made in building a 10,000 node evolved neural net artificial brain to control the behaviors of a life-sized robot. It can be can be downloaded from www.hip.atr.co.jp/~degaris.]

Ekman, P. and W. V. Friesen. "Detecting Deception from the Body or Face." *Journal of Personality and Social Psychology* 29:288–298, 1974.

Ekman, P., W.V. Friesen, M. O'Sullivan, and K. Scherer. "Relative Importance of Face, Body, and Speech in Judgments of Personality and Affect. *Journal of Personality and Social Psychology* 38(2):270–277, 1980.

Essa, I. A. and A. P. Pentland. "Coding, Analysis, Interpretation, and Recognition of Facial Expressions." *IEEE Transc. On Pattern Analysis and Machine Intelligence*, 19(7):757–763, 1997.

Ferrell, C. "Orientation Behavior Using Registered Topographic Maps." Massachusetts Institute of Technology, Artificial Intelligence Laboratory, 1996.

Fogg, B. J. and C. Nass. "Silicon Sycophants: Effects of Computers That Flatter. *International Journal of Human-Computer Studies* 46:551–561, 1997.

Knode, Steve. Steve Knode's consulting company at www.botknowledge.com will help individuals and companies build their own virtual human Web hosts and more.

Morgan Grover and David Makovoz. "Noise Cancellation: Reducing Noise with Software. *Speech Technology Magazine*, June/July 1999.

Isbister, K. and C. Nass. "Consistency of Personality in Interactive Characters: Verbal Cues, Non-Verbal Cues, and User Characteristics." *International Journal of Human-Computer Studies.* Forthcoming.

Isbister, K. "Reading Personality in Onscreen Interactive Characters: An Examination of Social Psychological Principles of Consistency, Personality Match, and Situational Attribution Applied to Interaction with Characters." Ph.D. dissertation, Communication Department, Stanford University, Stanford, California, 1998.

JDS Technologies, "Star Gate Operation Manual: WinEVM Event Manager Programming Guide, Revision C" (available for download at www.jdstechnologies.com).

Jones, G. A. "Andrea Active Noise Cancellation (ANC) Microphone Technology." A Microphone Study and White Paper prepared for Andrea Electronics Corporation by Digital Technologies, Inc., Pleasant Grove, Utah, 1996.

McFadden, Johnjoe. "Synchronous Firing and Its Influence on the Brain's Electromagnetic Field Evidence for an Electromagnetic Field Theory of Consciousness." *Journal of Consciousness Studies* 9(4): 23–50, 2000.

Lee, E-J. "Effects of Number, Ontology, and Representation of Influencing Agents on Public Compliance and Private Conformity." Ph.D. dissertation, Stanford University, Stanford, California, 1999.

Lee, E-J. and C. Nass. "Does the Ethnicity of a Computer Agent Matter? An Experimental Comparison of Human-Computer Interaction and Computer-Mediated Communication." *Proceedings of the Workshop on Embedded Conversational Characters Conference,* Lake Tahoe, California, 1998.

Massaro, D.M. *Perceiving Talking Faces: From Speech Perception to a Behavioral Principle.* Cambridge, Mass.: MIT Press, 1997.

Pell, M.G.B., M. Pollack, M. Tambe, and M. Wooldridge. "The Belief-Desire-Intention Model of Agency." *Proceedings of Agents, Theories, Architectures and Languages (ATAL).* Orlando, Florida, 1999.

Nass, C., Katherine Isbister, and Eun-Ju Lee. "Truth Is Beauty: Researching Embodied Conversation Agents." In Cassell, J. et al. (eds.), *Embodied Conversational Agents.* Cambridge, Mass.: MIT Press, 2000.

Nass, C. and K.M. Lee. "Does Computer-Generated Speech Manifest Personality? An Experimental Test of Similarity-Attraction." *Proceedings of the CHI 2000 Conference,* April 1–6, 2000, The Hague, The Netherlands, in press.

Pantic, M. and L.J.M. Rothkrantz. "Automatic Recognition of Facial Expressions and Human Emotions. *Proceedings of ASCI '97 Conference*, Delft University of Technology, Faculty of Information Technology and Systems (ITS), Delft, The Netherlands, 1997.

Pfeifer, R. "Artificial Intelligence Models of Emotion." In Hamilton, V., G.H.

Bower, and N. Frijda, eds. *Cognitive Perspectives on Emotion and Motivation*. Dordrecht, The Netherlands: Academic Publishers, 1988, pp. 287–320.

Rao, A. S. and M. P. Georgeff. "Modeling Rational Agents Within a BDI-Architecture." In Allen J., R. Fikes, and E. Sandewall, editors, *Principles of Knowledge Representation and Reasoning: Proceedings of the Second International Conference*. San Francisco: Morgan Kaufman, 1991, pp. 473–484.

Reeves, B. and Clifford Nass. "Perceptual Bandwidth: What Happens to People When Computers Become Perceptually Complex? *Communications of the ACM* 43: 65–70, 2000.

SzuÕcs, A., C.A.P. Varona, A.R. Volkovskii, H.D.I. Abarbanel, M.I. Rabinovich, and A. I. Selverston. "Interacting Biological and Electronic Neurons Generate Realistic Oscillatory Rhythms." Department of Physics and Marine Physical Laboratory, Scripps Institution of Oceanography, University of California San Diego, La Jolla, California, 1999.

Tian, Y., Takeo Kanade, and Jeffrey F. Cohn. "Recognizing Action Units for Facial Expression Analysis." Robotics Institute, Carnegie Mellon University, Pittsburgh, Pennsylvania. *CMURITR9940*. 23(2): 97–115, 2001.

Tian, Y., T. Kanade, and J. F. Cohn. "Robust Lip Tracking by Combining Shape, Color, and Motion." *Proceedings of the Asian Conference on Computer Vision*, 2000.

Traum, D. R. and James F. Allen. "Discourse obligations in dialogue processing." *Proceedings of the 32nd Annual Meeting of the Association for Computational Linguistics*, pp. 1–8, 1994.

Velásquez, J. D., Modeling *Emotions and Other Motivations in Synthetic Agents*. MIT Artificial Intelligence Laboratory, published by the American Association for Artificial Intelligence, 1997.

Winikoff, M., Lin Padgham, and James Harland. *Simplifying the Development of Intelligent Agents*. RMIT University, Melbourne, Australia, 2001.

Index